I0889745

Unfinalized Moments

Essays in the Development of Contemporary Jewish American Narrative

Shofar Supplements in Jewish Studies

Zev Garber, Editor

Los Angeles Valley College

Unfinalized Moments

Essays in the Development of Contemporary Jewish American Narrative

Edited by Derek Parker Royal

Purdue University Press / West Lafayette, Indiana

Printed in the United States of America.

Library of Congress Cataloging-in-Publication Data
Royal, Derek Parker, 1963-
Unfinalized moments : essays in the development of contemporary Jewish American narrative / Derek Parker Royal.
p. cm. -- (Shofar supplements in Jewish studies)
Includes bibliographical references and index.
ISBN 978-1-55753-584-9 (pbk. : alk. paper) -- ISBN 978-1-61249-162-2 (epdf) -- ISBN 978-1-61249-163-9 (epub) 1. American fiction--Jewish authors--History and criticism. 2. Jews--United States--Intellectual life. 3. Jews in literature. I. Title.
PS153.J4R69 2011
813'.54098924--dc23
2011036985

Dedication

To Daniel Walden, the grandfather of Jewish American literary studies.

Contents

Acknowledgments

First and foremost, I wish to acknowledge my gratitude to Daniel Morris and Zev Garber, co-editors of *Shofar: An Interdisciplinary Journal of Jewish Studies*. This volume actually began in a special issue I guest edited in 2004. Dan, in particular, was instrumental in helping to bring this about. I had attended graduate school at Purdue University, where Dan teaches, but I did not have the pleasure of taking a class with him while there. Still, we became friends and colleagues during my coursework, and it was Dan's encouragement and support that led to the guest editorship of that special issue of *Shofar* after my graduation. When I decided to develop that issue and expand it into a book-length collection of essays, I turned to Zev. In overseeing the Shofar Supplements series at Purdue University Press, he has been both a helpful editor and a source of collegial inspiration.

A hearty "thank you" as well to my editors and contacts at both the *Shofar* offices and at Purdue University Press. Nancy Lein, *Shofar*'s managing editor, was indispensible in pulling together the 2004 special issue of *Shofar*—indeed, she taught me what it means to step into someone else's shoes and guest edit a journal—and she has continued to help me in my various scholarly endeavors. Charles T. Watkinson, the director of Purdue University Press, has been supportive in a many ways, and not only in getting me to complete this volume. I also have the luck of working closely with him and his production editor, Katherine Purple, as the executive editor of *Philip Roth Studies*. Their keen insights and friendly working demeanor have made working on this manuscript a pleasure. I would particularly like to thank Rebecca Corbin and Dianna L. Gilroy at the press for all of the work they have put into this project. And a good part of that "work" has been putting up with my schedule and the hazards that come from my frantic multitasking.

I would like to acknowledge as well the many people who have contributed to my development as a writer and as a scholar. They are too many to list—and a number of them grace the pages of *Unfinalized Moments*—but I feel the need to mention a few names. Robert Paul Lamb, ol' Bob, was my mentor in graduate school, and even though Jewish American literary studies is nowhere near his field, he, more than anyone, encouraged me to pursue this community of writers in the early days of my graduate career. Others who have nurtured my passion for Jewish American writing include Daniel Walden, who gave me my first chance to publish on the topic; Victoria Aarons, a friend who has served as a role model of professionalism; Gloria Cronin, and the late Ben Siegel, who together tag-teamed to make sure I participated regularly in the (relatively small) community of Jewish American literary scholars; Jay L. Halio, the former director of University of Delaware Press, who helped to introduce me to the publishing business; and Sandor Goodhart, another of those graduate school professors whose scholarship in Jewish American literary studies has served as a beacon, and whom I can call friend.

The following essays in this volume were originally printed in the special issue on contemporary Jewish American narrative in *Shofar* (22, no. 3 [Spring 2004]), most in shorter form, and reprinted with permission:

> Susan Jacobowitz, "'Hardly There Even When She Wasn't Lost': Orthodox Daughters and the 'Mind-Body' Problem in Modern American Fiction."
>
> Michael Martin, "The Ethics of After: Melvin Jules Bukiet, Holocaust Fiction, and the Reemergence of an Ethical Sense in the Post-Holocaust World."
>
> Lee Behlman, "The Escapist: Fantasy, Folklore, and the Pleasures of the Comic Book in Recent Jewish American Holocaust Fiction."
>
> Adam Meyer, "Putting the 'Jewish' Back in 'Jewish American Fiction': An Allegorical Reading of Nathan Englander's 'The Gilgul of Park Avenue.'"
>
> Adam Sol, "'Were it Not for the Yetzer Hara': Eating, Knowledge, and the Physical in Jonathan Rosen's *Eve's Apple*."

Also, a shorter version of Michael Schuldiner's "The Second Generation Holocaust Survivor: Third-Degree Metalepsis and Creative Block in Art Spiegelman's *Maus*" appeared in *Studies in American Jewish Literature* (21 [2002]).

Unfinalized Moments: Essays in the Development of Contemporary Jewish American Narrative

Derek Parker Royal

In Jewish American fiction studies, it has become common practice to reference Irving Howe's pronouncement on what he saw as the waning influence of this literature—so much so, in fact, that the mere mention of it serves as a critical, if not hackneyed, rite of passage for those engaged in contemporary narrative. Indeed, the constant citation of it (present introduction included) begins to take on the cadence of an ironic mantra, one chanted to invoke the spirit of literary authenticity. One is even tempted, given our sound bite-laden culture, to encapsulate his views with the pithy phrase, "the Howe Doctrine." It all began in the introduction to his 1977 collection of Jewish American stories, where Howe broods over his belief that "American Jewish fiction has probably moved past its high point. Insofar as this body of writing draws heavily from the immigrant experience, it must suffer a depletion of resources, a thinning-out of materials and memories. Other than in books and sentiment, there just isn't enough left of that experience."[1] To a certain degree, such an outlook is understandable, coming from the author of *World of Our Fathers* (1976), a text whose foundation is the Jewish immigrant experience. Yet what makes this literary forecast uniquely poignant is that it introduces a first-of-its-kind manuscript, the collection of "contemporary" Jewish American narratives. In one fell—yet curious—swoop, Howe celebrates the centrality of Jewish American literature at the same time that he mourns its passing. It is as if a distinguished collector had displayed, for all his guests to see, a grand exhibition of significance. Yet in the process of doing so, he kills off the very subject of his admiration, much like a butterfly collector must place his specimens in ethyl acetate before they can be properly mounted and showcased. The very act of finalizing the literary moment secures its place in history, creating in the process an inert yet brilliant museum piece.

While such a simile may appear excessive on first reading, one should keep in mind that Howe was not alone in ringing the death knell, or perhaps saying Kaddish. In a 1976 article, Ruth Wisse, a critic that Howe himself cited to confirm his suppositions, uses rhetoric that is strikingly similar to Howe's. "The career of American Jewish literature would seem to have reached a turning point," she provocatively asserts, eventually concluding that "for those who take Judaism seriously as a cultural alternative, and wish to weave new brilliant cloth from its ancient threads, the sociological reality of the present-day American Jewish community would seem to present an almost insurmountable obstacle."[2] Perhaps even more dour, although not nearly as referenced as Howe's or Wisse's, is Leslie Fiedler's unequivocal assertion roughly ten years later that "the Jewish American novel is over and done with, a part of history rather than a living literature."[3]

These grim predictions serve as a backdrop, ironically enough, for what has become over the past several years an emergent body of scholarship on the most contemporary generation of Jewish American writers. The present work is a collection of essays that challenge Howe's and Fiedler's notions of finality. With a variety of forms and focusing on a diversely rich selection of writers, the contributors to this volume assert the ongoing vitality of Jewish American fiction. They find in authors such as Allegra Goodman, Michael Chabon, Tova Mirvis, Rebecca Goldstein, Pearl Abraham, Jonathan Rosen, Nathan Englander, Melvin Jules Bukiet, Tova Reich, Jonathan Safran Foer, Ruth Knafo Setton, Farideh Dayanim Goldin, and Ben Katchor an argument against the kind of conclusiveness reported by Howe, Wisse, and Fiedler. Or, to paraphrase another famous literary dictum, each of the essays in this collection underscores the fact that reports of the death of Jewish American fiction were exaggerated.

Since the late 1990s, there has been a growing critical awareness of what many have seen as a Jewish American literary revival. In 1992 Ted Solotaroff and Nessa Rapoport published *Writing Our Way Home*, a collection of short stories that emphasizes the postimmigrant as well as the postassimilation experience. This thematic focus, they argued, resulted in a new direction for Jewish American writing that promised to be fruitful. This energy, as the editors saw it, was fueled largely by a renewed interest in Jewish religion and culture. The centrifugal spin of assimilation gives way to a more centripetal pull toward ethnic definition. As Rapoport so succinctly puts it, "Having won our place in American culture, we are beginning to be confident enough to reclaim Jewish culture."[4] Although many of the writers that they pulled together represented an earlier generation whose publishing history had been established well before 1980—for example, Saul Bellow, E. L. Doctorow, Grace Paley, Bernard Malamud, Philip Roth, Cynthia Ozick, and Isaac Bashevis Singer—Solotaroff and Rapoport nonetheless included a variety of younger authors whose work seemed to exemplify what the editors saw as the new direction. Both Solotaroff and Rapoport point out that current fictionists such as Allegra Goodman, Allen Hoffman, and Daphne Merkin embrace Jewish culture and enthusiastically engage in dialogues with its history and orthodoxy.

Another significant critical moment in the exploration of this Jewish American "new wave" took place in the pages of *Tikkun* in 1997. In it, Thane Rosenbaum, the literary editor of that publication, collected a series of essays under the title, "The Jewish Literary Revival."[5] In his introduction to this literary symposium, Rosenbaum asks if Jewish American fiction is experiencing a new beginning, specifically in regard to that community of writers who inherited an ambiguous ethnic past. What burdens of culture and memory, he puts forth, contribute to the writings of this newer generation of Jewish American writers, and how might these writers—who were never particularly observant or who never experienced the horrors of the Holocaust—reenact those memories in ways that would represent the larger Jewish American experience? The various participants in the symposium looked at such issues as the influential shadows cast by the previous generation of Jewish American writers, the shifting mores of late-twentieth-century culture, the influences of faith, and, of course, the legacy of the Holocaust. The contributor lineup is impressive, a mix of artists and literary critics—Morris Dickstein, Nessa Rapaport, Mark Shechner, Rebecca Goldstein, Melvin Jules Bukiet, Steve Stern, and Sanford Pinsker—each of whom weighs in with their interpretation of the phenomenon. In his survey of the contemporary literary landscape, Dickstein argues that the identity politics of the 1960s helped set the stage for this revival, bringing a new vitality that people like Irving Howe had not foreseen: "The new emphasis on identity, the revival of interest in Jewish history, Jewish festivals, and sacred Jewish texts could not help but lead to a new Jewish writing that would confound the predictions of the critics."[6] Bukiet conducts a similar survey, but in his sweep of the contemporary scene he loosely groups Jewish American writers into two separate categories: mourners and machers. The former (e.g., Steve Stern, Thane Rosenbaum, Myla Goldberg, and Rebecca Goldstein—at least in *Mazel* [1995]) approach Jewish history through narratives of lamentation on, longing for, or at least recreating a past that exists only on the written page. Machers, on the other hand, use history to assert themselves, often with both enraging and comedic results. The in-your-face brashness of such authors as Saul Bellow, Philip Roth, and Erica Jong helped to pave the way for more recent machers such as Mark Helprin, Michael Chabon, and Francine Prose. What both camps of writers share is a spellbinding ability to chronicle their historical moments. Bukiet concludes, rather sardonically, that "if the critics are correct in believing that this literature will wither and die under the universal blending force of modernity . . . at least that death—sometimes lamented, sometimes defied—will go extraordinarily well-recorded."[7]

Equally sarcastic is Stern's contribution to the *Tikkun* symposium. Using his own background and literary subject matter as a "case in point" of Irving Howe's 1977 pronouncement, he prefaces his discussion of the contemporary scene by declaring, "It's certainly not my intention to question the authority of Irving Howe (who was an honorable man), for the evidence still remains more in favor of burying Jewish American fiction than praising it."[8] Stern acknowledges the shifting Jewish landscape in the past thirty years, but like most other symposium participants, he does not see the passing of the postimmigrant generation as the end of (Jewish American literary) history. Sanford Pinsker agrees, but in his piece he specifically focuses on writings that "creat[e] a new genre I call post-Holocaust fiction."[9] The thrust of this newer wave of Jewish American writing, he argues, comes from those narratives written not by Holocaust survivors (or their more fortunate brethren who escaped the camps) but by the children of that generation, younger writers who have become, in effect, the psychological and spiritual inheritors of the Holocaust. Pinsker sees what the others in the *Tikkun* symposium see, the ongoing presence of causal forces giving new (or sustained) life to Jewish American fiction.[10]

Other notable studies of this generation followed. Alan L. Berger, for instance, explored the burgeoning field of post-Holocaust writers in *Children of Job* (1997). Here he focused on what he called the second-generation witnesses to the Holocaust, the sons and daughters of survivors whose writings highlight the relationship between the Holocaust and contemporary Jewish American identity. Similar to Pinsker, but in a much more sustained manner, Berger explores the ways in which authors such as Barbara Finkelstein, Art Spiegelman, Thane Rosenbaum, J. J. Steinfeld, and Melvin Jules Bukiet point toward a new direction in Jewish American narrative by directly confronting the psychic legacy of the Shoah.[11] Other recent critical works have likewise concerned younger writers of fiction, but they have mostly done so within the larger context of post-1945 Jewish fiction. In *Jewish American and Holocaust Literature: Representations in the Postmodern World* (2004), Alan L. Berger and Gloria L. Cronin pull together a variety of essays on contemporary Jewish American writing.[12] Although a few of the contributions concern such authors as Thane Rosenbaum and Rebecca Goldstein, the vast majority of the essays focus on authors who came to prominence in the decades immediately following the Second World War. The same could be said of Janet Handler Burstein's *Telling Little Secrets: American Jewish Writing since the 1980s* (2006).[13] While her study is a useful introduction to literature over the past twenty years, it does not limit itself to the most recent generation of Jewish American authors, choosing instead to contextualize the work of younger writers alongside the previous generation of Philip Roth and Cynthia Ozick.

In fact, Burstein, along with other critics such as Sidra DeKoven Ezrahi, have noticed a new emphasis in Jewish women's writing on the re-creation of cultural origins through discourses on homecoming and home space. Such observations help to explain why many, if not most, of the younger Jewish American writers gaining notoriety are women, quite a shift from the previous generation dominated by the likes of Bellow, Malamud, and Roth.[14] Still, these studies tend to focus on an older generation of woman writers (e.g., Ozick, Marge Piercy, and Grace Paley), as does Lois Rubin's edited collection, *Connections and Collisions: Identities in Contemporary Jewish-American Women's Writing* (2005).[15] But perhaps the most significant study of the most contemporary generation of Jewish American writers, both male and female alike, is Andrew Furman's *Contemporary Jewish American Writers and the Multicultural Dilemma.*[16] In attempting to assess the place of Jewish American literature within the larger body of contemporary multiethnic studies (an all too uncertain place, unfortunately), he focuses almost exclusively on fiction writers whose publishing career began in the 1980s. His is the first fully developed critical examination of this group of writers—including discussions on Melvin Jules Bukiet, Thane Rosenbaum, Rebecca Goldstein, Robert Cohen, Allegra Goodman, Steve Stern, and Gerald Shapiro—and one that attempts to bridge the gap between multicultural studies in general and Jewish American literary studies in particular. The value of Furman's work is undeniable: he has helped to give critical form to an emerging body of writing whose significance should no longer be in question.

While the critics have been noticing and signifying this "new wave" of writing, editors have been active in collecting and anthologizing it, with impressive results. There have been at least seven significant collections of Jewish American literature since the publication of Solotaroff and Rapoport's *Writing Our Way Home*, all of it in some way focusing on the recent generation of writers.[17] In 1997, *Prairie Schooner* put out a special issue on Jewish American authors, later published in book form.[18] Although it includes both poems and essays, much of the collection is made up of short fiction by writers such as Faye Moskowitz, Rebecca Goldstein, Janet Sternburg, and Steve Stern. The following year saw the publication of two other collections. Ilan Stavans's *Oxford Book of Jewish Stories* (1998)[19] is notable for its scope—providing a diverse body of short fiction from North American, Israeli, and European Jewish writers from the nineteenth century to the present—but especially, in light of this present study, for the inclusion of the most contemporary group of American Jewish fictionists. Standing alongside such towering figures as Saul Bellow and Philip Roth are Stern, Goldstein, Bukiet, Goodman, and Janice Eidus. Indeed, two writers from this younger generation have been editors of their own collections of contemporary Jewish fiction. In his volume, Gerald Shapiro looks specifically at American Jewish writers, beginning with the works of Abraham Cahan and Anzia Yezierska and wrapping up with Stern, Bukiet, Goodman, Lev Raphael, Robin Hemley, and Helen Schulman. Melvin Jules Bukiet and David G. Roskie's *Scribblers on the Roof: Contemporary Jewish Fiction* (2006) is even more ambitious and wide ranging, gathering the stories of such young writers as Jonathan Ames, Myla Goldberg, Ken Kalfus, Binnie Kirshenbaum, Jonathan Levi, Mary Morris, Sonia Pilcer, Jonathan Rosen, Norma Rosen, Lucy Rosenthal, Lynne Sharon Schwartz, and Aryeh Lev Stollman, authors who for the most part tended to get overlooked in the previous anthologies.[20]

Perhaps the most curious recent compilation of fiction is another by Bukiet, *Neurotica: Jewish Writers on Sex* (1999).[21] At least half of the selections are written by the younger wave, including Nathan Englander, Binnie Kirshenbaum, Cheryl Pear Sucher, Benjamin Taylor, and S. L. Wisenberg, as well as many already mentioned. Bukiet contributes still another collection, this one with a much less facetious tone. Springing from the editor's blunt assertion, "In the beginning was Auschwitz," *Nothing Makes You Free* (2002) brings together international writings from Alan Berger's "children of Job," including selections from Rosenbaum, Art Spiegelman, Barbara Finkelstein, Eva Hoffman, and Joseph Skibell.[22] W. W. Norton also weighs in with their first ever anthology of Jewish American literature.[23] Jules Chametzky, John Felstiner, Hilene Flanzbaum, and Kathryn Hellerstein attempt to cover the entire history of the Jewish American literary experience—from 1654 to the present—and even in this death-defying scholarly sweep they still find it necessary, in their section significantly titled "Wandering and Return," to include writings from Stern, Bukiet, Goodman, and Spiegelman. More recently, Paul Zakrzewski, editor of *Heeb* magazine, added to the growing "new wave" with his collection of even younger writers.[24] Only four of the twenty-five contributing authors published their first book before 1998, and sixteen of the collection's stories were copyrighted in 2001 or later. This makes Zakrzewski's *Lost Tribe*—with pieces by first-time novelists and short story writers Myla Goldberg, Nathan Englander, Tova Mirvis, and Jonathan Safran Foer—the "greenest" compilation of Jewish American writers to date. And in an added twist on this phenomenon, my own edited special issue of *Shofar* focuses on the growing significance of comics and graphic novels in recent Jewish American narrative studies, a field with a rich history yet one that is just now beginning to receive its due.[25]

All of this creative and critical work, impressing in its scope, establishes an imposing context. Even though the scholarly field is as young as the writers it canvasses, it has already received a significant amount of attention. However, there is certainly room for fresh analytical voices, and the essays in the present collection provide a necessary and unique contribution. Unlike earlier anthologies and critical works, these essays focus solely on the community of writers who published their first book after 1988 (even Furman's impressive study begins with an analysis of Philip Roth). What is more, it is the first substantial collection of critical essays on this subject matter, the most recent generation of Jewish American authors, written by a variety of scholars in the field. As such, the volume does not attempt to foreground any one critical agenda—such as post-Holocaust writing, engagements with Zionism, feminist studies, postmodern influences, or multiculturalism—other than its intended focus: the presence of a robust and ever-evolving body of Jewish American fiction. Indeed, one could argue that the need to assign a precipitating cause to a literary phenomenon—a tendency all too common in academia—does unintended critical harm, unnecessarily limiting our understanding of the literature and truncating our appreciation of texts that may fall outside of our intellectual schema. In taking to task Howe and his ilk for failing to envision a Jewish literature much beyond the immigrant experience, some recent scholars may fall prey to similar critical strategies. Understanding (and explaining) contemporary Jewish American writing *only* thought the lens of post-Holocaust studies or *only* through the generational desire for cultural or religious return can be just as restrictive as reading it primarily though the immigrant experience. Yet, as the essays and interviews in this volume so clearly demonstrate, recent Jewish American fiction has taken a variety of forms with its negotiations of orthodoxy, representations of a post-Holocaust world, reassertion of folkloric tradition, explorations of postmodernity, reevaluations of Jewishness, alternative delineations of ethnic identity, engagement with visual narrative and various forms of new media, accommodations with multiculturalism, and even (in the case of recent Russian émigré fiction) reemphasis on the immigrant experience. The conditions underlying the recent flowering of Jewish American writing are multifold, and we would do well to broaden our understand of this literature so as to account for its varied expressions.

The title of the volume, *Unfinalized Moments*, bears out this multifaceted quality of contemporary Jewish American fiction. It is a reference to one of Mikhail Bakhtin's central critical concepts, "unfinalizability," the idea that characters (in real life as well as in fiction) are constantly in the process of making themselves, thereby resistant to any finalizing definition or end point of understanding. As he writes in *Problems of Dostoevsky's Poetics* (1929), "Nothing conclusive has yet taken place in the world, the ultimate word of the world and about the world has not yet been spoken, the world is open and free, everything is still in the future and will always be in the future."[26] The ability, or the sheer necessity, of characters to surprise readers through confounding expectation is central to Bakhtin's poetics. No matter what the determining factors—psychological, sociological, economic—texts and the characters they contain, much like real individuals, can never be ultimately pigeonholed. There is always something left over, what Bakhtin aptly calls a "surplus of humanness."[27]

Such a concept pertains directly to the state of Jewish American fiction, especially when previous critics have lamented that its characters have become nothing more than "stock literary fixture[s]" (Wisse 10). The fictional creations had never really become stock fixtures, and neither have their authors. As Howe, Wisse, and Fiedler have unwittingly demonstrated, some past scholars of Jewish American fiction were too quick in ringing a finalizing death knell. They, as well as others, have understood this literature as a result primarily of one or two cultural phenomena (e.g., Jewish immigrant experience). However, the current volume assumes a more eclectic argument, accounting for the rise in recent Jewish American fiction through a number of diverse and interconnected cultural and literary events. These include, but are certainly not limited to, the presence of an already established canon of Jewish American writing; the second generation or postassimilationist "return" to Jewish religious and cultural practices; the rise of identity politics in the 1960s through the 1980s; the legacy of feminist movements since the 1960s and its current third-wave manifestations; the proliferation of critical race theory and queer theory studies and the ways in which these have influenced Jewish American writing; the flourishing of second generation survivor literature, fiction written by children of Holocaust survivors; the inheritance of postmodernism and the ways in which its literary strategies contextualize the Jewish subject; a broadening of understanding what is Jewish and how American literature has been shaped by forces other than Ashkenazi; and the growing awareness, from a writer's point of view, of the cultural significance of Israel. What is more, and perhaps more significant, the sheer diversity within this literary field exemplifies its always already process of (re)definition. This can be seen in the subject matters of the various essays that make up this collection, which range from emphases on orthodox communities to studies of eating disorders; from journeys into Holocaust-marked Eastern Europe to meanderings through the postassimilated streets of lower Manhattan; from studies on more traditional and realistic forms of narrative to explorations on the uses of fantasy and the graphic novel; and from discussions on authors whose fictions are steeped in *Yiddishkeit* to new readings of those writers who have previously chosen not to reference their Jewishness.

It is appropriate that this collection begins with examinations of the past and the ways in which it manifests itself through the writings of the younger generation. The first section, "Dialogues with Orthodoxy and History," explores some of the different ways in which Jewish tradition and the weight of history have become such prominent themes in many of these narratives—an emphasis that would have been unheard of, with one or two exceptions, in fiction of the 1960s and 1970s. Each one of the contributors to this section, five in all, acknowledges the dominance of memory and the past, especially as it relates to religious and cultural tradition. Susan Jacobowitz and Maya Socolovsky examine the work of recent narratives by women and how orthodoxy plays a part in their sculpting a Jewish identity. Both Michael J. Martin and Michael Schuldiner map out the contours of a post-Holocaust world, although each does so through vastly different textual media: Melvin Jules Bukiet's fictional narratives as a way to an "after" (after the Holocaust, after postmodernism), and Art Spiegelman's comics as a metaleptic strategy to frame identity in the wake such horrors. Jennifer M. Lemberg's contribution also focuses on the world after Auschwitz, but does so by looking at literal journeys back to the places of horrific origin, a theme found in the writings of both Thane Rosenbaum and Jonathan Safran Foer. As Alan Berger and Sanford Pinsker have persuasively argued, much of contemporary literature reflects post-Holocaust concerns, and this is a notion to which the contributions of Martin, Schuldiner, and Lemberg certainly bear witness.

The essays in the second section of the text, "Folklore, Fantasy, and the Metanarrative," all deal with fictional discourse and the ways in which the fantastic intersect with the real. Lee Behlman, Alexis Wilson, and Monica Osborne look at the ways in which writers such as Rosenbaum, Michael Chabon, Nathan Englander, and Steve Stern have appropriated folklore and fantasy—a rich tradition indeed—in ways that help signify the Jewish American present. Tracy Floreani concludes this section with a discussion on Foer's bestselling novel, *Everything Is Illuminated* (2002), and how he employs metafictional strategies to represent what many see as an unapproachable subject. In the third section, "(Re)inscribing Jewish Text and Identity," the contributors investigate the ongoing process of defining the Jewish American subject and demonstrating how some of the most recent writers have resisted any pre-fixed notions of Jewishness. As such, these writers are, in essence, redefining our understandings of Jewish American literature. Both Adam Meyer and Adam Sol confront the question of what makes a text Jewish, but they do so in divergent ways. Whereas Meyer uses Englander's Jewish subject matter as way of illustrating the return to a cultural and religious heritage, Sol focuses on the ethnically defining uses of food and the body in the fiction of Jonathan Rosen. Joe Kraus spotlights the writing of S. L. Wisenburg, an author who has received little critical attention, and how she brings a fresh approach to Jewish writing, integrating both fiction and creative nonfiction. And it is appropriate that Bart Lievens ends this section by contrasting Pearl Abraham with some of the most prominent representatives of the previous generations of Jewish American writers.

The final section of the manuscript, "Authors in Their Own Words," is made up of interviews from several contemporary Jewish writers who have traditionally been marginalized within the criticism. Both Ruth Knafo Setton and Farideh Dayanim Goldin reflect on the genesis of their works, the state of contemporary Jewish American writing, the uncertain position of Sephardic and Mizrahi American fiction, and their unique perspectives as Jewish writers on the periphery. Ben Katchor, perhaps one of the most notable comics artists in America today, discusses his work, picture-stories, and the current state of cultural production, especially as it applies to graphic narrative and his particular urban perspective. His interview is significant, in that it (along with Schuldiner's contribution on Spiegelman) demonstrates the growing importance of comics studies within the academy and its links to recent Jewish American narrative. Both of these interviews not only allow the authors to speak for themselves, but they offer alternative glimpses into Jewish American writing today. They demonstrate how new paths are being forged, yet at the same time these same trajectories—whether it be Katchor's American urban landscape, Knafo's journey into Morocco, or Goldin's memories of Tehran—suggest a return to the kind of challenges facing previous generations of Jewish authors.

Yet, as inclusive as this survey of contemporary Jewish American writing may be, it is by no means exhaustive. There is only so much one can include between the covers of a book, even if its individual contributions are broad in scope. Indeed, it is my hope that the essays and interviews in this collection, diverse and embracing in their own right, will serve as inspirations and springboards for further and more ambitious studies of current Jewish fiction. The literary landscape is fertile terrain. There are many contemporary authors not covered in this collection: Elisa Albert, Aimee Bender, David Black, Amy Bloom, Gabriel Brownstein, Judy Budnitz, Ethan Canin, Joshua Cohen, Robert Cohen, Janice Eidus, Jyl Lynn Felman, Myla Goldberg, Neil Gordon, Harvey Grossinger, Ehud Havazelet, Robin Hemley, Joshua Henkin, Dara Horn, Judith Katz, Binnie Kirshenbaum, Nicole Krauss, David Leavitt, Joan Leegant, Adam Levins, Sam Lipsyte, Michael Lowenthal, Lesléa Newman, Ellen Pall, Ben Schrank, Sarah Schulman, Dani Shapiro, Gerald Shapiro, Joseph Skibell, Aryeh Lev Stollman, and Evan Zimroth . . . among others. There is much more work to be done, not only with authors who use their fiction to frame their Jewishness, but also—and perhaps more significantly—with writers who problematize or intentionally erase Jewish subjectivity. And there is the very recent phenomenon of the arrival of Russian Jewish émigrés. Writers such as David Bezmozgis, Olga Grushin, Michael Idov, Sana Krasikov, Ellen Litman, Anya Ulinich, Lara Vapnyar, and especially Gary Shteyngart are redefining the thematic contours of Jewish American fiction. A more complete study of contemporary Jewish American narrative would certainly have to take into account some of America's most recent immigrants and how their subject matter recalls early-twentieth-century Jewish writing.

And discussions of return and the immigrant past bring us once more to Irving Howe. At the end of his introduction, he speculates on the resistance that many younger writers of his time might have toward his grim predictions. "They would argue," he adds,

> that there is a post-immigrant Jewish experience in America which can be located in its own milieu, usually suburbs or middle-class urban neighborhoods; that it has virtues and vices distinctly its own; and that it offers a body of experience which a serious writer can draw upon in creating fictions. Is not their phase of Jewish life in America as authentic and interesting as that of the earlier immigrants? Do they not have a right, also, to make of their involvements and confusions with Jewishness the foundation for stories and novels?" (17)

To those of us reading in the early twenty-first century, the answer to these questions is, but of course! The essays composing this volume demonstrate how right Howe's imagined writers would have been, how the historical moment in Jewish American writing is all but finalized. And each serves as an illustrative example of the current trends in literary studies. Their subject matters concern many of the major issues that have come to define this brand of writing, from an interest in its late-nineteenth-century immigrant roots to its most recent expressions in the new millennium. What is more, many authors that are discussed here are some of today's most significant American writers of fiction. Allegra Goodman's reputation continues to grow, and Art Spiegelman and Michael Chabon have both received the Pulitzer Prize. Furthermore, Thane Rosenbaum, Jonathan Safran Foer, Nathan Englander, and Ben Katchor have each won (respectively), the Wallant Prize, the National Jewish Book Award, the PEN/Malamud Award, and the MacArthur Award. Readers interested in theories of ethnicity—Jewish or otherwise—and its relation to postmodernism or contemporary critical studies will find in this volume a useful case study in the ways in which the two interact. Of particular interest to such readers will be the chapters concerning Spiegelman's and Wisenburg's untraditional uses of narrative form, Goldstein's and Mirvis's engagement with gender, Stern's and Foer's appropriation of magical realism and romance writing, and Rosen's and Abraham's unique articulations of the ethnic self. Overall, this manuscript provides another chapter within the general area of American literary studies, and those readers interested in this—whether they are students of Jewish American literature, Holocaust studies, multicultural canons, or postmodern fiction—will discover in *Unfinalized Moments* an illustration of those tendencies that have helped to define American literary history. Taken as a whole, its contributors provide an instructive journey through the ongoing literary, critical, and cultural debates within Jewish American studies, as well as detailed readings of the authors who most clearly illustrate its various contemporary forms.

In a 2001 interview, Cynthia Ozick (one of the more formidable writers from the previous generation) comments on Howe's belief that Jewish American material was disappearing: "I always thought that the subject matter would always be there, because the issue is existential, not sociological. Now along comes this next generation of Jewish writers, and sure enough, they are interested in the existential questions of Judaism. It's very unexpected; if Howe were alive I think he would be amazed."[28]

An unfinalized moment indeed.

Notes

1. Irving Howe, Introduction, in *Jewish-American Stories*, ed. Irving Howe (New York: Mentor-New American Library, 1977), 16. Hereafter cited parenthetically within the text.
2. Ruth Wisse, "American Jewish Writing, Act II," *Commentary* (June 1976): 40, 45, hereafter cited parenthetically. It is interesting to note that almost fifteen years later, in *The Modern Jewish Canon: A Journey Through Language and Culture* (New York: Free Press-Simon, 2000), the "youngest" or most recent Jewish American authors Wisse discusses are Philip Roth and Cynthia Ozick. At no point does she mention, even in passing, the more prominent writers born after 1933. Even the older "young" writers at that time—e.g., Max Apple, Mark Helprin, Nessa Rapoport—fall short of citation. This is a notable omission, given the fact that by 2000 many of these writers, including the younger Allegra Goodman and Michael Chabon, had already been

collected, anthologized, and seriously critiqued for quite some time. Wisse would not necessarily have to place these writers within her Jewish "canon" (and of course, the issue of canonicity is problematic in and of itself). However, it would have been useful for her to note the growing presence, however minimal in her eyes, of a generation of writers coming after, yet highly influenced by, Roth and Ozick. The closest she comes is to state in a postscript that her book "is only a signpost on an unfinished road" (347).

3. Leslie Fiedler, "Growing Up Post-Jewish," in *Fiedler on the Roof: Essays on Literature and Jewish Identity* (Boston: Godine, 1991), 117.
4. Nessa Rapoport, "Summoned to the Feast," in *Writing Our Way Home: Contemporary Stories by American Jewish Writers* (New York: Schocken, 1992), xxx.
5. Thane Rosenbaum, "The Jewish Literary Revival," *Tikkun*, November-December, 1997, 33. According to Janet Handler Burstein, in "Recalling Home: American Jewish Women Writers of the New Wave," *Contemporary Literature* 42 (2001): 802-03, Rosenbaum was the first to apply the term "new wave" to Jewish American writing of the 1980s and 1990s. However, such an easily applicable term is many times applied to a new creative phenomenon.
6. Morris Dickstein, "Ghost Stories: The New Wave of Jewish Writing," *Tikkun*, November-December, 1997, 34.
7. Melvin Jules Bukiet, "Machers and Mourners," *Tikkun*, November-December, 1997, 76.
8. Steve Stern, "After the Law," *Tikkun*, November-December, 1997, 47.
9. Sanford Pinsker, "Post-Holocaust Literature," *Tikkun*, November-December, 1997, 50-51. The term "post-Holocaust fiction" was in common use well before Pinsker's piece, sometimes but not always applied to the writings of survivors' children. For an alternative way of signifying this fictional genre, see Marianne Hirsch's use of the term "post-memory" in "Family Pictures: *Maus*, Mourning, and Post-Memory," *Discourse* 15, no. 2 (1992-93): 3-29.
10. The one possible exception to this is Mark Shechner. While acknowledging renewed emphases in contemporary Jewish American writing, he notes ambivalently that "the present situation . . . can be read as a diaspora Babel and a token of deterioration, or as a sign that in the long progression from tribe to culture to civilization the Jews have at last attained the diversity, the complexity, and the inner dynamism of a full civilization. The corollary is that we are not likely to again see anything like a unified vision of culture from our writers or even a 'Jewish' school of writing." Mark Shechner, "Is This Picasso, or Is It the Jews?: A Family Portrait at the End of History," *Tikkun*, November-December, 1997, 41.
11. Alan L. Berger, *Children of Job: American Second-Generation Witnesses to the Holocaust* (Albany: State University of New York Press, 1997).
12. Alan L. Berger and Gloria L. Cronin, *Jewish American and Holocaust Literature: Representations in the Postmodern World* (Albany: State University of New York Press, 2004).
13. Janet Handler Burstein, *Telling Little Secrets: American Jewish Writing since the 1980s* (Madison: University of Wisconsin Press, 2006).
14. Sidra DeKoven Ezrahi, *Booking Passage: Exile and Homecoming in the Modern Jewish Imagination* (Berkeley: University of California Press, 2000); and Janet Handler Burstein, "Recalling Home: American Jewish Women Writers of the New Wave," *Contemporary Literature* 42 (2001): 800-24.
15. Lois Rubin, ed., *Connections and Collisions: Identities in Contemporary Jewish-American Women's Writing* (Newark, DE: University of Delaware Press, 2005).

16. Andrew Furman, *Contemporary Jewish American Writers and the Multicultural Dilemma: Return of the Exiled* (Syracuse: Syracuse University Press, 2000).
17. And this number does not even reflect recent collections that are strictly genre-based. See, for instance, mystery fiction collections by Lawrence W. Raphael, ed., *Mystery Midrash: An Anthology of Jewish Mystery & Detective* Fiction (Woodstock, VT: Jewish Lights, 1999) and Lawrence W. Raphael and Laurie King, eds., *Criminal Kabbalah: An Intriguing Anthology of Jewish Mystery & Detective Fiction* (Woodstock, VT: Jewish Lights, 2001); Jack Dann's edited collections of science fiction/fantasy, *Wandering Stars: An Anthology of Jewish Fantasy and Science Fiction* (Woodstock, VT: Jewish Lights, 1998), and *More Wandering Stars: An Anthology of Outstanding Stories of Jewish Fantasy and Science Fiction* (Woodstock, VT: Jewish Lights, 1999); and even the adolescent fiction found in Sandy Asher, ed., *With All My Heart, With All My Mind: Thirteen Stories About Growing Up Jewish* (New York: Simon & Schuster, 1999). In his *Tikkun* piece, Mark Shechner mentions the prominence of Jewish romance fiction, so perhaps this is another genre in which we may soon see a compilation.
18. Hilda Raz, ed., *The* Prairie Schooner *Anthology of Contemporary Jewish American Writing* (Lincoln: University of Nebraska Press, 1998).
19. Ilan Stavans, ed., *The Oxford Book of Jewish Stories* (New York: Oxford University Press, 1998).
20. Gerald Shapiro, ed., *American Jewish Fiction: A Century of Stories* (Lincoln: University of Nebraska Press, 1998); Melvin Jules Bukiet and David G. Roskie, eds., *Scribblers on the Roof: Contemporary Jewish Fiction* (New York: Persea, 2006).
21. Melvin Jules Bukiet, ed., *Neurotica: Jewish Writers on Sex* (New York: Norton, 1999).
22. Melvin Jules Bukiet, ed., *Nothing Makes You Free: Writings by Descendants of Jewish Holocaust Survivors* (New York: Norton, 2002).
23. Jules Chametzky, John Felstiner, Hilene Flanzbaum, and Kathryn Hellerstein, eds., *Jewish American Literature: A Norton Anthology* (New York: Norton, 2001).
24. Paul Zakrzewski, ed., *Lost Tribe: Jewish Fiction from the Edge* (New York: Harper, 2003). One of the collection's main marketing strategies is apparently the Lower East Side-flavored "raw, dark, sometimes outrageous" content of its stories (back cover). True or not, this attitude reflects the feel of *Heeb* magazine, which calls itself "The New Jew Review." As its Web site describes it, the magazine is "an ambitious antitrust investigation into the monopoly on God. It is a sweaty prizefight between hip-hop and sushi in this corner and klezmer and kugel in the other. It is the bastard love child of Emma Goldman and Lenny Bruce. It is a plague on modern day pharaohs replete with miraculous jailbreaks and a nice little riot or two. It is a Carnival cruise to the Garden of Eden with all-you-can-eat cheesecake and Parliament as the house band. Hallelujah." Or, put more succinctly, as the editors say of themselves, "We're the kids your rabbis warned you about" ("What Is?" *Heeb Magazine*, Nov. 10, 2003, http://www.heebmagazine.com/whatis.php).
25. Derek Parker Royal, ed., *Jewish Comics*. Special issue of *Shofar* 29, no. 2 (2011).
26. M. M. Bakhtin, *Problems of Dostoevsky's Poetics*, ed. and trans. Caryl Emerson (Minneapolis : University of Minnesota Press, 1984), 166.
27. M. M. Bakhtin, *The Dialogic Imagination: Four Essays*, ed. Michael Holquist, trans. Caryl Emerson and Michael Holquist (Austin: University of Texas Press, 1981), 37.
28. Quoted in Calev Ben-David, "Guardian Angel," *Jerusalem Post Magazine*, June 1, 2001, 10.

Part 1

Dialogues with Orthodoxy and History

"Hardly There Even When She Wasn't Lost": Orthodox Daughters and the "Mind-Body Problem" in Contemporary Jewish American Fiction

Susan Jacobowitz

In *The Mind-Body Problem* (1983), Rebecca Goldstein sets out to explore what she describes as the "mind-body problem," the dichotomy between being perceived as either attractive or intellectual when the two are polarized and seen as mutually exclusive. Her protagonist, Renee Feuer, is a graduate student in philosophy who comes from an Orthodox Jewish background. On a superficial level, her problem revolves around not being taken seriously in the secular, academic world because she is attractive. One of her friends, Ava, addresses this problem by resorting to "intentional uglification." She doesn't want to look "pretty" or "feminine" because "feminine is dumb."[1] Ava has internalized the mind-body problem and come up with her own solution. She feels that she must sacrifice being attractive in order to be taken seriously.[2]

Renee is very attractive, so it is questionable whether or not gaining fifteen pounds or wearing an unbecoming hairstyle would provide the answer for her. But Renee, like Ava, has been very successful as a student, graduating summa cum laude from Barnard and getting accepted into a doctoral program at Princeton. She seems to feel a little overwhelmed and describes feeling "marginalized" as a first-year graduate student, but she doesn't cite any specific examples as to how she has been dismissed or denigrated because she is a woman. The problems that lead to her abandoning her program seem to have more to do with her own feelings of ambivalence about studying philosophy. She never seems clear about what kind of contribution she would like to make within her field, or how she envisions fitting into the world of philosophy as a practitioner. Despite Renee's constant references to various philosophic theories, there is a striking lack of commitment; her interest seems almost desultory. There is never any discussion after she marries about whether or not she will continue with her training. Her husband doesn't voice any objection, yet she seems almost eager and relieved to have an excuse to give it up. Again, the mind-body problem is something that Renee has internalized; it doesn't have to be imposed. Even though she feels marginalized and self-conscious about being a woman in a "man's world," nobody is refusing to take her seriously. Renee refuses to take herself seriously. Her problem seems to stem from something that she hasn't resolved from the past.

This culturally induced internalization seems to be the significant mind-body problem at the heart of *The Mind-Body Problem*, and it is a problem which is not unique to Goldstein's work. Just as Ava feels that women must choose mind or body and present themselves as one or the other, Renee sees the rest of the world in terms of mind or body. She chooses a husband for herself who is almost pure mind, pure secular Jewish mind.[3] Renee experiences the world as polarized. One of the significant divisions for her has to do with religion, with its Orthodox (Jewish) and secular binary. She comes from a tradition that instilled in her a mind-body problem, a tradition that privileged the former over the latter and tended to associate, arguably exclusively, men with mind and women with body. Renee's Orthodox parents weren't hoping for a daughter who would be mentally impaired, or who would experience some kind of low functioning or incapacitation. But they did raise her in an atmosphere in which female independence, achievement, and ambition were all viewed as problematic. Renee can escape the Orthodox world in which she was raised but it's much more difficult, if not impossible, for her to escape the value system she has internalized and which, in turn, she projects out into the world around her.

Into the world of fiction then, slowly, come the daughters of the Orthodox, the inheritors of Esther Singer Kreitman's eponymous figure in *Deborah* (1946) and Anzia Yezierska's Sara Smolinsky in *Bread Givers* (1925).[4] Deborah and Sara struggled to understand their roles and the expectations of them as Jewish daughters while trying to make choices that acknowledged their own desires, choices that brought them into confrontation with the traditional Jewish world. Daughters like Renee and Rachel, the protagonist of Goldstein's short story, "Rabbinical Eyes" (1993), are estranged either from Judaism, their families, or both. Often the daughters of the Orthodox are depicted as confused and deliberating and almost all of them are in at least some degree of emotional confusion and pain. These modern authors try to analyze and enter into a deeper understanding of the roots of that pain. In short stories by Sarah Hamer-Jacklyn ("My Mother's Dream" [1954 in Yiddish; 1994 in English]), Pearl Abraham ("The Engagement" [1995], later expanded into *The Romance Reader* [1995]) and Tova

Reich ("The Lost Girl" [1995]) we meet the daughters of the "ultra-Orthodox."[5] These authors take up where the chroniclers of Jewish "daughterhood" from an earlier age left off. Yet the issues remain the same: What are the expectations of Jewish daughters? How are they valued, and how do they perceive their own roles? What are the choices and opportunities afforded daughters? Contemporary authors explore these dilemmas through their reenvisioning and reanalysis of the mind-body problem.

The estrangement of women from Judaism may trace back to the very beginning, to the central event that established the Jewish people: the giving of the Torah and the entry into the covenant at Sinai. In Exodus 19:15, Moses warns, "Be ready for the third day; do not go near a woman." Judith Plaskow labels Moses's admonition a paradigm of what she has called "the profound injustice of Torah itself," arguing, "Although the verse hardly can be blamed for women's situation, it sets forth a pattern recapitulated again and again in Jewish sources. Women's invisibility at the moment of entry into the covenant is reflected in the content of the covenant which, in both grammar and substance, addresses the community as male heads of household. It is perpetuated by the later tradition, which in its comments and codifications takes women as objects of concern or legislation but rarely sees them as shapers of tradition and actors in their own lives."[6] Women are often treated within Jewish law, within *halakhah*, in terms of their bodies rather than in terms of their minds.[7]

Orthodox feminist Blu Greenberg suggests that part of the problem in terms of *halakhah* seems to be women's "exemption" from observing the "fixed-time" commandments.[8] She writes, "From the exemption of women from *tefillin* the rabbis derive several other exemptions: counting the *omer*, hearing the *shofar*, and reciting the *Shema*. That women were not considered part of the *minyan* also is derived rabbinically from the laws of women and *tefillin*" (82). From the point of view of many women, exemption equals exclusion.[9] Intelligent, committed Orthodox Jewish women often feel marginalized when it comes to leadership roles within their own communities: they cannot be counted as part of a *minyan*, cannot be ordained and cannot read from the Torah at the *bimah*. The fact that women's less central position is encoded in the interpretation of Jewish law reinforces the magnitude of the problem. It explains why it has been so difficult for even very accomplished women to try and fight for equal status and the right to equal participation within traditional communities.[10] This may be one reason why Ava and Renee despair of ever being taken seriously in the world of academe; they come from a tradition where their status has been viewed as lower than that of the "adult free male."[11] They would never even have tried to push for equality in the Orthodox Jewish communities in which they were raised, as such a thing would have been understood to be impossible.

Just as Plaskow traces the alienation of women within Judaism back to the very birth of the Jewish people as a people, for female protagonists in works of fiction and memoir the alienation often traces back to their understanding of their own births and their receptions within their own family systems. In *The Mind-Body Problem*, Renee recounts, "My mother has probably worried about my virginity since the moment the doctor announced I was a girl (and after she had prayed for nine months for the blessing of a male firstborn)."[12] In traditional Judaism, the birth of a son is celebrated with a *brit milah* (ritual circumcision) at eight days and with a *pidyon ha-ben* (ransoming ceremony) as well if the son is a first son; there are no established rituals to mark or celebrate the birth of a daughter.

In Hamer-Jacklyn's story, "My Mother's Dream," a woman in the Old World living among the Hasidim is under tremendous pressure to produce a son after giving birth to several daughters. Her mother-in-law tells the pregnant woman's oldest daughter, "If your mother has another girl, your value will diminish."[13] The child feels immense pity for her father, who collapsed, "confused, bitter, silent" (67), upon receiving the news of the last daughter's birth. With terrifying prescience, the child's grandfather tells her that she should be praying not for a brother, but for her mother to come through her pregnancy safely (68-69). Knowing there is something wrong, the mother starts to teach her oldest daughter how to be a *baleboste* (maid, housekeeper), her replacement. She dies after a terrible hemorrhage (72-73). Instead of getting together to grieve or sit *shiva* (the traditional period of mourning) with the family, a group of Hasidic men come to hold a ceremony, a "trial" (73), over the dead body of the woman, to command her to give up the body of the child still inside her. In death, as in life, the woman's status as body is confirmed. She is nothing more than a vessel containing what might have been life and, perhaps even more importantly, potential male life.

In Goldstein's *The Mind-Body Problem*, Renee is a graduate of a religious *Bais Ya'akov* secondary school. In Abraham's "The Engagement" and Reich's "The Lost Girl," religious secondary schools for women feature prominently as well. One protagonist is a teacher at such a school while the other is a student. The women have access to and are involved in education, ostensibly involving the mind, but it is not enough to get them over their binary problem, the problem of being perceived as either mind or body.

In her fiction, Goldstein deliberately creates female protagonists who are high achieving in the secular world. For example, Renee's scholarly achievements are paralleled in "Rabbinical Eyes" by Rachel's success at Harvard Law School and as an attorney. Both women love their fathers, which should perhaps also signal a love for and acceptance of the God of their fathers. Yet both reject Judaism in a sense as they intermarry: Renee with Noam, a completely a-religious assimilated Jew, and Rachel with Luke, a Christian "Semitophile"[14] and son of a minister. The high achievement in the secular world is meant to contrast with the traditional position of women in Judaism, particularly with regard to religious education. According to Jonathan Sacks:

> The Talmud (Kiddushin 29b) cites a verse from the Shema, "And you shall teach them to your children." But the sages chose to interpret the word

> *beneikhem* as "your sons" rather than "your children," although the word might mean either . . . In the Mishnah, Ben Azzai rules *Chayyav adam lelamed et bito Torah*, "It is incumbent upon every individual to teach his daughter Torah" (Sotah 3:4). But Rabbi Eliezer says, *Hamelamed et bito Torah, melamdah tiflut*, "Anyone who teaches his daughter Torah is teaching her immorality" or "nonsense." Although this is the same Rabbi Eliezer ben Hyrcanus who lost another important debate with the sages, in this case it was his opinion that was adopted as normative by the halakhah.[15]

Rabbi Eliezer writes, "The words of the Torah should be burnt rather than be taught to women."[16]

In *The Mind-Body Problem*, Renee's brother Avram learns in a *kollel* as an adult, but it was always Renee who showed academic promise when they were children. Her mother used to hide her report cards so as not to discourage Avram (75). Renee's mother felt that Renee's scholastic achievements were attributable to some kind of flamboyance or showing off; she could only understand and approve of Renee's intellectual gifts in the context that they had been given to her so that an intelligent husband might be attracted to her (57). Renee feels that her mother always favored Avram, and that she could never please her (169). Rather than exclusion and discrimination bringing about solidarity between the two women, it seems to result in their being alienated from each other, perhaps because Renee wants to avoid being grouped with her mother and sharing her fate through replicating her life choices. When Renee longs for her Jewish roots, it is her father's world she visualizes (123). Her father was a teacher of young boys who worked at preparing them for the *bar mitzvah* ceremony, and his specialty was hard-to-teach boys, boys with emotional and behavioral problems or learning disabilities. At the same time, he had a brilliant daughter at home whom he did not teach. The implication is that the most unpromising or most severely challenged boy is eligible for participation and acceptance in Jewish communal life in a way that the most capable girl is not.

In Abraham's "The Engagement," about a match made for a seventeen-year-old Hasidic girl who teaches secular subjects at a Hasidic girls' school, the protagonist's mother has to field pointed questions from the *shadkhan* (marriage broker) about her daughter's intelligence.[17] Rachel's reading, symbolizing her mind, isn't her parents' only problem. A more serious situation arises around body when Rachel is caught wearing pantyhose without seams. Rachel's father is shocked by her immodesty and feels that her reputation has been compromised to such an extent that she will have to accept a marriage proposal from the first man who comes along (38).

In "Rabbinical Eyes," Rebecca Goldstein's protagonist Rachel's father is not afraid to teach his daughter Talmud. Growing up in a remote, rural area, Rachel and her brother rely on their parents to teach them all of the Jewish subjects. She recounts:

> My father studied Talmud with me just as hard and as long as with Gideon. I know that Orthodox Jews are rumored to be sexist. Hell, it's no rumor . . . I've read some of the angry literature that's been put out recently by Jewish feminists. And truly there seems to be a lot to be angry about. All I can say is that the kind of mindless dismissal of girls that seems to typify certain parts of the Orthodox Jewish world simply wasn't my experience at all. If anything, my father worked me a little harder than he did Gideon, because I had so much *sitzfleisch*, staying power.[18]

In Rachel's case, it hardly seems to matter. The religious education she has received and participated in the development of her mind does not keep her from being perceived as body. Her father does not teach or include her in everything. In fact, he leaves out something very essential: the connection to Judaism and God that he experiences through the ritual of daily prayers.

In the same way that Renee can't re-create a *Shabbat* atmosphere through preparing a traditional meal of *cholent* and *challah* in *The Mind-Body Problem*, Rachel in "Rabbinical Eyes" can't re-create the atmosphere of her father in prayer because she doesn't know how to pray. She describes "catching" him in the morning when she has to enter the dining room to retrieve a textbook that she needs for school. He seems so emotional; she wishes she had asked him "what it was he did when he prayed."[19] Her father taught her Talmud, but he did not give her the kind of inclusive education he would have given her had she been a boy and truly mind over body. There is something essential about Rachel's father's faith that he has not been able to share with his daughter.

In Judaism, God is often described as "the God of our fathers."[20] Rachel and Renee are not only estranged from the God of their fathers, they are both estranged from their literal fathers. In "Rabbinical Eyes," Rachel's family rejects her when she intermarries. They sit *shiva* for her as if she had died. The estrangement takes on an especially tragic dimension when Rachel and Luke's daughter is born with Jewish eyes, the same "rabbinical eyes" that Rachel has, but with some kind of mysterious ailment that cannot be named or diagnosed. The baby looks perfect, but does not and seemingly will not develop. Because Rachel and her father did not pray together, she is cut off from a certain kind of hope and comfort her religious tradition might have provided had she been able to tap into the source. Rachel dreams that her father's acceptance of her husband and family could somehow restore her child to health and so to her.[21]

There is such an emphasis on body for the Jewish woman in *The Mind-Body Problem* that Renee, like Rachel, swings the other way and tries to focus almost exclusively on mind. "I had always thought of intelligence as power, the supreme power," she admits (96). Renee sees that women are in an inferior position with regard to the spiritual and the intellectual. "For Jews," she relates, "learning is the highest spiritual activity, but one from which women are barred" (64). She focuses on learning and the mind, albeit in a secular setting, to such a degree that she becomes estranged from her own body. "I was every bit as unsexual as Noam," she relates, "more so really, since *my* body, in which I was lodged like an ice cube in a furnace, never took over" (89). It seems that Renee sacrificed body for mind. Although she tries to reject her mother's conservative sexual views, she internalizes them as well. When her Orthodox brother and his bride Tzippy hold a handkerchief over the *mechitzah* (partition) at their wedding, she writes: "I watched them and was filled with disgust at my own life, which, in the glow of their purity, seemed dirty and sordid" (65).

Aviva Cantor has theorized that one of the reasons why Jewish patriarchy oppressed women with such vigor was because of the emasculation of the Jewish male.[22] The three fathers presented in *The Mind-Body Problem*, "Rabbinical Eyes," and "The Engagement" all reflect a kind of emasculation; they are somewhat out of touch with the modern world, ineffectual and incompetent as breadwinners. In Goldstein's novel, Renee writes, "My father's lack of ambition was an acid eating at my mother's life" (58). Rachel's father in "Rabbinical Eyes" is a Holocaust survivor, a remnant of a defunct *yeshiva*, who didn't really fit in anywhere and so was itinerant, unable to find a permanent place or secure a strong foothold within a community. Feigie Singer, in Tova Reich's "The Lost Girl," is the last of thirteen children, with a poor father who barely makes enough money selling fruits and vegetables door to door to enable his family to survive. Housewives buy from him "out of pity."[23]

Some argue that Orthodoxy validates the importance of the woman's role within the family. One example of this might be Avram's wife Tzippy in *The Mind-Body Problem*; she is romanticized as an Orthodox woman who is ignorant intellectually but doesn't need education or access to power since she has faith and is very loving. Others find women's unequal status disturbing. Both Orthodox men and women live according to a number of codified rules and restrictions, yet the restrictions for women focus almost exclusively on their physicality and sexuality.[24] In "The Engagement," Rachel contemplates rebellion. She doesn't tell her parents, but she decides that after she is married, she won't wear a hat over her wig. "I don't even want to wear a wig," Rachel muses. "I think if all women refused to shave and cover their heads, the rabbis would have to rethink the laws, change them. But I don't know anyone who agrees with me" (42).

Sam Heilman, in his ethnographic work amongst the Hasidim, observed a kind of relentless focus on the body.[25] The necessity to control sexual desire and urges created a tradition of early marriage and a society in which almost everyone had to marry. Rachel in "The Engagement" experiences the process of having a match made for her as depersonalizing. "I used to think things would be different for me," she muses. "That my life would be different. But it isn't. I teach grade school like all the others. I'll get engaged like all the others. Get married. Maybe it's better doing things the way everyone does. You know exactly how it goes . . . Married is the only way to live on my own, in my own apartment" (43). A match is made for Rachel in exactly the same way as it was made for her mother. Nothing awaits a girl who will not marry; she knows that there is no future for her outside of marriage, and that if she refuses one potential bridegroom, she could be saddled with another who might be even worse (38-39). Her future is dictated by her body, not her mind. She wishes she could abdicate mind in order to feel less of a conflict, less ambivalence and less frustration about being perceived as body.

The lack of individuality or sameness and the interchangeability of young women comes into play in Reich's "The Lost Girl." A girl from a Hasidic school goes missing during a Lag B'Omer outing. Rabbi Berman, the principal of the school, makes an unfortunate remark to a reporter from the *New York Times*. Because the reporter has a Jewish name, the rabbi assumes the reporter will be sympathetic and understand his point of view:

> "Look, Shmiel," he said, "we went into the woods with 300 girls and came out with 299. Now, you learned arithmetic. If you consider all girls equal, so that each one is worth the same amount of points, on a final exam that would give you a score of about 99.7 out of 100, a sure A, maybe even an A plus. Not a bad showing in anybody's book, am I right?" (62)

Rabbi Berman wonders that the disappearance of a girl like Feigie Singer could illicit such a fuss. Reich reveals, "this was a girl who scarcely made any impression at all. You barely noticed her, she was hardly there even when she wasn't lost. It was a wonder, in a way, that they even realized she was missing" (62).

Rabbi Berman is surprised that there is such excitement and exultation when Feigie is found, three days later. He urges her parents to collect notarized letters and affidavits from doctors and other "examining authorities" testifying to the fact that nothing compromising had happened to her during the three days she was alone in the woods (62). He is interested only in the lost girl's body. It is the only interest Rabbi Berman really takes in Feigie, or in any of the girls. He checks to make sure they are wearing stockings and that their earrings aren't too dangly. When he tries to make small talk to Feigie, asking her how her older sisters are doing, she knows he doesn't really remember them, that he doesn't know their names. For Rabbi Berman and, by implication, for much of the community, one young girl is pretty much like any other. His interest is intrusive and invasive. He embarrasses Feigie by asking a pointed question about what she plans to do about her pimples (63). He has a proprietary interest in Feigie's body. Everybody knows what is going on with a woman's body.[26]

In a world where women are perceived mainly through the lens of body, marriage, as Rabbi Berman and Rachel's parents in "The Engagement" envision, should provide a kind of answer or solution for women. In *The Mind-Body Problem*, even when Renee has left the traditional Jewish world of her family for Princeton, she imagines that marriage will bring status and security, that it will somehow address the things that are wrong with her life. At twenty-two, she marries a man of thirty-eight. Her husband, who has a patina of glamour due to having been a math prodigy, is in reality a depressed and insecure man who is washed up professionally; he basks in the glory of a very early mathematical breakthrough that represents a height he knows he can never again attain. In "The Engagement," Rachel agrees to marry because of the independence she imagines it will bring. "I don't care whom I marry," she thinks to herself. "Once married, I at least won't have to worry about it. Married, I'll do and wear what I want. I'll be who I am" (38). Unfortunately, she is body. Her optimism gives the tale a hopeful tone but the story's expansion, in *The Romance Reader*, shows that marriage leaves her feeling even more alienated and dependent. Her husband takes the place of her father, even adopting his distinctive style of suit. Rachel feels even more dominated and suffocated, suspecting that her husband and father are a team, even calculating when her husband should have relations with her in order to get her pregnant. Her marriage ultimately fails.

In "Rabbinical Eyes," Goldstein's Rachel marries for love, but her marriage to a Christian brings estrangement and separation from her family. She severs herself from the world of her childhood and feels somehow incomplete, full of yearning, not unlike Renee, who feels an absence and lack of fulfillment in the secular world, particularly when she thinks about the Jewish world she associated with her father. Renee tells stories of how Orthodox Jews live, what they believe, to Noam to entertain him, almost so that he can make fun of the irrationality of the world from which she comes. But she also has a fantasy of fulfillment, of bringing home a Jewish groom to her family who, with his beard and the way he moves, almost *shuckling*, as if *davening*, comes close to making her feel as if her mother's dream for her in marriage (symbolized by her first serious boyfriend, Hillel) had somehow been realized. Rachel also tells her husband Luke stories about Judaism that captivate him. He is intrigued and respectful. He offers to convert. But Rachel knows that a quick and easy Reform conversion wouldn't mean anything to her religious family. She wants her family to accept her husband as he is, and to accept her choice.

Marriage, embracing a kind of fulfillment through the destiny of body, does not seem to be the answer. It brings challenges and disappointments of its own. In "Rabbinical Eyes," the problem Rachel encounters in her marriage is that her child is born with some kind of undiagnosable defect which means that she cannot thrive. Even though her "rabbinical eyes" seem to speak of some kind of inheritance or connection to Judaism that should have been hers, she is just a body. This drives a wedge between Rachel and Luke, as Luke seems better able to accept his daughter's limitations. In Goldstein's novel, there is a wedge between Renee and her husband as well. Their marriage is sterile in more than one sense. In addition to having affairs, she gives up the idea of having a child because her husband claims that a wife is "distraction enough" for a mathematician and that a child is "out of the question" (180). There is nothing procreative about either her work, which she abandons, or her marriage, which she remains in, expressing resignation and ambivalence. Rachel in "The Engagement" is no happier in *The Romance Reader* after her marriage; she runs away, has a nervous breakdown and ends up receiving a *get* and moving back into her parents' home. Instead of embracing independence, she finds herself reinfantilized. None of these women experience through their roles as wives or mothers the longed-for completion or fulfillment.

Renee and Rachel in "Rabbinical Eyes" also experience estrangement from the Orthodox worlds of their youth. It is a world where they experience rejection by their fathers because they are daughters. Writes a woman who grew up Lubavitch:

> When I was little, I was allowed to enter the men's section with my father. Some other fathers brought in girls older than myself. When a little girl looked a little too old to be in the men's section, around ten years old, the men would become very agitated. Sometimes someone would say something to admonish her, and the big little girl would understand that she was too old to be with the men.[27]

Goldstein's protagonists, Rachel and Renee, both felt close to their fathers when they were young but became estranged from their tradition as they got older. They chose the life of the mind as characterized by higher degrees in philosophy and law. Feigie in "The Lost Girl" and Rachel in "The Engagement," born and raised in the Hasidic world, find it difficult to escape body as fate. They have nowhere to go.[28]

Renee, with all of her achievement and intelligence, seems to want to fuse mind and body, head and heart. She wants to experience faith as something organic, something heartfelt. She wants something to believe in something close to the kind of faith her father or sister-in-law Tzippy exhibit, but something that she can also tell herself is rational and of the mind. She wants an experience of faith that doesn't make unreasonable demands of her because she is a woman or impinge upon and invalidate her sense of individuality. This, within the confines of perhaps any traditional or fundamentalist religion or sect, seems impossible.[29] In addition to the problem of women being viewed primarily as body, the physical demands made of women are overwhelming as well. For Renee, it seems that they fall under the rubric of "unreasonable demands."[30]

In the Orthodox world, women experience other kinds of painful exclusions. Thena Kendall's alienation from her British Jewish community became complete when Orthodox men blocked the way to her father's grave, insisting that a woman could not be present at a burial. She made her way there using an alternative route. "With every clod that was thrown onto my father's coffin, another link that connected me to the Orthodox tradition was broken," she writes. "I would have liked to have said Kaddish for him, for he had left no son, but no Orthodox congregation would countenance a woman reciting a prayer in front of the congregation."[31] For many, the barriers to participation and acceptance prove extremely painful. As Judith Rotem argues, "The women's section in the synagogue is a symbol, and an example, of the invisible but real partition that exists in every arena of life" (138). For Rachel in "Rabbinical Eyes" and for Renee in *The Mind-Body Problem*, it's hard to envision that there could be any breaching of that wall, any road that they could find back or any tools that they could use to forge a different kind of more fulfilling relationship with the traditional Jewish worlds they were a part of when they were young.

Renee envies the certainty her brother and his wife Tzippy seem to represent. Renee is married to Noam, a Jewish man, but he is not religiously observant. Curiously, she both romanticizes and abhors her tradition and what its values dictate. The certainty expressed through religious life and the meaning observance can bring in the presence of such belief has no exact correspondent in the secular world. Those who are secular ("rational") are left embracing the unknown and longing at times for the kind of certainty they might once have known in the worlds of which they might once have been a part. This kind of romanticizing of an imagined past may be one reason for the recent "*baal teshuvah*" movement which motivates some secular Jews to "return" to a more traditionally observant Jewish life. For women, this often means relinquishing the challenges of mind in favor of the perceived simplicity of body.

Jewish daughters are not the only women facing the mind-body dilemma. But in the depictions of the daughters of the Orthodox in modern American fiction, reservations and dilemmas are given voice and made real. The mind-body dilemma, which can also be characterized as a religious-secular dilemma, is never fully and satisfactorily resolved. Without balance or resolution, none of the protagonists seem completely comfortable with their choices or hopeful about the future. For Renee in *The Mind-Body Dilemma* and Rachel in "Rabbinical Eyes," embracing mind means abandoning body. There is no joy in sex for Renee, who is involved in a loveless and barren relationship about which she feels powerfully ambivalent. She has mixed feelings about Judaism, rejecting the world of her parents while also longing at times for the world represented by her more observant brother and his wife. She does marry a Jewish man but, because her husband does not want children, there will be no perpetuation of Judaism through descendants.

Rachel in "Rabbinical Eyes" is left in a similar situation. Even though her father taught her Talmud and they learned together, her relationship to her religion is problematic. She never entered into her father's emotional and sustaining world of prayer. Not wanting to be seen only as body, she embraces the world of the mind represented through Harvard Law School. Yet she seems cut off from the fulfillment of body in that her family rejects her when she marries and she seems unable to produce a healthy child. Her daughter's impairment in some ways seems to reflect the opposite dilemma. Rachel is mind without body; her daughter is body without mind. The metaphor of a female infant born seemingly perfect physically but unable to develop suggests it is unhealthy to categorize women as pure body. The infant represents the impairment of body without mind, similar to the image of the dead mother in Hamer-Jacklyn's "My Mother's

Dream." There can be no full life or any delivery of life where the mind and being are not also present. The dilemmas of both mother and child seem to suggest that, without acknowledgment and acceptance, women in Judaism cannot be seen to be or made to be fully whole, alive and functioning. Rachel cannot find a balance between the world of the mind and the world of the body, and so she suffers. She fantasizes that her two families, her birth family and the family she creates with Luke, could be joined. She dreams that her father's embrace—the embrace of her past, her religion, her heritage—and acceptance could somehow heal and restore her daughter so that there could be a deeper connection between mother and daughter as well as the possibility of inheritance between father and daughter. But she also knows that what she longs for is impossible.

Rachel in *The Romance Reader* is left to find a place in her conservative religious family and community as a divorced woman, a kind of pariah. Her future seems very uncertain; she seems almost to lurk in the household of her youth, observing from a distance the matches being arranged for her younger siblings. In terms of embracing either the life of the body or the life of the mind, Abraham's Rachel seems almost to be in stasis, to be undecided. Having rejected the marriage that was arranged for her, it is uncertain what might come next for an intelligent young woman who was always questioning and struggling, reading voraciously, teaching secular subjects at a religious girls' school by the age of seventeen, and somehow even managed to evade the strictures of her father and her community long enough to become certified as a lifeguard and work at a public pool. Rachel's world seems to hold out little hope for the possibility of balance between mind and body. Neither does Feigie's; she seems to radiate a poignant hopelessness and despair. As Rabbi Berman puts it, such young women are hardly present even when they aren't lost.

A more recent text could stand as a possible coda to this mind-body problem. In Allegra Goodman's *Kaaterskill Falls* (1998), Elizabeth Shulman is an observant Jewish woman from Manchester, England, living in America. She is forced by a *rav*, the religious leader of her community, to give up a grocery store and catering business she built and loved in their summer community of Kaaterskill Falls. Like Rachel in "The Engagement," Elizabeth is a voracious reader of literature who sometimes has to defend her passion. Like the mother in "My Mother's Dream" who dies while pregnant, Elizabeth gives birth only to girls. When she delivers her sixth, she knows her husband is disappointed. Goodman writes:

> Elizabeth is disappointed too. She feels it more than she used to, the difficulty with girls, the confining of expectations. The difficulty that they are expected to be careful always and responsible, practical, nothing more . . . The Kehilla is a tight little world, and a tighter one for women. A narrow place. Always safe and binding.
>
> Elizabeth looks at the infant lying there. She is sound asleep, even though her parents do not have a girl's name. Of course, the baby does not care that

> she has no name. She sleeps there with all her life before her. And yet so much has already been decided. Elizabeth feels that now.
>
> On other nights like this she felt differently. What futures she had imagined for her daughters. What careers. They seem in retrospect like wild fantasies. She gave her girls English names, grand, she thought, sophisticated. Annette, and Margot, Roweena, Sabrina, and Bernice. It seems quixotic now, the way she used to sit with the children in the dark. On the edges of their beds she used to dream about her daughters; she used to spin lives for them out of books. As if the girls could be part one thing and part another, take flight from the rooftops of the brick apartment buildings and soar through the night sky—journalists, travelers, philosophers—and then somehow return home, floating down as in fairy tales, gliding down over the Heights, television aerials barely touching their feet.[32]

Elizabeth feels the mind-body dilemma within her community: she chafes under but accepts its prohibitions, restrictions, and limitations. Her perceived purpose is not entrepreneurial but domestic. Her relationship to Judaism is different from her husband's. "The Rav's authority is not a matter of politics to Isaac," Goodman writes. "And following the Rav is, and always will be for Isaac, an issue of aspiring to the best life. Elizabeth had been innocent like this, but curious. She envies her husband his devotion" (310). The way in which the Rav shut down Elizabeth's business, in effect, stifling her, challenged her faith. But unlike Rachel in "Rabbinical Eyes," Elizabeth had a deeper connection to her religion through prayer:

> Elizabeth will pray in the house as soon as she can, in the time she finds. She will not put on tefillin, but, like Isaac, she will bind herself with the commandments. She will not fold herself in a tallis, but like him, she will fold herself in prayer. She will never cast the life away. But when, she wonders, will she view the pattern of her days as brightly, or say her prayers as gratefully? When will she observe the holidays with the pleasure of past years? When will she cook again with such joy? (294-95)

Elizabeth will not break from her community, but she imagines that her daughters will test and even breach the boundaries that she has accepted for herself, and that makes her feel hopeful.

Elizabeth has dreams for her daughters. Like her other five daughters, the new baby is given a Hebrew name, Chaya. But eventually Elizabeth goes to the hospital to fill out the baby's birth certificate. When asked how she wants the baby's first name to appear, she says, Celia. Goodman writes, "They will never use the name. No one will say the name aloud, but in sharp black print the registrar is typing onto the official New York state birth certificate, the English name Celia. C-E-L-I-A" (297). In a world full of new and better possibilities, Elizabeth's girls might have the chance to be "part one thing and part another." Mind and body might fuse; from the two parts may come wholeness. If so, Celia will be more than "hardly there"; as a "new" Jewish daughter, she will have the potential to be fully present at last.

Notes

1. Rebecca Goldstein, *The Mind-Body Problem* (New York: Penguin Books, 1983), 193-94.
2. In one sense, Ava is taken seriously even though she is a woman: her competence and intelligence so impress her advisor in graduate school that he wants to keep her as his assistant indefinitely so that she can ghostwrite his academic publications. Ava's fear seems to be that she will always be forced into a subordinate role because she is a woman in what has traditionally been viewed as a man's field.
3. Noam is so estranged from Jewish practice that he listens transfixed and incredulous as Renee tells him stories about the traditional, observant Jewish world.
4. Esther Singer Kreitman, *Deborah* (New York: St. Martin's, 1984); Anzia Yezierska, *Bread Givers* (New York: Persea, 1975).
5. Sarah Hamer-Jacklyn, "My Mother's Dream," in *Found Treasures: Stories by Yiddish Women Writers*, ed. Frieda Forman, Ethel Raicus, Sarah Silberstein Swartz and Margie Wolfe (Toronto: Second Story Press, 1994), 65-76; Pearl Abraham, "The Engagement: A Story," *Commentary* 100, no. 1 (1995): 36-44; Tova Reich, "The Lost Girl," *Harper's Magazine*, August 1995, 60-66.
6. Judith Plaskow, *Standing Again at Sinai: Judaism from a Feminist Perspective* (New York: HarperCollins, 1991), 25-26.
7. Some men object to this as well. As Jonathan Sacks puts it, "The contemporary failure of *halakhah* to respond to the rights of women . . . is a symptom of its alienation from life." *Crisis and Covenant: Jewish Thought after the Holocaust* (Manchester: Manchester University Press, 1992): 164.
8. Blu Greenberg, *On Women and Judaism: A View from Tradition* (Philadelphia: The Jewish Publication Society of America, 1981), 81. Hereafter cited parenthetically.
9. Blu Greenberg writes, "Although both positive and negative reasons have been advanced, it seems that the principle and practice of exemption generally yielded negative self-images of women regarding a discipline of steady prayer. What tilts the balance perhaps is the language of the principle itself: 'Women, slaves, and children are exempt' (Kiddushin 1:7). Of course, women are not equated with slaves or to children, but the phrase subtly suggests that, in the eyes of the *Halakhah*, women shared with slaves and children a status lower than the adult free male. Not lost on women, surely, was the realization that individual slaves and male children could grow up or out of these ascribed categories, but the entire class of women forever retained a status of 'exempt,' 'released,' 'unaccountable'" (85).
10. There is now a yearly conference in New York put on by a group called the Jewish Orthodox Feminist Alliance that tries to address some of these issues. See also Phyllis Chesler and Rivka Haut, eds., *Women of the Wall: Claiming Sacred Ground at Judaism's Holy Site* (Woodstock, VT: Jewish Lights Publishing, 2003) for descriptions of the struggles of observant Jewish women who want to pray at the Western Wall in Jerusalem and accounts like Loolwa Khazzoom's "United Jewish Feminist Front," in *Yentl's Revenge: The Next Wave of Jewish Feminism*, ed. Danya Ruttenberg (Seattle: Seal Press, 2001), 168-80.

11. Religious leaders may advocate more intense devotion to prayer for women, but women praying together at the Western Wall still get routinely harassed and attacked by their male counterparts.
12. Goldstein, *The Mind-Body Problem*, 66. Hereafter cited parenthetically.
13. Sarah Hamer-Jacklyn, "My Mother's Dream," in *Found Treasures: Stories by Yiddish Women Writers* ed. Frieda Forman, Ethel Raicus, Sarah Silberstein Swartz and Margie Wolfe (Toronto: Second Story Press, 1994), 67. Hereafter cited parenthetically.
14. Rebecca Goldstein, "Rabbinical Eyes," in *Strange Attractors* (New York: Penguin Books, 1993), 193.
15. Jonathan Sacks, ed., *Orthodoxy Confronts Modernity* (Hoboken: Ktav Publishing, 1991), 89.
16. Vanessa Ochs, *Words on Fire: One Woman's Journey into the Sacred* (San Diego: Harvest/Harcourt Brace Jovanovich, 1990), 1.
17. Pearl Abraham, "The Engagement: A Story," *Commentary* 100, no. 1 (1995): 40. Hereafter cited parenthetically.
18. Rebecca Goldstein, "Rabbinical Eyes," in *Strange Attractors* (New York: Penguin, 1993), 205-06.
19. Ibid., 212-13.
20. Melvyn Jules Bukiet, "In the Beginning Was Auschwitz," The Chronicle Review, *The Chronicle of Higher Education* 48, no. 26 (2002): B10.
21. Goldstein, "Rabbinical Eyes," 216.
22. Aviva Cantor, *Jewish Women/Jewish Men: The Legacy of Patriarchy in Jewish Life* (San Francisco: Harper San Francisco, 1995), 14.
23. Tova Reich, "The Lost Girl," *Harper's Magazine*, August 1995, 64. Hereafter cited parenthetically.
24. Maurie Sacks, ed. *Active Voices: Women in Jewish Culture* (Urbana: University of Illinois Press, 1995), 148.
25. Samuel Heilman, *Defenders of the Faith: Inside Ultra-Orthodox Jewry* (New York: Schocken Books, 1992), 308-09.
26. Observant Jewish women endure a high level of scrutiny. Some describe going to the *mikveh* (the ritual bath) as a humiliatingly public event. The *mikveh* is often right across the street from a synagogue, yeshiva, or kollel. Orthodox women are amongst the few who refuse hormone replacement therapy after they enter menopause. Freed from the duty of going to the *mikveh*, they don't want the responsibility to resume along with their restored periods.
27. Shoshana Gelerenter-Liebowitz, "Growing Up Lubavitch," in *Daughters of the King: Women and the Synagogue,* ed. Susan Grossman and Rivka Haut (Philadelphia: The Jewish Publication Society of America, 1981), 238.
28. Some religious girls' schools have no twelfth grade, to keep graduates from having the full transcripts they would need to request were they to apply to college. Some religious boys' schools discourage the earning of high school degrees for the same reason, not wanting young men to forsake *yeshiva* and *smicha* for an undergraduate degree. See Lis Harris's *Holy Days: The World of the Hasidic Family* (New York: Simon and Schuster, 1985), 239.
29. It has been argued that even men sacrifice identity and individuality in the Hasidic world. Lis Harris, who spent time amongst the Hasidim to write *Holy Days*, experienced something similar to Renee. Her rational self would "stand apart," but another part would "drift along." After attending High Holy Day services, she wrote, "For the first time, I understood why the Hasidim did not mind sacrificing their identities to

their communal world; that world *was* their identity and in the synagogue that day the congregation was so identified with God, his people, and the Torah that, like the *kabbalistic* image of a supernal man/woman larger than the universe, it seemed to fill all imaginable space" (224).

30. In just two examples, both Chaim Grade in *My Mother's Sabbath Days: A Memoir* (New York: Schocken, 1986) and Thena Kendall in "Memories of an Orthodox Youth" in Susanah Heschel's *On Being a Jewish Feminist* (New York: Schocken, 1995), 105-19 recount the grueling preparations required by their mothers with regard to getting ready for the holidays. Grade's mother and the other women in his community in Vilna were too exhausted by their preparations for Purim to attend the required *megillah* readings. Kendall's mother, also suffering from exhaustion, would fall asleep during the Passover *seder*. As one Orthodox woman in Judith Rotem's *Distant Sisters: The Women I Left Behind* (Philadelphia: The Jewish Publication Society, 1997) told her husband, "The holidays were given only to you, the men. We were given the work" (148).
31. Thena Kendall, "Memories of an Orthodox Youth," in *On Being a Jewish Feminist: A Reader*, ed. Susannah Heschel (New York: Schocken Books, 1983), 101.
32. Allegra Goodman, *Kaaterskill Falls* (New York: Dell Publishing, 1998), 282. Hereafter cited parenthetically.

Southern Discomfort: Revisiting the Jewish Question in Tova Mirvis's *The Ladies Auxiliary*

Maya Socolovsky

In January 1929, an essay entitled, "Why Are Jews Like That" appeared in *American Magazine*. The writer, a Jewish man named Lewis Browne, composed it as a response to his non-Jewish friend who had asked him, as they walked among a Jewish crowd in Manhattan, "Say, Browne, why are Jews like that?" His friend later clarified the question: "I wasn't thinking of their language or their beards. Those things, I realize, are superficial. . . . Nor was I thinking of their manners, either. No, it wasn't their manners that bewildered me, but their manner. . . . There was a queer light in their eyes, and a sort of tenseness in their bodies; *that* was what made me put my question to you." Browne's friend then addresses him further and says, "For you, too, show those characteristics to a degree. . . . You are all somehow different from the rest of us. And I'd like to know why."[1] The anxious Jewish question that tried to identify the mark or stain of even a secular and assimilated Jew such as Browne, and tried to precisely identify the signifier of difference, surfaces again and again in the late nineteenth and early twentieth centuries. The image of "the Jew" commonly appeared and developed out of journalistic, literary, and social-scientific sources as paradoxically both white and racially other, and vulgar yet highly cultivated,[2] and Jewish American writers such as Anzia Yezierska depicted their own and the mainstream's anxiety about the threat of this chameleon and shape-shifting identity in their work. The question of whether Jews could be full citizens of the state, despite their somewhat residual loyalty to something or somewhere else, has since then manifested itself, sometimes in a ghostly fashion, throughout twentieth-century Jewish American literary works: in responses to the immigrant experience, in postwar philo-Semitism and cultural assimilation, and in the narratives of lamentation that look back at the stain of the Holocaust and try to countenance its legacy for future writers. Now, in assessing the place and direction of Jewish American literature in both the canon and the classroom, literary critics have begun to notice a new trend; Derek Parker Royal, for example, writes that there is an energy in new writing that is fueled largely by "a renewed interest in Jewish religion and culture" and that "the centrifugal spin of assimilation gives way to a more centripetal pull toward ethnic definition."[3] Recent critics have also noticed a new emphasis in Jewish women's writing, specifically, a "re-creation of cultural origins through discourses on homecoming and home-space,"[4] and indeed, much of the critical work on writers such as Allegra Goodman focuses on the interplay of orthodoxy, domesticity, and feminism in her texts. While Goodman builds a reputable market for Jewish American literature in both mainstream and smaller literary circles, and forces us to recognize the uncertain place of Jewish American literature in multiethnic studies, she also creates a space—a postmillennial literary landscape—from which a newer writer such as Tova Mirvis can pose and rephrase the Jewish question.[5]

Because Mirvis sets her debut novel, *The Ladies Auxiliary* (1999) in Memphis, Tennessee, her characters inhabit an American landscape that is peripheral to the Jewish American imagination. In asking us to leave Goodman's New York and enter the South, where Jews are a tiny minority, Mirvis moves in mostly uncharted territory; historians agree that despite a long presence in the South, there is relatively little historical research on Southern Jews, and critics have commented on the paucity of texts coming out of the region.[6] Writing in 1993, Eli N. Evans asks, "Since the history of the Jews in the South is such a rich one . . . why hasn't there been more written about it? Where are the poets and playwrights, the essayists and novelists? Only a handful of novels have been written on the southern Jewish experience in the last decade . . . compared with the tremendous outpouring from the centers of Jewish life in America, it's almost negligible."[7] In crucial ways, early twentieth-century images of the Jew as paradoxically American and foreign, deviant yet normative, still haunt the Southern literary imagination and surface in Mirvis's work as questions of home and exile. *The Ladies Auxiliary* is a story about Orthodox Jewish women in Memphis whose tight-knit and closed community is thrown into disarray with the arrival of Batsheva Jacobs, a convert to Judaism. Throughout, the Ladies themselves narrate the novel, through a plural first-person "we." When Batsheva, together with her small daughter Ayala, move into the neighborhood, the Ladies are confused and upset by her strange mixture of strict orthodoxy and liberal social behavior. The novel traces the women's wary acceptance of Batsheva, and their rejection of her after her urbane approach to life and her friendship with the rabbi's son, Yosef, seem to encourage their own daughters' adolescent rebellions.

While in one way the novel presents obviously clear binaries—restrictive orthodoxy versus joyous interpretative orthodoxy, Southern conservatism versus

Northern liberalism—it also more subtly presents itself as a textual examination of the label "Jewish American." If the struggle for Jewish Americans has been to reconcile their sense of nationhood with their Judaism, in the South that struggle is readdressed as a particular source of tension between Southernness and Jewishness. Mirvis rephrases the question of what it means to be a Jew in America: what does it mean to be Jewish in the American South, with legacies from Europe, Northern America, and of course the South's own steeped history, haunting you? As the narrative voice describes it, Jewishness and Southernness blend to make "a strange new combination," and that "strangeness," reminiscent of Browne's acknowledgement of a Jewish body that is ill at ease, tense, and with a different light in its eyes, works to reassert the Southern Jew as continually in exile.[8] At the same time, true to a particular Southern desire to repress such a discomfort of exile, the community that Mirvis presents appears at first to have completely reconciled such tensions. In fact, their comfort in Memphis is so complete that there is barely a whisper of difference or anxiety, and one could argue that in this way, Mirvis already answers the Jewish question of the South: to be Jewish in the South means ignoring the question itself and refusing to acknowledge its pertinence, even and especially amidst a majority culture (the Bible Belt) that defines itself as Protestant Christian. That is, instead of confronting Southern Jewish identity as problematic, the women write it as a site of cultural assimilation. For example, the basket of food that Mrs. Levy prepares for the Sabbath and presents to Batsheva is filled with "challahs, a fried chicken, two kugels, and a dish of her famous hush puppies" (15). The novel's main action—the plot device of Batsheva's stormy arrival—upsets the complacency of the community, revealing the rippling tensions beneath the surface of their lives. Fundamentally, that tension lies in the paradoxical doubleness of the Jew seen in early twentieth-century literature, and resurfacing in the South today. In an interview, Mirvis reiterates these tensions, describing her experiences of growing up Jewish in Memphis: "We've lived here for many generations and yet, we feel a sense that we too are outsiders in some way. . . . Typical of being Southern and Jewish. So many Southern Jewish communities are very well established and go back so many years, and yet still it seems like they don't quite fit here. . . . I grew up feeling very aware of being different. At times, this was uncomfortable, always feeling like an outsider. But still, I feel deeply connected to Memphis."[9]

The novel illustrates this contradiction of connection and exile, and shows how the two oppositional forces eclipse each other. For example, when Helen Shayowitz goes shopping she feels awkward about asking the salesgirls for any help: "It was too hard to explain why her skirts needed to cover her knees, why she didn't wear dresses that dipped low in the front or that revealed her back and shoulders. It was better to be on her own" (56). She continues, "That way, no one would know that she was different from any other Memphis lady. Orthodox women could pass easily" (56). Her desire to "pass" switches on as she crosses the "city" walls of her fortressed community into mainstream Memphis, where for her, secularity functions as normative Christianity. By remaining silent, as she shops, Helen performs a form of passing, but like all gestures of passing the act is by definition imbued with a trace of difference and alterity. Because the laws of modesty prevent Helen from showing off her figure, she can only dream of "walking into shul in a tight, sequined dress or wearing a strapless gown to the school's Annual Scholarship Banquet" (58). In an extension of this fantastical scenario, she imagines how "everyone would marvel at how young Helen looked. They would exclaim that at the age of sixty-one, she looked as beautiful as she had as a teenager" (58). In this moment, her body becomes a site of longing, and in its yearning recalls the "tenseness in body" that Browne's friend detects in the Jews of early twentieth-century New York. Helen, we read, encourages her husband to wear a cap over his yarmulke when they are in public: as she says, "'It's easier this way. You don't have to worry what people are thinking. It's not like we live in New York.' In New York, there were men in yarmulkes everywhere. But not in Memphis, where most people had never seen a yarmulke. It was easier to blend in" (56). It is the act of blending and passing, however, that creates a moment of uncomfortable Southern Jewishness here, as their bodies work to make something—what that imperceptible something exactly is, is never clear—vanish. Consequently, the women walk around both at home in and exiled from their surroundings.

The tension of home and exile is also evident at the level of the text's narrative voice, as Mirvis adopts, from time to time in the novel, a particular anthropological stance that seems to explain rather than simply present Judaism to her readers. The collective narrative "we" describes the various Jewish holidays, customs, traditions, and laws as if to strangers or outsiders. This rhetorical strategy complicates Allegra Goodman's statement about her own fiction. Goodman says she herself writes, "from the inside, taking . . . an idiom in which ritual and liturgy are a natural part of my fictional world, and not anthropological objects to be translated and constantly explained,"[10] and indeed, the "Jewishness" of her New York Orthodox characters in *Kaaterskill Falls* (1998) is naturalized. In contrast to this, in Mirvis's novel Judaism is stylized, is assumed to be foreign to its readers, and with this assumption, is made foreign and other. However, although the text does not naturalize or even normalize Jewish orthopraxis, it does nevertheless centralize it by speaking it from the point of view of a first-person narrator. That is, Judaism can be described, taught, and understood, although Jewishness—as a historically anxious and racially specific body practicing Judaism in the South—still hovers uncertainly as foreign and othered.[11] For example, when Batsheva first makes an appearance, it is almost Friday night and the narrative voice slips into its explanatory descriptive mode stating, "We put on flowing skirts, silk blouses and fresh make-up. Our weeks waited for Fridays. We were commanded to set the Sabbath apart and make it holy. We have clothing we wear only on Shabbos . . . We don't turn lights on or off, don't listen to music, go to work, use our ovens, our telephones, our cars. We reserve the day for God and for family, spending those twenty-five hours between Friday's sundown and Saturday's dusk in a peaceful pattern of prayers, meals, and relaxation. The outside world vanishes, even if only for that one day" (19). In contrast, Goodman's Sabbaths in *Kaaterskill Falls* are conveyed through the characters' experiences rather than explanatory acts: as one of the men, Isaac, comes home after Friday night services, he finds the apartment "so warm and bright, the table dazzling white, the toys put away, the candles lit. Every Friday he is amazed at the transformation. The apartment is more than clean; it glows with warmth and safety."[12] Although both texts present orthodox communities, Mirvis's Southern Jewish narrative voice, explaining the letter of the law—with an emphasis on restriction—situates itself and perpetuates its own outside status, even as it speaks in the first person.

Mirvis's decision to narrate the story through a plural "we" rather than a single "I" allows the narrative voice to implicitly perform the complexity of being both at home in and alien from the South. The "we" of the orthodox Southern Jewish woman is connected to the past, and thus can feel linked to those around her through their shared cultural and racial history. Batsheva's assessment of what it means to be religious, for example, could well be a comment on the beauty and security of speaking in a communal voice: "By being Jewish, you're connected to a tradition that goes back thousands of years. You're always part of something larger than yourself" (135). Like a fortress built to protect their outsider, foreign status from outside foreign forces, the women can speak together, in apparent harmony. As the story unfolds, however, we begin to sense the various "I"s within the plural "we" and the bond of community is revealed to be, in many cases, a bind that silences difference and opposition. Naomi Eisenberg, for example, is described as being contaminated by the outside, having somehow "breathed in another world," even though like most of the women she had "gone to the Torah Academy with us, attended Stern College in New York, and after getting married, moved back home" (38). Even Jocelyn Shanzer, an otherwise exemplary woman in the community, has an anxious secret. Being observant "comes naturally to her" (61) but a remnant of her unorthodox Jewish upbringing haunts her: "there was one small thing that she couldn't bring herself to give up: shrimp salad. She ate it in secret, whenever she had the urge. She had a separate treif pot and knife she used, and she kept the finished product in a special container in the freezer, behind the frozen veal chops and broccoli florets. No one, not even her husband, knew" (61). Alternately critical, judgmental, and humorous, the narrative voice somehow understands itself to be a victim of its own plurality: articulate, outspoken, and trapped.

In only being able to articulate the women's alienation from one another by speaking in a plural voice, Mirvis reveals the limitations of such a narrative strategy, and suggests that these limitations illustrate an essential conundrum of Southern Jewish identity. That is, in building a community and home, and steeping oneself with tradition, the individual's anxiety and isolation has been eclipsed, and her exile from her own home space becomes shadowy and indistinct. Crucially, it is a Jewish exile that she can never speak of openly, as it is always shrouded behind a communal and pleasantly Southern "need to emphasize the positive" (205). Ultimately this represents the extent to which the Jewish community of the novel has assimilated into Southern culture; their mock-assimilation of manners disguises their legacy of homelessness and difference. In particular, the text figures Memphis as a Southern-Jewish home space into which the women have assimilated. Memphis becomes a Zion, the promised land of the wandering lost Jews of the South. Topographically and spiritually, Memphis is protected: "built on a bluff, a high-rising strip of land that overlooks the Mississippi River, shielding us from the tornados that sweep across Arkansas every year just as spring is around the corner. When the warning sirens ring, winds hurl and rain pounds against our thick roofs, we breathe easier up here on this God-given piece of land" (9). Here, the narrative voice signals a natural connection between man and land, creating a Southern-Jewish agrarianism in which God has chosen this holy part of Tennessee as the Jewish homeland.[13]

The descriptions of this peaceful and religious inheritance of land form the foundation of the text, smoothly combining Southern ambiances with Jewish ways of life. In the novel's Memphis, where dogwoods, magnolias, and oaks create a "thick canopy" as if to protect the community's "shul and school," and the community's houses "circle around them in homage to what is most important" (12), Southernism and Jewishness harmonize, making the Jewish question seem irreverent and paranoid. The intimate connection between land and community creates a confidence in these Southern Jews: far from being tense or uncertain in their bodies, they know and are at ease with themselves and one another. The women claim, "we knew the city as well as we knew our own faces, could map each turn and bump in the roads the way we followed the curves of our own chins" (9). For as long as their community remains undisturbed by the external forces of modernity, there is no experience of exile, and no acknowledgement of an exiled history. The narrative voice explains, "We saw ourselves as the Jerusalem of the South, our families part of a chain of Jewish Memphians that would extend into the future forever, as long and as far away as God in Heaven" (10). Memphis is so rooted in the community's sense of identity that they cannot even "imagine" what it would be like to live anywhere else (9). And like the Jerusalem of Israel—necessarily absent from this text—Memphis exerts a powerful and mythical pull that extends far beyond the region. Batsheva herself has moved from New York to Memphis in order to try to reconnect to the beauty of the safe and Southern childhood that her recently deceased husband experienced, and to provide such a home for their daughter Ayala. She says, "Before I decided to move to Memphis, I had a dream that I was standing in front of a map of the United States, closing my eyes, and placing my finger wherever it fell. No matter how many times I did it, it always landed on Memphis" (71). The Zionistic pull of

Memphis thus seems to gather its exiles home, and the text performs an alternate history in which the South becomes, in effect, the Jewish homeland.[14]

With this gesture, Mirvis's novel becomes a literary example of the kind of preordained Southern-Jewish love affair that other writers have articulated. Evans emphasizes this when he writes that "Jews and Southerners are alike—stepchildren of an anguished history" and that from the period before the Civil War, "southerners have used Old Testament analogies to portray themselves as 'the chosen people,' surrounded and outnumbered but destined to survive and triumph against overwhelming odds."[15] Furthermore, the "Southern idea of place, so rooted in the Bible, and the Jewish attachment to homeland, as old as civilization itself" easily combine, while "Christian fundamentalist passion has linked the South and the Holy Land psychologically in the soul of the South."[16] Indeed, Mirvis's characters seem to unconsciously merge Christian and Jewish Southern history and genealogy, accommodating both in order to reassert their rightful place in the South. In the text, Bessie Kimmel says, "we, of course, are from Memphis . . . Fourth generation. Our family came down right after the civil war [sic]. They were among the first Jews here, maybe even the very first, and we've been here ever since" (40-41). Bessie is not alone in driving home her birthright of this piece of Southern land. Mrs. Levy, a formidable force among the women of the community, likes to say with pride that her family "was *from* Memphis. Not just living here for a generation or two, but deeply and certainly from the innermost core of this city" (88). Insofar as these families have sprung from the earth of Tennessee, they also depend on their religious leader, the rabbi, to forge eternal links to the land. They assume that his son, Yosef, will succeed his father, "the rabbinate passed down like the kingship from David to Solomon" (37), in this way sealing the holy covenant of their Memphis homeland.

The narrative voice's construction of Memphis as Zion, its insistence on the natural, eternal, and biblical connections between selves and land, and its intimate collapse of the geography of city and body, all illustrate the Southern Jewish desire to dispel exile, even to eliminate the state of exile from history, and thus to smooth the transition to southern living. However, although the women blame Batsheva for the breakdown of their community and for their daughters' rebellions, both their exile and their denial of that exile are as deep rooted as their Jewish history in Memphis. Similarly, while Evans describes the similarities between Jews and Southerners, he also reluctantly expresses a discomfort with being Jewish in the South, and longs to resolve the conflict that, he states, "is deep in me." In his writing, Evans outlines the paradoxical position of the Jew in the South: a figure that historically has passed for white yet remained an outsider, and with related confusion, Evans seems unable to decide whether the South is a place of philo- or anti-Semitism. He states that "Jews were not aliens in the promised land" but then concedes the essential ambiguity of the Southern Jew: "I am not certain what it means to be both a Jew and a Southerner—to have inherited the Jewish longing for a homeland while being raised with the Southerner's sense of home."[17]

Mirvis's novel presents this clash of exile and rootedness when Batsheva, as a stranger and outsider, is first introduced into the Memphis community, and then later ostracized from it. In the process, the community is forced to speak of its exclusion from the mainstream South as well as its estrangement from itself. In effect, it is less important to determine whether or not the literary South loves or hates the Jew, and more interesting to acknowledge the presence of such contradictory anxieties at the edges of Mirvis's text and to read her Jewish characters' responses to this implicit doubleness. That is, even as Memphis is proclaimed to be home, it is also understood as a place of exile. Mrs. Levy, for example, has to live with the fear that none of her grown children have chosen to return to Memphis as adults. Although she talks of the practical reasons for their departures from Memphis, she "sometimes felt a fleeting fear that at the heart of these reasons lay a dissatisfaction with Memphis, that her own children found something missing in this community she had worked her whole life to build" (55). As soon as she has this thought she pushes it away: "Dissatisfied with Memphis? It was impossible" (55).[18] But the cracks are there. Other women talk more explicitly about the alienness of home: Edith Shapiro thinks to herself, "this was the South, after all; as at home as she felt down there, it didn't have the reputation for being the most accepting of regions" (157). And ultimately, the women are reminded by their much-loved rebbitzin, Mimi, that "the Torah says once someone converts, you aren't allowed to single her out and make her feel like a stranger, because we too were once strangers in the land of Egypt. And living here in Memphis, we could certainly relate to that" (92-93). As a symbol for the nonplace of Southern Jewishness, Memphis is both Jerusalem and Egypt, home and place of exile.

Yosef's departure at the end of the novel also forces the women to articulate the sense of discomfort that has always been with them: "Instead of viewing the roots we had set down here as nourishing and supporting, we tried to imagine seeing them as twisting round and round each other in overly close, strangling connections" (301). Furthermore, because community and Orthodox practice are so closely bound, having their sense of home shaken creates moments of exile from Judaism too: "All the moments of doubt that we had had over the years came together now, and we thought about how hard it sometimes was to be religious, how elusive this God of ours could be, how lonely it was to always be different" (301-02). Because the women's experience of Judaism is based largely on prohibitions, they define their Jewishness through an oppositional identity, rather than through a celebratory focus on spirituality. Specifically, the world hovering on the edges of this tightly knit community is one of normative Christianity, and it is against this world that the women continually measure themselves. For example, when describing their synagogue the narrative voice proudly asserts that it was "built by the first Jews who came to Memphis more than a hundred years before" but that this is "no ordinary shul. Instead of the simple buildings that exist in Jewish communities twice our size, we have the equivalent of a cathedral that rivals the magnificent steepled structures decorating every corner of this Bible Belt city." It "stands proudly at the center of our world like a beloved oldest son" (26). This center of home, described in terms of family and community, is also crucially signified through reference to churches and to the heavy presence of Christianity all around them.

In this way, the text suggests that the Memphian Jews are not entirely at ease either with their Jewishness or with the South; just as their women try to pass as ordinary Memphis ladies, so does their synagogue attempt to pass as a church in its architectural imitation of the mainstream. That is, the "body" of the community—the literal bodies, and the buildings that form a foundational connection to the land—exists at odds with, in tension with, and also strangely at peace with its neighboring Christian symbols.[19] Even as the women fear a certain contamination from the outside world, they absorb and assimilate aspects of the gentile Southern world. Leanna Zuckerman recognizes the irony of the community's insularity, and reads it as a form of Southern xenophobia. She thinks to herself, "maybe we were like any small town, with small town ideas and small town fears" (220). Their homogeneity and desire to protect themselves from "outsiders," while motivated by Judaic law, seems to mimic a Southern intolerance of difference. In this way, Judaism and Southernism become metaphors for one another, creating a simulacrum where, despite the adherence of each to tradition and history, there are no origins. The narrative voice observes that "we exist as a city within a city, with fortress walls surrounding us on all sides . . . The only thing that has seeped in is a southern flavor, creating a strange new combination. And after living here for so long, who can remember what originally was ours and what was theirs?" (10). In such moments of oppositional identity, the women figure themselves as minorities against a majority culture, feeling that the South has a longer history than their own Jewish history and feeling alienated from their beloved Memphis.

The narrative voice articulates many of these moments of alienation with humor, as if to understate or lighten the ladies' experience of the Bible Belt Zion that surrounds them. In one episode, the narrative voice recounts Tziporah Newburger's fear of shopping at the Piggly Wiggly. At the very thought of the place, she shudders: "She never shopped at Piggly Wiggly. Even if the store carried products that were certified kosher, she was not sure that the very name rendered the entire operation treif. She had been there once, and it was as bad as she had feared: there were giant pictures of smiling red pigs on the walls, on the shopping carts, even on the milk containers. She had felt as if they were trying to tempt her into tasting just a little bit of bacon, a single slice of ham. Her heart had raced uncontrollably and she had had to flee the building" (81). The humor of this paragraph reveals Tziporah's perception of mainstream culture as gentile, threatening, and alien. As one of the older Southern grocery chains, Piggly Wiggly's very name renders it foreign to her, and as a symbol of Southern culture, it threatens to infect her. Specifically, it is the word "pig" that signifies the store as a forbidden place. Although Tziporah is depicted as more fanatical in her adherence to orthodoxy than most of the other women, the episode nevertheless points to the various acts of translation between the Jewish and Christian worlds that all the women, to some extent, have to engage in. While Helen's response has been to try to pass herself off as a regular Memphis lady, and to participate in a moment of Christian drag, Tziporah's is to flee what she reads as the Christian world's desire to proselytize. As images of pigs smile at her from all directions, her body physically reacts as if to danger: she shudders and her heart races.

Tziporah's oppositional identity clearly defines itself through items of American popular culture that are prohibited by Judaic laws. When she sees one of the women's daughters, Shira, sitting in McDonalds eating a cheeseburger with a non-Jewish boy, she recoils: "That it was McDonalds made it worse. Big Macs seemed more nonkosher than any other food, singled out by God as the one thing above all else that we were not supposed to eat" (196). Like the phrase "Piggly Wiggly" and its associated images of pigs, the words "McDonalds" and "Big Mac" become as forbidden as the things they signify. Just as pictorial representations of pigs seem inherently unclean, so do the words themselves—the language of mainstream culture—become taboo. For Tziporah, it seems that an ancestral threat of forced conversion still hovers and threatens the very survival of her family, her religion, and her community, making her somewhat paranoid. Other women in the community, however, take on icons of popular culture and convert them to Judaism. Mrs. Levy is pleased to order, each year around the time of Sukkot, decorations from a catalog that specializes in out-of-season Christmas ornaments, thinking to herself that "no one would guess that the blue-and-white metallic stars she hung were intended for something else entirely" (147). Similarly, she starts organizing an annual Memphis-in-May Kosher Barbeque Contest because "the rest of Memphis had its contest the first weekend in May, and chefs came from all over the world to prepare hundreds of pigs for the roast. Mrs. Levy had spent years watching the city go all out for an event that, because we were kosher, we couldn't be part of, and she hated being left out of such a big to-do" (238). Rather than feeling terrorized by the sound and connotations of the word "barbeque" Mrs. Levy organizes her own contest where they barbeque brisket.

Despite their different responses to the Christian world on the edge of their own, both Mrs. Levy and Tziporah engage in forms of oppositional identity. Mrs. Levy's mimicry of popular culture assumes an origin based on normative Christianity; the very act of copying the mainstream, by definition, reminds her that the authentic item at the center of the world she imitates has to remain prohibited and beyond her reach. And Tziporah's own religious fervor becomes ironically expressed through the very language of Christian evangelicism that she so fears. When she sees the daughters of the community straying, Tziporah thinks to herself, "Perhaps the recent problems with the girls were even God's way of telling us that we were too lax." She imagines that "by pointing this out, [she] could strengthen her own position of communal role model. She would be like a commander in God's army, offering sustenance and support to His weary troops" (208). Although she trembles at the words "Big Mac," she envisions herself as the military leader of an army of God, a Christian rather than Jewish trope, and has to be reminded by Mimi that "there's a difference between working on our own observance and working on other people's observance" (209). For Tziporah, the former's Jewish spirit has merged with the latter's Christian influence.

Batsheva's arrival in the small Jewish community of Memphis forces the women's experience of alienation out into the open, despite their attempts to draw even tighter lines around the mythical stance of Memphis as Zion. On the surface, Batsheva's threat is that of difference; beneath the surface, she frightens the women as her presence reveals the unknowability of everything they have always found most familiar. Her dress, although still adhering to orthodox rules of modesty, is more provocative than theirs, and her "white-blond hair" (12) stands out. Right away they know that "Batsheva wasn't one of us" (12). Their anxiety is in part fuelled by suspicion at her being a convert to Judaism: she is rootless, apparently from nowhere and everywhere (she says, "I'm a mix of a lot of different places" [40]), and despite her adherence to the laws of Judaism, she fails, in their eyes, to belong. Implicitly, the narrative voice suggests that her failure to fit in is due to their impenetrable mix of Southernism and Judaism. Nevertheless, Batsheva is an Orthodox Jew, and thus her presence forces them to face versions of the Jewish question that they have up until now repressed: How can Batsheva be a Southern Jew if she was not born a Southern Jew of long lineage? Is Southern Judaism refigured as a "race," a religion, a practice, or a culture, and how does it manifest itself against the mainstream? How does a Southern Jew reconcile the state's definition of itself as Christian with his or her own practice of Judaism? Batsheva represents a frightening ambiguity, and her doubts, questions, and self-perception lead to confusion among the women, who think, "people were supposed to be either religious or not; we had never before entertained the possibility of an in-between category, never considered any shades of gray" (207).

In trying to pinpoint Batsheva's difference, the community refers both to her racial non-Jewishness—which by default becomes, for Southerners, a native Christianity—and to her northern ways. Early on in the text, one of them says, "I heard that she is definitely a convert" and adds, "I don't know about the rest of y'all, but I knew she wasn't Jewish the minute I laid eyes on her" (30). When Batsheva unashamedly sings loudly in synagogue, they respond, "maybe that's how they do it in church. Not that I've ever been inside one, but I would guess that they do a lot of singing" (30-31). If, according to Daniel Itzkovitz, conversion to Judaism "means renouncing one's former religion and race,"[20] then in Memphis, conversion to Judaism means somehow forging ties to the South and creating an ancestry, lineage, and family out of thin air. Batsheva's Jewishness makes the community's own practice and understanding of Judaism more ambiguous. When, towards the end of the novel, Shira has run away with her non-Jewish boyfriend, and Yosef has left Memphis full of doubts about his place in orthodox Judaism and the South, the women turn against Batsheva, deciding that she has had a negative influence on their children, and voting against her reappointment as the art teacher in their local school. However, what surprises the women is that the vote is very close, and consequently, "we realized that we didn't know anymore what anyone felt. We were split . . . This realization made us see each other for the first time, and it was as shocking as looking at our faces in a mirror and seeing, suddenly, a stranger" (277). The fractured community, "an unraveling group of people turned in against itself" (278) now has to live with "a gnawing sense that nothing was as simple and clear-cut as it had once been" (280). Although Batsheva will no longer be teaching their children, the process of trying to protect themselves from her, and ostracizing her, has left them all essentially alone. For the first time, the narrative voice describes a Jewish holiday, Pesach, as laced through with doubt and isolation. Batsheva and her daughter celebrate it alone, and Mrs. Levy, surrounded by her children who visit her for the holiday, has an angry (and consciously un-Southern) confrontation with Batsheva that leaves her even more isolated. After she shouts at Batsheva, "all we wanted was to keep our children religious" (290), she sees her children's shocked faces and realizes that "her children's practical reasons for living away were excuses" and that "the truth was, they wanted no part of her, no part of Memphis" (290). In effect the leader of the women, Mrs. Levy undermines her authority in the community with her outburst, and she is left rejected by all. The narrative voice notes the betrayal and strangeness all around her: "No one came over to her, not her son or her daughters, not her grandchildren, not even Irving or Helen . . . They let her stand there all alone" (291).

During the course of the narrative, Batsheva is shown at times as a temptress figure, awakening desires in all parts of the community.[21] The dresses she wears to synagogue seem too loose: they "lacked the propriety of the tailored dresses and summer suits we wore, and . . . made us all too conscious of her body underneath, her long legs and thin torso" (29). Batsheva comes to represent, for both the women of the community and their teenaged daughters, a world of limitlessness, "the outside world" (162). The narrative voice remarks, "Hearing Batsheva speak about the life she had emerged from was like looking out a window at a place we would never go" (162). She becomes, for the women, a safe way of knowing what they cannot really know. For their daughters, she becomes a confidante, offering counsel and a space where they can express some of their more untoward desires and anxieties. The girls, like their mothers, also imagine alternate selves, although they go further with their flights of fancy. For example, at Batsheva's house, inspired by photo albums of Batsheva's former life, they imagine themselves in provocative clothing: "Ariella Sussberg in black spandex, Aviva Berkowitz in a halter top, Hadassah Berner in fishnet pantyhose, Nechama Sheinberg in a sheer red blouse, and Shira Feldman in a skin-tight mini-dress" (134). The clash of worlds encapsulated when the Orthodox Jewish names are paired with descriptions of racy clothing symbolizes the shifting potential of language; words (their names) are dressed up in provocative clothes and their meanings changed, albeit momentarily. Such longings later become translated into actual performances when Batsheva chaperones the high-school girls' trip to Gatlinburg. Let loose, more or less, in a city far away from home, they go out one night wearing makeup and are "freed . . . to put on their tightest blouses and to roll up their skirts so they looked even shorter" (191). In this holiday space, the Jewish body that the girls at times long to discard sheds its tenseness and difference. During this brief evening of drag, they are able to perform as other to themselves and to try on alternate personas.

For some of the girls, however, this vicarious or borrowed experience of the outside is not enough. One of the climaxes of the story occurs during Purim, the holiday, which, the narrative voice explains, celebrates the deliverance of Queen Esther, Mordechai, and the Jews of Persia from the wicked Haman (243). On this day, Jews are commanded to "let loose" (243), to wear costumes, send baskets of food to the poor (and to one another), and have festive meals with singing, dancing, and drinking until "we no longer know the difference between righteous Mordechai and evil Haman" (243). It is a topsy-turvy, upside-down holiday, and an apt backdrop for Shira's escape. Purim sets the scene for carnival and mayhem, and illustrates how permitted revelry, regulated and contained on a specific day, can spill over from performance into reality. On one level, Purim speaks to the Memphis Jewish community in a way that none of the other Jewish holidays can. It is commonly believed to be the first recorded instance of anti-Semitism in history because Haman was shown to hate the Jews as a nation and a race, and as a remembrance of the Jews' escape from annihilation, Purim stirs up the women's anxieties about their own home in the South. The holiday comes after the trip to Gatlinburg and after Batsheva has already upset the community in various ways, and so the narrative voice recounts, "this year, . . . the story was transformed, and we saw Memphis as a modern-day Shushan" (246). As the children become unrecognizable in costume—boys dressed as girls, girls as boys—the teenaged girls "transformed themselves into punks, their hair teased high above their forehead, spray-painted with glitter and temporary dye" (248). They wear leather jackets, neon dresses, multiple strands of silver necklaces, and there is nothing their mothers can say. On this day, through their performance as punks, the girls dabble in a version of identity that is constructed rather than essential, and amidst this confusing freedom, Shira runs away. Her escape represents the other girls' struggles of identity. Although these episodes of drag are brief, they introduce the possibility of ambiguity into their otherwise religious and heavily prescribed lives, so that even the most conservative of the girls begins to express moments of doubt and frustration with her life in Memphis, where the options for socializing and engaging in a wider range of teenage activities is limited because of the tiny size of the Orthodox community.

Yosef's shocking decision to leave, and his implicit rejection of the security and tradition of the South, Judaism, his family, and the community further illustrates the claustrophobic nature of the community. His departure comes almost at the end of the novel, after a period of suspicion and gossip during which the narrative voice is unable to find out exactly what is going on with him. More interesting than the fact of his departure, however, is the narrative strategy for talking about it. Because none of the women actually see Yosef leave (they hear about it the next day), they are limited to their imaginations as they try to picture it: "In our minds we imagined the scene of Yosef leaving, over and over again, like a movie projected on a giant screen set up on our lawns" (304). This repetitive imagining—suggesting the traumatic effect of his departure—is the closest the women will come to experiencing departure from the life they know. In other words, his struggle is also theirs, but his is articulated and actual. As the narrative voice struggles with its "imaginings" it demonstrates the limitations of its communal stance. The collective "we" has, throughout the text, allowed the reader to enter every character's thoughts except Batsheva's and Yosef's. They remain closed off from the narrator's comprehension, and the final pages of the book illustrate an action, Yosef's departure, that the "we" can barely understand, and can only mourn. Being limited to the imagination suggests, ultimately, the inevitable presence of foreignness among the familiar faces of the community. The narrative "we" assumes and perpetuates the community's homogeneity, and is both bothered and stirred by signs of difference and disruption. In reconstructing Yosef's departure, the narrative voice says, "the next morning, when it was time to leave, he would sling his bag over his shoulder and walk out the door . . . He pulled the door shut and stepped outside into the early morning light, the time of day when anything feels possible" (306). The possibilities are endless, and the freedom limitless. But the narrative voice sends Yosef into exile, imagining him leaving Memphis, but not arriving anywhere else: "We didn't envision him ever arriving anywhere" (306). Ultimately, this limitlessness is a form of exile that, through Yosef's departure and the upheaval caused by Shira's rebellion, manifests itself in the middle of their neighborhood. In stark contrast to the safe "Jerusalem of the South" described at the beginning of the novel, Yosef's absence "created a hollowness in the middle of our neighborhood . . . a pit" which grew each day "until our houses circled dangerously close to its edges" (306). This abyss of absence, strangeness and otherness now lies at the heart of this Southern Jewish community, opening up questions about identity, history, and nationhood.

In the novel, Mirvis figures this process of questioning, ambiguity, and doubt as a positive thing. Despite Batsheva's disruptions, the text is clearly sympathetic towards her version of orthodoxy, and through the gentle influence of Mimi, the rabbi's wife, the narrative suggests that ambiguity itself is necessary for a thoughtful and renewed faith that will inspire the next generation of Southern Jews. To the discomfort of the other women, Batsheva openly talks about the imminence of God and focuses on the beauty of, rather than the limitations of, Judaic law: "When I converted," she says, "one of the ideas that moved me the most was that there was beauty in restraint, that you can feel more free by setting limits than when everything in the world is wide open to you" (170). After Batsheva is warily accepted into the community (and before she is ostracized at the end), the ladies find her presence surprisingly inspiring and refreshing, even in its more liberal moments. For example, during Christmas Batsheva builds and unveils a huge menorah on her front lawn. Initially the women are skeptical: "we came up with all the problems it presented: it was ostentatious, showy. Even though we were commanded to publicize the miracle of Chanukah, we were different enough from our non-Jewish neighbors, and we didn't need this in their faces more than it already was" (184). While Batsheva celebrates difference, the women somewhat ashamedly try to disguise it. Ultimately, however, her menorah makes a statement that touches them affectively, allowing them to experience a rare moment of spiritual connection to Judaism: "we couldn't stop staring at how tall and proud this menorah stood against the darkening blue-gray sky, how pure and simple it was. It brought this miracle from so long ago into our front yards" (184). Furthermore, Batsheva's menorah, in celebrating rather than hiding Judaism, allows them to define themselves through the presence of Judaism rather than through their absent Christianity: "we no longer had to stare longingly at the Christmas decorations in the rest of the city. We finally had something of our own to look at" (184). With Batsheva, Judaism takes center stage: "she was singing her heart out and didn't care if her voice floated down the street, through the neighborhood, clear across town" (184).[22]

During Sukkot, Batsheva similarly brings God closer to the community. As the women sit in their sukkot they hear the singing from Batsheva's garden: "their singing floated toward us, filling our air with a sweetness that was fresh, like a new fruit we had never tasted before" (150). Batsheva instills an unexpected newness and freshness into the celebration; but as always, there is a doubleness to her influence and its reception in the community. The "fruit" that they have never tasted before is surely kosher, suggesting that there are possibilities for renewal even within Halakhic laws. At the same time, the fruit recalls the sinful forbidden apple of Eden that was prohibited because of the questions it could unleash, and the yearning and knowledge it would inspire. The metaphor demonstrates Batsheva's impact on the women of this traditional community; Batsheva's very newness is interesting, and yet also seductive and threatening.[23] In her interpretive Judaism, Batsheva comes up against the rigid ties to orthodoxy that are as essential to the women as their ties to Memphis. Helen Shayowitz and Mrs. Levy, for example, speak about "the importance of obedience and discipline, of following all parts of a rigorous system, of being connected to the past" (49). When Mrs. Levy thinks about Batsheva's conversion, she has trouble understanding why someone would voluntarily choose to adopt Jewish practice, with all its prohibitions (90). In the text, the community's fearsome and restrictive orthopraxis tries to counter the unarticulated ghosts of exile; their wish for their daughters is "to avoid the confusion of the modern world . . . to always feel rooted in their tradition, to be close to their families, their community, and God" (137).

The clashes between Tziporah Newburger and Batsheva illustrate the text's inquiry into various strains of Jewish practice. Arguing over the proper use of the *mikvah*—Batsheva uses it even though she is widowed and presumably not having sexual relations—Batsheva asks, "How can it be bad if it makes me feel more religious?" and adds that to do it "only because it's commanded would take the joy out of the mikvah" (68). In response to this, Tziporah thinks, "Judaism wasn't about self-interpretation; it wasn't a new age religion where you were supposed to create your own meaning. It was a very old tradition with very old laws" (69). For her, changing the tenets of Judaism means violating the integrity of divine revelation at Mount Sinai. At the end of the book, after Yosef has left the community and the text outlines various women's responses to the shocking event, we see Tziporah's almost fanatical reaction: "maybe now," she thinks, "everyone would realize that once you start down the slippery slope, there was no escaping its icy descent . . . The only answer was to pull inside as tightly as possible, to build an ark around her family which would protect them from the flood of hard times that lay ahead" (303). Even as Tziporah figures orthodoxy as an ascent, she does so by imagining an utter isolation for herself and her family. As the text describes the beginnings of such a collapse in this community, it performs the tensions seen in contemporary American Jewish literature, where, according to Victoria Aarons, there now remains "little connective cultural tissue to pattern and shape the lives of the characters."[24] Furthermore, she writes that this shift from community to isolation is caused by a worship of popular culture, which is itself in defiance "of any authorizing covenant, a covenant that, of course, promises protection through a community."[25] Without the protection of the covenant, and the security of community, the individual returns to exile.

Traditionally, diaspora Jews, insofar as they are in exile from a homeland, perceive the state of exile as a threat to Jewish survival, and through study and Halakhah (observance of Jewish law) they counter this threat of extinction. However, in *The Ladies Auxiliary*, only the male characters—who barely participate in the narrative chain of events—study, while the women focus on Halakhah. Ultimately, Batsheva introduces a form of Jewish feminism into the community that presents an alternative space for Southern Jewish women: a space of learning and study that, in challenging the women's traditional and patriarchal orthodoxy, may be the only productive way to ensure the community's survival. While orthodox women hope that, as Susannah Heschel puts it "something can be done within the framework of *halakhah* to create a strong sense of pride in women coupled with the conviction that what they do is religiously significant,"[26] Mirvis's text shows how all the "significant" tasks of the women actually center around their men, families, and the rest of the community. That is, women are peripheral to Jewish law, and as such, are, according to Rachel Adler, "educated and socialized toward a peripheral commitment." The Jewish woman's "major mitzvoth aid and reinforce the lifestyle of the community and the family, but they do not cultivate the relationship between the individual and God. A woman keeps kosher because both she and her family must have kosher food. She lights the Sabbath candles so that there will be light, and hence, peace, in the household. She goes to the *mikvah* so that her husband can have intercourse with her, and she bears children so that, through her, he can fulfill the exclusively male *mitzvah* of increasing and multiplying."[27] As if to support this, in the novel Tziporah's use of the mikvah makes her anxious as she feels she is cleansing herself only physically, not spiritually; as she brushes her hair she imagines being intimate with her husband and it is only this focus on the male of the household that helps her fulfill the commandment.

Throughout the text we learn that the men's domain is one of thought and learning while the women's is based on the physical. Adler notes that in Jewish praxis it is perhaps "most damaging that the woman's meager *mitzvoth* are, for the most part, closely connected to some physical goal or object. A woman's whole life revolved around physical objects and experiences—cooking, cleaning, childbearing, meeting the physical needs of the children."[28] In Mirvis's novel, the women have to look to their men to find an affective connection to the past: "We didn't study Talmud; that was a world reserved for men. Our only knowledge of these sacred texts came from the snatches of conversations overheard from our fathers, husbands, brothers, and sons" (228). They are only voyeurs to the experience of learning, which, at its best, creates a "dialogue with the generations of scholars before them," into which the men vanish, "lost inside this ancient world that remained closed to us" (228). Most troubling, Adler writes, is that "without any independent spiritual life to counterbalance the materialism of her existence, the mind of the average woman was devoted to physical considerations; marriages, deaths, dinners, clothes and money."[29]

Significantly, one of the most striking and distressing aspects of the plural narrative voice in *The Ladies' Auxiliary* is its often harsh, judgmental, or gossipy tone, and its misguided focus on the superficial (what the women wear to synagogue, what people might think, etc.).[30] Constrained by both Southern conservatism and Jewish orthodoxy, the narrative voice has too much intellectual energy, and too little opportunity to channel itself towards something other than suburban trivialities. Batsheva has clearly been sent, in a sense, to save the women from their growing exile from one another, their daughters, their city, and their Judaism. Almost immediately, Batshava, by the sheer fact that she is a woman living alone with her daughter, represents an alternative way of being Jewish and a woman. When she arrives, the women watch as "she tried to unload the tarp [from her car], a job that we would have left to our husbands" (13), and when Batsheva first meets Mrs. Levy, she shakes her hand, "like two men at a business meeting" (15). Her gender-bending behavior causes discomfort among the women of the community: she by necessity leads the prayers in her own house, takes charge of her own and her daughter's Jewish education, and resists being matched up with any eligible young men in the community.

When Batsheva invites the women to her house for a Rosh Chodesh celebration in honor of the new moon, they respond with suspicion: "It seemed like some feminist innovation that we, thank God, didn't have to think about living down here" (124). Because the South is directly associated with their reluctance or inability to liberate themselves from a confining Judaic practice, freeing themselves as Jewish women means lifting themselves away, even momentarily, from the rootedness of Memphis. Initially, when they follow Batsheva's dance steps, their steps are "measured, slow and precise" but they are quickly inspired by Batsheva's body, "so fluid, her arms like two birds flying off." (129). The women long to be like her, "loose and free inside, not worried about how we looked or what anyone thought of us" and specifically, they dream of not being tense in their bodies: "We imagined . . . some small piece of us that was usually hidden away would escape from the tight casing that held our bodies together and fly away unencumbered" (129), and feel themselves mentally undressing, longing "to be rid of our coifed hair, unloosen our respectable, ladylike clothing, remove our sturdy bas and sensible underwear" (130). Batsheva defies the trivial, the domestic, and the mundane, exemplifying the Jewish woman's body both as a site of pleasure and as a weightless entity by which she is no longer defined or restrained. Although the dancing is physical, it becomes infused with spirituality, and allows all the women a brief but necessary moment of transcendence: "In the dim lighting, we could just make out the outlines of one another's faces, all lines and angles softened into each other, and we felt, for that one second, that we had slipped out of who we usually were" (130).

Ultimately, Mirvis's text promotes a renewed Southern Jewish feminism while at the same time illustrating the ambiguous mixture of discomfort and pleasure that such feminist practices provoke. Just as the women's moment of dance connects them affectively to their past, so Batsheva's studying sessions with Yosef opens them up to the possibilities of learning. Helen realizes that "learning had come into fashion for women" and wonders "if it was too late for her, or if, like Batsheva, she also might have the chance to catch up. . . . She tried to imagine it: Helen Shayowitz, Torah Scholar. But then she laughed. She was sixty-one years old. Who knew if it was still possible?" (109). Insofar as study has been the traditional male response to the threat posed by exile, the desire for women's learning in the text points to an awareness of the threat facing women and girls in Judaism, particularly in the South, as they struggle to reconcile their traditionalism with their desire to be more intellectually fulfilled. In the book, the women's inability to recognize and address this struggle in their daughters reflects the largest threat to survival of all. Essentially, study and learning might, if adopted by the women, replace Memphis as the identifying marker that holds the Jewish people together in exile. Learning, that is, might allow the women to exile (or free) themselves from the bond (or bind) of the Jewish South.

It is significant that the book closes with Shavuot, the Festival of Weeks that commemorates the end of the Children of Israel's wandering in the desert and their creation of a Jewish nation at Mount Sinai. With this ending, Mirvis poses, but does not fully answer, all the questions that have simmered in her text. Just as the neighborhood, fragmented and isolated, is forced to call into question its own religious and national identity, so it is forced to prepare for a holiday which celebrates the coming together, rather than the falling apart, of a people. The text crescendos as Mimi gives a class for the women where she recounts the story of the Book of Ruth, through which she "reminded us that the kingship of Israel was passed down through Ruth. Even though she had initially been regarded with suspicion because she was a descendent of Moav, God saw fit to reward her for her righteousness by having the future kings of Israel descend from her" (309). After this lesson, the women look up at the night sky, recalling that at midnight every year on this night the sky is supposed to open and reveal a flash of heavens. As they crane their necks upwards, they see lightning, and then, instead of what they expect—storybook images of Mount Sinai and the desert and the Jews—they see themselves: Memphis, the Mississippi River, their houses and the synagogue and school and restaurant, as well as a "chain of hands" linking them back to their female ancestors. When they look forward, however, their daughters are in the distance, some close and some further away, "and only if we stretched out our arms as far as they would go could we maybe begin to reach them" (311). Crucially, God is imminent in this Southern community not because of its status as the "Jerusalem of the South" but because its women can forge ancestral links, connected by "the daily routines of our lives" (311). The novel suggests that to survive in the South, however, the women must infuse those daily routines—physical acts of Judaism—with intellect, study, and learning. To do so requires a physical and mental "stretching" that will continually bring them into an anxious area of discomfort: a site of ambiguity, self-doubt, and questioning. Ultimately, the challenge for Southern Jewish women that the text presents in this moment is the same challenge that faces Southern Jewish American literature: to survive, to create an ongoing literary presence and legacy, it must recognize its exiled status within an already marginalized site, accept the ambiguous task of renewing Judaism and Jewish practice in a literature based outside mainstream Orthodox spaces, and use the discomfort of home and place in order to create a significant literary and canonical identity.

Notes

1. Lewis Browne, "Why Are Jews Like That?" *American Magazine*, January 1929, 7-9, 104-06.
2. Daniel Itzkovitz, "Passing Like Me," *South Atlantic Quarterly* 98, no. 1/2 (1999): 38.
3. Derek Parker-Royal, "Unfinalized Moments in Jewish American Narrative," *Shofar: An Interdisciplinary Journal of Jewish Studies* 22, no. 3 (2004): 1-11, 2-3.
4. Ibid., 5.
5. Although Mirvis's second novel, *The Outside World* (New York: Alfred A. Knopf, 2004) is set primarily in New York, it too leads us again to Memphis when the main

character, Tzippy, moves there as a newlywed with her husband Bryan. Compared to New York, Memphis, in fact, represents a place where dreams can come true. For both Tzippy and Bryan it offers a new beginning away from their parents, where they can forge their own interpretation of Orthodox Judaism. Significantly, it offers Tzippy a space where she flourishes intellectually (she takes classes at the university, and considers options for herself as a career woman as well as a wife and future mother).

6. Eli N. Evans, in *The Provincials: A Personal History of Jews in the South* (New York: Simon & Schuster, 1997), points out that the South itself is a complex region: "Perhaps there is no 'South' anymore, other than the geographical and historical South, but psychologically it is a region of such complexity that sweeping generalizations about it are foolhardy and naïve" (275). Evans notes that, for example, "Rural Mississippi and Alabama . . . differ so markedly from the rest of the South that they surely rate special attention; for too long they have distorted the national view of the Southern psyche" (275). To add a history of Southern Jews to the already complex region means, therefore, stepping into even more ambiguous territory.
7. Eli N. Evans, *The Lonely Days Were Sundays: Reflections of a Jewish Southerner* (Jackson: University Press of Mississippi, 1993), 6.
8. Mirvis, *The Ladies Auxiliary* (New York: Ballantine Books, 1999), 10. Hereafter cited parenthetically.
9. Ibid., interview at end of the novel. n.p.
10. Allegra Goodman, "Writing Jewish Fiction In and Out of the Multicultural Context," in *Daughters of Valor: Contemporary Jewish American Women Writers*, ed. Jay L. Halio and Ben Siegel (Newark: University of Delaware Press, 1997), 268-74, 270-71.
11. Structurally, the novel's plot follows a Jewish calendar year, starting with Batsheva's arrival on a Sabbath eve, descriptions of the kosher laws, the laws of modesty and use of the mikvah, and the community's participation in and observance of the High Holy Days (Rosh Hashana, Yom Kippur and Sukkot) in the Fall, Chanukah in the Winter, Purim in early Spring, Pesach in later Springtime, and Shavuot—the festival of God's choosing the Children of Israel as a nation with the giving of the Torah at Mount Sinai—closing the text. The text in effect introduces the action by situating it within the context of the particular Jewish holiday or season that is about to start.
12. Allegra Goodman, *Kaaterskill Falls* (New York: Random House, 1998), 157.
13. Leonard Dinnerstein and Mary Dale Palsson, in Introduction, *Jews in the South*, ed. Leonard Dinnerstein and Mary Dale Palsson (Baton Rouge: Louisiana State University Press, 1973), write that one of the three potentially powerful forces that Southern Jews experience that Jews of the north do not face is the agrarian tradition. They state that "the rural nature of the region always constituted a foreshadowing of what the South would be like" and that "the predominantly agrarian society in the South helped conserve a typically American bias that favored the producers rather than the financiers" (3-23, 9). In the 1820s, one of the objections voiced by Southern Jews in Maryland in the *Niles Weekly Register* was that the Jews "will not sit down and labor like other people—they create nothing and are mere consumers. They will not cultivate the earth, nor work at mechanical trades, preferring to live by their wit in dealing, and acting as if they had a home nowhere" (9. Originally cited in John Higham, "American Anti-Semitism Historically Reconsidered," *Jews in the Mind of America*, ed. Charles Herbert Stember [New York: Basic Books], 1966, 248). Although we don't see Mirvis's characters literally cultivate the earth, their connection to the land

is deeply enough engrained as to seem to counter their people's legacy and identity of homelessness.

14. Evans notes that, "Jews in the South were not strangers to the idea of a homeland for the Jews" and that in fact "at one time, the South itself was considered as a possible site for the Jewish state. The silk-hat banker Jacob Schiff, concerned about the conditions on the East Side of New York . . . pledged half a million dollars in 1906 to the 'Galveston Project' which helped direct more than ten thousand East European immigrants through Galveston into the South and Southeast" (*The Provincials*, 97). The Am Olam movement, a "back to the soil" movement in Russia that advocated immigration to America (not as a "nonproductive" commercial middleman, which the movement believed to be one of the causes of anti-Semitism, but as productive farmers) planned to establish in the U.S. a "Jewish state based on socialist and collective ideals" with farming as its base (98).
15. Evans, *Lonely Days*, xix.
16. Ibid., xx.
17. Ibid., xxii.
18. The novel also more than hints that Mrs. Levy's children's rejection of Memphis, as well as Yosef's exile and Shira's escape, all signal a rejection not just of the Jewish community, but also of the stereotyped overbearing Jewish mothers that the text presents. The text's depiction of Jewish mothers (including Batsheva's own laid-back mothering skills) would make a fascinating study, in particular read in light of the Jewish mothers that have come before them in literature, and with the thought that the mothers in this text are an integral part of the new trend in Jewish American women's writing.
19. Mirvis remarks in an interview that "one of the best compliments I've received about the novel was from someone in Mississippi who told me that she knows very little about Judaism but she could have sworn this book was about her mother's Methodist church" (interview at end of *The Ladies Auxiliary*, n.p.). This suggests not only that Mirvis has attracted a readership in the South, but also points to a certain translation of Judaism into the language of the Southern mainstream. One could either describe this as a way to talk across cultures, or as a way of anthropologizing Judaism to such an extent that it once again disappears into the normative Christianity of the South.
20. Itzkovitz, 42.
21. A separate study could read Batsheva as a Lilith figure. Although Lilith's crimes are obviously more extreme than Batsheva's—Lilith allegedly kills child-bearing women, injures newborn babies, and exiles men in their sleep, taking their sperm to manufacture demon children to replace her own—in essence "all these crimes embody crucial male fears . . . and a threat to survival." See Aviva Cantor, "The Lilith Question," *On Being a Jewish Feminist: A Reader*, ed. Susannah Heschel (New York: Schocken Books, 1995), 40-51, 46). Bearing in mind that the Lilith myth became more prominent in exile, and that "Lilith is . . . in some ways a metaphor for Exile itself" (48), Batsheva's threatening exilic effect on the Memphis community, and her feminist independence, could be read as a feminist revision of the Lilith myth.
22. It is, of course, ironic and crucial that it is Batsheva—a convert, originally a non-Jew—who shows the women how to be less ashamed. To understand the implications of this it is tempting to return to Browne's early twentieth-century discussion of the Jew. Browne, after raising and summarily dismissing various explanations for Jewish "difference" (such as biological race, religiousness, and nationality), fi-

nally defines the "distinctive" Jewish "manner" as a result of "the inescapable feeling that you Gentiles still consider us 'outsiders'" (9). Browne notes that the feeling of estrangement is in effect an "inherited wisdom" (105)—a learned behavior passed down through the generations, and might theorize that a convert to Judaism lacks this distinct manner. In converting, moving from insider to outsider status, Batsheva does not so much estrange herself as legitimate, with her presence, the foreignness of Judaic practice. With her zeal of the converted, she doesn't just offer a refreshing insight into and love for Judaism; she also permits it.

23. Mirvis herself, in talking about creating the character, says that, "She walks the line and sometimes crosses it" and that "I wanted to blur the line between propriety and impropriety. I didn't want her to commit any grave, clear-cut offenses that would definitely put her outside the self-constructed walls of the community, but I also didn't want her to be too perfect." (Interview at end of *The Ladies Auxiliary*, n.p.).
24. Victoria Aarons, "The Covenant Unraveling: The Pathos of Cultural Loss in Allegra Goodman's Fiction," *Shofar: An Interdisciplinary Journal of Jewish Studies* 22, no. 3 (2004): 12-25, 24.
25. Ibid., 24.
26. Susannah Heschel, Introduction, *On Being a Jewish Feminist: A Reader*, ed. Susannah Heschel (New York: Schocken Books, 1995), xxxvi.
27. Rachel Adler, "The Jew Who Wasn't There: Halakah and the Jewish Woman," *On Being a Jewish Feminist: A Reader*, ed. Susannah Heschel (New York: Schocken Books, 199), 12-19, 13-14.
28. Ibid., 15.
29. Ibid.
30. For example, the narrative voice notes that while Mimi cooks well for the Sabbath, "for many of us, this kind of cooking was part of a competition over who could make more, who could be fancier, more like a gourmet restaurant. But Mimi never looked like she was doing it for those reasons; she seemed to be doing it out of a love for Shabbos" (97).

The Ethics of After: Melvin Jules Bukiet, Holocaust Fiction, and the Reemergence of an Ethical Sense in the Post-Holocaust World

Michael J. Martin

After the defeat of Nazi Germany and the liberation of the death camps in 1945, a great emergence of discussions occurred concerning any relationship between the Holocaust and a developed ethical sense. A dominant belief that evolved from this atrocity is that the Holocaust was and is an "uncharacteristic" blip on the screen of a developing humanity, a full disruption of an evolving, humanistic, ethical sense. However, as Zygmunt Bauman has argued, it remains possible that the Holocaust was nothing but the logical outcome of the modernist moment: "The truth is that every 'ingredient' of the Holocaust . . . was normal; 'normal' . . . in the sense of being fully in keeping with everything we know about our civilization, its guiding spirit, its priorities, its immanent vision of the world—and of the proper ways to pursue human happiness together with a perfect society."[1] Despite Bauman's argument, there exists a continuance in the search for a disrupted ethical sense, and in many cases this search forces the individual to return to a pre-Holocaust modernist moment.

This question of ethics can be seen as a central concern in, for example, Tadeusz Borowksi's collection of stories *This Way for the Gas, Ladies and Gentlemen* (1959).[2] Whereas one might argue that Borowski recognizes the dismantling of an ethical sense in "The People Who Walked On" and the need for a new understanding of ethics and concern for humanity in "The January Offensive," one can maintain that after the Holocaust, Borowski returns to the modernist-humanist world of the past in search of this new ethics. In the final story of his collection,

Borowski writes of the world he encounters after his liberation and describes the rebuilding, in all senses of the term, of the old world. Similarly, Victor Frankl recognizes the horrors of the Holocaust and the extreme dehumanization that the Jews encountered in the world of the death camp, and yet his own logotherapy stresses the need for the patient, that is, the survivor, "to find meaning in his life."[3] The danger that is present in such texts or the belief that the Holocaust was an uncharacteristic historical blip is that, if Bauman is correct, then nothing has been nor can be learned from the Holocaust. While the Holocaust has been traditionally characterized as an ineffable event from which one can gain neither meaning nor understanding, I would argue that the time for this characterization has ended and the continuance of such a belief is dangerous.

In terms of the theoretical paradigms such as deconstruction and postmodernism that emerged in the post-Holocaust world, there also came a need for the complication of traditional philosophical notions, and the acceptance of language and ideology as social or cultural constructions. While some may argue that postmodernist theory and understanding served no greater purpose than free play and endless meanings, the opposite is true.[4] One particularly important postmodern sensibility is the desire for and the need to dismantle a dominantly held world belief in the metanarrative. As such, one can then make sense of Bauman's argument. To a certain degree, the humanist philosophy that emerged in the early and mid-twentieth century, particularly in Nazi-controlled Europe, was nothing short of a metanarrative. As Martin Heidegger, among others, was to display in his work, particularly in his essay, "The Age of the World View"[5] and his work on *das man*, a metanarrative of power and control gained great credence in the modernist world.[6] As Bauman suggests, this metanarrative was in keeping with everything we understood about our world and how to develop the perfect society. However, society also came to learn the dangers of such a metanarrative and, in a sense, halted such a belief at the Nuremberg Trials.

During the proceedings of the Nuremberg Trial, most of those accused either denied the accusations or plead innocence based on the belief that they were only following orders. It is only through a belief in and acceptance of the dominant world view and metanarrative that a defense such as the latter, innocence due to orders, could be developed and employed. If we blindly accept that *das man* both creates the world picture and metanarrative that all follow, then these individuals were not guilty. However, the court did not acknowledge such a defense and insisted that every individual is responsible for his or her actions. Thus, in a sense, the decree handed out at Nuremberg acknowledged the danger and collapse of modernist-humanist philosophy.

At this same time, and as demonstrated through the works of Borowski and Frankl, many subscribed to a belief in the return of a potentially liberating philosophy and metanarrative that was simply disrupted by the Holocaust. In contrast to such individuals and ideas, the postmodern moment worked to deconstruct many of those sensibilities and beliefs that emerged from modernism in an effort to "enlighten" individuals to the dangers of metanarratives and interpellation. In dismantling, interrogating, and problematizing such notions, postmodernism decreated the world, while simultaneously teaching the individual to question commonly held assumptions about such issues as truth, language, interpretation, and ethics, and revealing how each of these can be, and most likely is, tied to a greater metanarrative. However, while such activities remained productive throughout the second half of the twentieth century, the postmodern moment, having encountered questions and concerns that move beyond postmodern sensibilities, wanes.[7] Definitively unnamed as of yet, the writing and philosophy of this new paradigm has been titled and openly heralded in both fiction and theory by numerous authors, but most importantly, for the context of this discussion, by Melvin Jules Bukiet.

On the surface, Bukiet may seem as unlikely a herald of the coming paradigm as Ben Alef and his sociopathic, murderous band of apostles were of the millennial change in *Signs and Wonders* (1999).[8] Much of Bukiet's writing seems to embrace the sensibilities of postmodern fiction as discussed by such scholars as Linda Hutcheon—historiographic metafiction—and Brian McHale—the developed nuance recognizing the difference between the epistemological and the ontological.[9] Importantly though, one must understand that a shifting paradigm does not simply dismiss that which preceded it. Thomas Kuhn writes of paradigm shifts, "Since new paradigms are born from old ones, they ordinarily incorporate much of the vocabulary and apparatus, both conceptual and manipulative, that the traditional paradigms have previously employed. But they seldom employ these borrowed elements in quite the traditional way. Within the new paradigm, old terms, concepts, and experiments fall into new relationships one with the other."[10] Thus, amidst the installation and subversion of such grand issues as what constitutes reality and what is the impact of the individual on the world—seemingly traditional, postmodern considerations—a much larger discussion can be found.

Of importance to this discussion are two pieces that Bukiet published in 1996. The first was "Crackpot Realism: Fiction for the Forthcoming Millennium," followed by his novel *After*.[11] While seemingly disparate works, I find it of great value to read them dialogically. The theoretical notions that Bukiet develops in his article provide a key for the reading of *After*. Furthermore, each work, in its own way, proposes a developing post-Holocaust ethical sense that Bukiet argues is emerging at the end of the millennium.

From the outset of "Crackpot Realism," Bukiet contrasts the work of the crackpot realist with the works of other literary contemporaries, that is, postmodern authors. "Beyond the welter," he writes, "of random, inchoate experience, they [crackpot realist authors] find pattern and meaning. For every code, there is a cipher. There's danger and danger's nemesis, truth. If crackpot realism begins with subversion and suspicion, it takes a spiritual journey in a rocketship all the way to salvation" (15). From this description alone, the movement within and past the postmodernist moment is obvious. Whereas the crackpot realist may develop as intricate and dangerous a plot as Thomas Pynchon in *The Crying of Lot 49* (1965), the crackpot realist would never leave Oedipa Maas passively awaiting a discovery that will never come. Instead, the work itself would explore the cipher of the impervious mail system and lead Oedipa to salvation. But, simply because the crackpot realist will offer the cipher and once again find salvation, this is not salvation in the traditional sense. The crackpot realist is the by-product of the postmodernist, and will use and abuse (a postmodern sensibility in and of itself) postmodern thought to lead readers to new understandings.

Interestingly, postmodernist and crackpot authors use their work to respond to the world around them and complicate traditional understandings of historical and human events. However, whereas the postmodernist author may choose to look at a variety of possible topics in a transgressive manner—the assassination of JFK in Don DeLillo's *Libra* (1988), the emergence of virtual reality in Richard Powers' *Plowing in the Dark* (2000), or contemporary rewrites of canonical works in Kathy Acker's *Don Quixote* (1986)—the work of the crackpot realist is more centered as "the human response to the Jewish trauma of this century" (20). This is not to say that the postmodernist author has not chosen to look at the Holocaust in his or her work. In fact, readers of postmodern literature will recognize that World War II and the Holocaust, to varying degrees and for differing purposes, have been commonly adopted as historical vantage points or reference markers for the postmodernist author. One example of such is the use of the Hitler studies backdrop in DeLillo's *White Noise* (1985). The difference remains that whereas certain contemporary authors, according to Bukiet, "allow themselves to be silenced by the insane energies of willful genocide, they [crackpot realists] look to perfervidly fecund notions of regeneration" (21). In other words, contemporary authors, including the postmodern, may find it imperative to recognize and explore how such an event disrupted traditional notions of understanding or they may interrogate meanings of silence; whereas, the crackpot realist will choose to look, simultaneously, into and beyond this period in hopes of discovering a new key to humanity. The key to understanding this new humanity "is the assumption that some of us are shaping our world," and "the crackpot believes that ideas create his reality" (18).

The place of Bukiet, beyond that of theoretician, in this new humanity exists in his role as an author of crackpot realism. Prior to the release of *After*, Bukiet argued, that "crackpots dive into the underlying madness of the war [the Holocaust] itself. Yet none of the preeminent practitioners of this genre is Jewish, with the recently surprising exception of [Joseph] Heller" (20). My interest here is that while Bukiet insists that "the crackpots' is the human response to the Jewish trauma of this century," he nonetheless notes that little of the work he has come to consider crackpot realism either centers on the Holocaust or is written by a Jew. However, in the same year of this article, St. Martin's released Bukiet's *After*, a dark, sardonic, and yet hopeful interrogation of the world created after the liberation of the death camps. Thus, whereas no author or text fully fits with his understanding of crackpot realism, his own novel fills this void.

In *After*, readers encounter a band of Holocaust survivors who have migrated to a small German town where they come together and engage in "business." Initially, the group makes money through the trade of cigarettes, forged passports, copies of maps, and the highly lucrative and yet false military need for DPIDs (Dead Person Identification Cards). Throughout the novel, however, the primary goal of the group's leader, Isaac Kaufman, is the "liberation" of an eighteen-ton gold ingot—made, of course, from the extracted teeth of Jews once in the camps—from a United States Military encampment. In the course of the many dealings and problems encountered by this group, readers are invited into a subtextual discussion and understanding of the crackpot view of the world at hand.

The hope for and need to return to a modernist world view that governed all before the war becomes quite obvious at the start of the novel. When the American soldiers, "Hershey's advance men," liberate Isaac's concentration camp "home," the sign hanging above the gate is changed "with a hand-lettered plywood sign strung ungrammatically over its first word, to read, TANKS MAKES ONE FREE" (7). After one survivor reacquires three diamonds that he had hidden in the lining of a coat that was confiscated upon his arrival, Isaac comes to realize that for all that the war changed, the belief that money equals power and freedom remained. As Isaac witnessed, the survivor "was immediately granted anything he wanted on the bourse based on his own word" (15). This belief assumes so much power among those liberated that, once again, they change the sign, but this time to read, "$ MAKES ONE FREE" (17). Realizing this point, Isaac decides to leave the "safety" of the liberated camp and journeys to Regensburg where he will meet other liberated Jews and begin his struggle to become the free, rich man able to participate in all activities of the world.

In following the initial encounters of Isaac and his band of survivors, readers will realize that for those who survived the war, the world remains unchanged. Instead of looking at the Holocaust as a social and philosophical rupture and thus a call for a new world view and understanding of humanity, these survivors attempt and hope, as do many of those non-Jews living throughout Europe, to return to an untainted, pre-World War II, modernist world view. This hope is illustrated effectively at two distinct points in the novel.

After converging as a group and beginning their business in the black market, Isaac and his gang pass many evenings at a local nightclub. On one particular night, as the evening's entertainment ends, the emcee takes the stage and gives his farewell, asking, "So what say every twenty years we have a little excitement and then After, we have a lot of fun. See you at the next set" (93). Those in the audience respond quite differently. While the foreigners are described as clapping and stamping their feet, the locals barely notice the emcee's words or the show because "they had seen the show before" (93). On the surface, this may simply mean that since entertainment after the war was less of a priority, the show provided was the same day to day and held little interest for those who came in nightly to drown their sorrows. Subtextually, however, the emcee has opened a discussion of the modernist world view. Those who clap and stamp their feet, the outsiders, seem to enjoy the show and the unspoken sentiment that every twenty years, a rough estimate of the time between World Wars, they will encounter a distant country and emerge victorious. For these victors (those outsiders), there is no need for change because the "righteous" will always emerge victorious. For the locals and the Jews, there is little interest in the end of the show because it is a "rerun." Only twenty years earlier, they had seen their country demolished, and witnessed the same victory parties. And, for the Jews, this "rerun" is simply another instance of unending Jewish persecution that had plagued Europe for centuries. For all, however, there is a common theme: the rerun. In twenty years time (metaphorically), the locals will once again wish to gain a larger place in global politics, a war will come about, and the foreigners will once again invade, emerge victorious, and work to reestablish the status quo. For Isaac and his band, they take the side of the foreigners in hopes that the status quo will allow them the time and money needed to become successful and depart before the next show, that is, World War. For this emcee and for those who attend the night's events, no individual or action will be able to change the rerun of history.

This idea is further cemented later in the novel when Isaac meets with another survivor, Der Schreiber, Benya, at a carnivalesque party, where the two discuss the ability to write and understand the Holocaust. Benya has penned a memoir of his life in the camps and has been asked to teach a seminar in Paris based on the work. Annoyed with Benya's popularity and his continued immersion in the world of the Holocaust, Isaac sarcastically suggests that Benya may have something to teach all the survivors, but Benya does not agree: "I have nothing to teach you Mr. Kaufman. I was rather hoping that you could teach me" (259). Taken aback by this response because he has done everything possible to rid himself of the Holocaust and his status as survivor, Isaac reminds Benya that he is not a scholar, and yet that is exactly why Benya needs his help. Benya's attempt to work through the Holocaust in his text is based on a philosophy that cannot explain this past world: "'That's why I thought you would know better. I seem to be able to describe, but I still can't understand. I guess that I can survive. I have, like a . . .' He raised both arms to display himself. 'But I need help. The problem is that life is not like a book; I think you know that'" (259). For Benya, his hope is that his work will not simply describe the world of the lager, but that a reader can come to understand the lager through reading his work and thus work to end the possibility that it may occur again. Benya draws the early and yet important conclusion that has become more dominant at the end of the twentieth century: memory alone is not enough. He remembers the lager, but cannot something more be learned? Benya recognizes that Isaac is not the "typical" distraught survivor, and thus turns to him in hopes that Isaac will guide him to the understanding of what one can learn from this period of history. Isaac, however, has not yet reached the greater understanding for which Benya is looking. Isaac has not come to understand that he, as an individual, can impact the world at large at all. Instead, he only understands that the purpose of life is to have fun, become rich, and recreate normalcy, not to look for a new world.

Isaac, throughout much of the novel, remains the antithesis to the philosophy of Bukiet. For the crackpot realist, there must exist a key to understanding the insanity and discovering salvation. While in terms of the Holocaust, understanding may not be possible, if one refrains from ever working towards discovering deliverance, then one is completely lost. Thus, the salvation of the Holocaust is found when one comes to a new belief in the possibility of the individual voice when expressed among dissenting opinions. Immediately following the Holocaust, this possibility was lost in the return to the old world, and when writing *Night* (1955),[12] Elie Wiesel originally penned a conclusion that called attention to this fact. In the published conclusion, the work ends with Wiesel's skeletal reflection staring back at him. Originally, however, the conclusion continued past this point with Wiesel breaking the mirror, discussing the rebirth of the German state and army with war criminals wandering the streets, and contemplating the silence that has come after the Holocaust.[13] Because of this silence, Wiesel wonders whether he should have broken the mirror and shared his story. Whereas Wiesel has regularly questioned the ability of his books to honor the dead and many times concluded that silence may have been the greater honor—the same answer that Isaac has chosen—I would argue that for the crackpot realist, such silence is what has hindered deliverance. While silence has served a purpose in Holocaust study, this silence must end and the individual voice must be heard anew among dissenting opinions. In heralding the individual voice of dissension, the crackpot realist seems to push the world forward into a new realm of ethics and understanding.

The importance of the individual voice, the kind espoused by Bukiet and other crackpot realists, is a notion quite similar to that of radical democracy as defined by Chantal Mouffe. Radical democracy, like crackpot realism, is modern, postmodern, and something completely new. It is postpostmodern in that it continues to work towards fulfilling the project of modernity, while still acknowledging contemporary postmodern theoretics and erasing the "epistemological perspective of the Enlightenment."[14] Mouffe continues arguing that it is important to forego a return to the Enlightenment for reasons that such a movement hinders an understanding of "those new forms of politics, characteristic of our societies today, which demand to be approached from the nonessentialist perspective."[15] The end goal of this new democracy is "making possible a new form of individuality that would be truly plural and democratic."[16] In other words, the goal is to set up competing voices in an open, dialogic relationship in an effort to discover the commonalties of those divergent voices and reach new understandings. This becomes possible, in terms of the Holocaust, when, instead of being silenced or ignored, the Jewish trauma of this past century is reinterrogated in such a "crackpot" light.

While Isaac is the individual who clings to the world of the old and hinders the possibilities that the crackpot realist desires to achieve, another survivor, Fishl, acts as the voice of the new world view. In the context of Isaac's band of black marketers, Fishl remains the clumsiest and most "useless" member of the group, and yet he is constructed as the perfect contrast to Isaac. Early in the novel, Isaac, Morgenstern, and Fishl spend an evening drinking wine and waxing philosophic. At one point, Fishl asks what kind of God would give the world to the Germans and persecution to the Jews. Before he is able to complete his thoughts, Isaac interrupts:

> "Dreck and claptrap," Isaac declared. "He gives dreck and I have never heard such self-indulgent claptrap in all my life." He stood and slammed his empty glass down on the straw-covered table. "If this is what freedom brings, then put me back in the lager where I can understand what people are saying. At least you knew where you stood and what you needed. The last thing I needed then and the last thing I need now is theology." (121)

Interestingly, Isaac insists that theology can offer no understanding of the physical world and insists that if the world turns to theology, he would rather remain in the lager. The paradox seen here is that while Isaac insists that the lager made sense, many argue that the lager was a base for insanity. In the lager, one could never be exactly sure of how to react in any situation because there were no defined rules that guaranteed life. However, as Isaac insists here, he believes that if one can learn to read the world, alone and without thinking of others, as he did in the lager, then one can survive. Theology, he argues, does not teach the individual how to live in the world: it teaches blind trust in the world. In many ways, Isaac is the postmodernist who recognizes that theology is dangerous in that it is a metanarrative that demands blind faith. However, while Fishl does seem to call for a return to a theology, the fact that he questions God illustrates his new relationship to theology.

As the conversation continues, Isaac is again confronted with theology, despite his attempts to silence this issue. As the three discuss what each physically wants at this moment, the answers remain divergent. Morgenstern wants enough money to move to Australia where he can travel for many miles without seeing another human. Isaac asks for nothing and everything: "It's not what I'm interested in; It's when. I want nothing for tomorrow. I want anything you've got, however, today. Skoal!" (122). Finally, Fishl asks for a Torah so that he can see the word of God before he dies.

In each case, although to varying extremes, the liberated Jews want nothing more than to forget. For Morgenstern, the avoidance of humanity would allow him to erase the fact that he was ever interned because he would never see anyone and thus have no need to speak of his life. For Isaac, the past and future do not matter. It is only the moment that matters, and in the case of this novel, Isaac's moment is one of money and enjoyment. As his initial statement points out, the lager, the most insane place in the world, made sense to him because he did not question who he was or what he needed. Sadly, that world made sense to him because it was black and white, life and death. In the lager there was no sense in thinking past the moment, and thus Isaac continues to live only in the moment. Fishl, however, finds that the world of the moment is the same world that led to the lager; therefore, he must break free of this thought. In asking for a Torah, Fishl is struggling both to find the key to insanity and to understand how to live beyond the moment. While Fishl has begun to progress past Isaac, at this point in the novel, each character, to varying degrees, maintains some desire to hold onto a world view that is centered in an ideology outside of the self that will never lead one to the key. For Fishl, however, this point of view changes rapidly.

During one assignment, Fishl reunites with his wife, Rivka, who has also survived the Holocaust. Upon bringing her back to the band's home in Regensburg, Fishl and Rivka begin to build a new life: Fishl returns to his life of religious study and Rivka becomes pregnant. While the two continue to rebuild their lives and find their place in this new world, they continue to live with Isaac and the other Jews but spend less time engaged with the activities of the gang. It is the birth of Fishl's child and the stealing of the gold ingot that cements each survivor's understanding of the world.

Near the novel's end, Bukiet provides a grand description of the planning and actual heist of the gold ingot, but it is a plan that does not go smoothly. As Isaac and his crew devise their own plan for the robbery, so have the American soldiers who are about to be sent home. For all involved, this gold signifies a world of wealth that, no matter the circumstances, can change an individual's life for the better. After a series of mishaps, Isaac and his crew make it out of the American compound with the gold and place it on the getaway truck. Before escaping, they are almost stopped by a third American party that also seeks to steal the gold, but Fishl—with Rivka and the baby in the truck—speeds away and disappears with the gold. After the disappearance of Fishl and the gold, Isaac and his crew are brought to trial but released due to lack of evidence.

In the novel's last pages, Isaac and the others remain at their apartment, trying to decide what new "business" to begin, when Fishl finally returns. Fishl explains that when he escaped that night, he just kept driving until he stopped under an arched gate that read "ARBEIT MACHT FREI." He tells Isaac that he buried the gold here, on sacred ground with the dead, and Isaac insists that they dig it up. Fishl responds, "It's all that's left of them. They're buried now. You can't unearth the dead" (381). In a sense, Fishl has begun and ended the silence. In his description of where he buried the gold, he tells Isaac, "The grass. It was growing. It was alive. And I was alive too, so I said Kaddish" (383). Fishl has come to understand that he needed to honor the dead, and he did so by returning the gold, gold that once belonged to the victims. In doing so, however, he also noticed the return of life and came to see that he can no longer live in the moment of the lager, but must move ahead. The Kaddish allowed him to do so. After Fishl's description of his actions, Bukiet ends the novel with a final, extended line that I quote in entirety to illustrate the importance of the final movement this novel takes:

> After it was all over, after the murders, after the rapes, after the old people were stripped and the children were starved, after the Torahs were torn to shreds and the shreds burned, ashes scattered, and the synagogues converted to stables for the cavalry and the graveyards were desecrated, after the living were turned dead and the dead denied dignity, after everything, one could hear a whisper rising out of the forest and the fields and the universities and the churches and out of the bunker in Berlin, the still unfulfilled prayer born of the knowledge that Isaac and Marcus and Fishl and Der Schreiber and Miranda were in Regensburg and others were in Amsterdam and London and Toronto and Buenos Aires and Capetown and Melbourne and Bombay and Shanghai and New York and Jerusalem and the last Jew, wherever he was, was still breathing, and the whisper was sighing, "No, nein, not After," but that other, age-old, heartfelt eternal resolution: "Again." (383-84)

As Bukiet suggests of the crackpot novel, not only must salvation be reached at the end, but the protagonist of such a novel also needs to learn that the external world is the embodiment of his own discontent. Throughout the novel, Isaac and the others have struggled to become part of the commercial world and simply ignored or silenced their past. In doing so, it should become obvious for the reader that these Jews will never accomplish their goals; they participate in the new world and hope to become rich so that they will never suffer again. In this silence, however, there exists only the possibility for the rerun that the emcee suggested earlier. As Fishl reminds them, they may avoid suffering only in remembering a past world, assuming their responsibility to speak of that world, and, finally, taking a role in creating a new world.

The new world that Fishl discovers growing out of Auschwitz and becoming part of his own life is that same new world that the crackpot struggles to discover. As Bukiet writes in "Crackpot Realism," "The crazed, wishful thinking crackpot realist has faith in a nature that keeps procreating, renewing itself in further generations of lunacy and murder, trying again and again to get it right. If the last page of any of these [crackpot realist] books announces the end with terrifying clarity, we turn immediately to the next page 1. Perhaps this time it will read, 'A sighing comes across the sky'" (22). This is what Fishl learns and hopes to teach Isaac and the Jews of Regensburg. The emcee is correct to suggest that every twenty years or so there will be madness, but one must struggle through this madness. In reliving the rerun of life—if the individual has not turned away from or returned to the past—the individual can bring a new vision to the events of the world and this time attempt to get it right. Lunacy and murder may repeat, as it has in terms of genocide since the Holocaust, but with each repetition a new world is created that brings about the hope of a better future. For example, in response to the differing genocides that occurred during the twentieth century, tribunals have emerged to prosecute war criminals in hopes of telling all humanity that such actions will not be tolerated. Thus, as the Jews of Regensburg finally separate and the reader exits the novel, no one can look at the world or life as After: all must now look at it as Again with hopes of getting it right.

Two years following the publication of both Bukiet's essay and novel, Dalkey Archive Press published Curtis White's *Monstrous Possibility: An Invitation to Literary Politics.*[17] As the title alone suggests, White, like Bukiet, is interested in the interconnection between literature, politics, and the individual. Furthermore, again like Bukiet, White is an author of the postmodern moment and yet in this text, he reopens the interrogation of issues that many postmodernist thinkers tend to dismantle and then ignore. Specifically, I am intrigued by White's discussion of literature in terms of politics and how it connects to Bukiet and the world of *After*.

In the context of the work, White argues that the exemplary writer of the postmodern moment will "confront postmodern problems on postmodern grounds" (63). What are these problems? Speaking more specifically to theory than literature, White defines the postmodern condition as such: "The postmodern moment is one of great and very rare opportunity. All is fluid. But as the molten intellectual magma cools, one particularly frightening possibility begins to take form: in the time after the end of ideology, literature has outlived its usefulness. The new word is 'performance.' Make your means suit our ends or else" (67). The danger that White recognizes is that the creation and study of literature, in the moment that will follow the postmodern, will serve no greater purpose than that of a service to the university interested in producing a literate culture. Thus, the task for the writer and poet is to fight because, as the tradition of the writer and poet—not the English department—holds, "the study of the literature of the past and production of the literature of the future requires two things fundamental to human sociality: a critical awareness of where we are and how we've gotten to where we are, and the creation of our own future" (68). In the end, every "new work of fiction or poetry is the presentation of a world within which we might choose to live" (68). As a pedagogy, the teaching of this literature "fulfills the real purpose of humanistic training: the growth of the capacity for critical inquiry" (30).

The postmodern moment allowed those who studied the Holocaust to realize the complicated discussions that arose from this atrocity. Furthermore, in recognizing the role that ideology, a single world view, and a modernist ethical sense played in the construction of this horrific event, postmodern sensibilities awakened authors and readers to the impossibility of returning to a pre-Holocaust, modernist understanding of the world. It was only through the deconstruction of modernist and Enlightenment understandings of an issue such as ethics that critical readers and citizens of the world could come to understand how we arrived at the point we are at: the post-Holocaust world where genocide continues to occur. Now, it is the role of the current Holocaust author to continue to push one forward, past the deliberations and deconstructions of ideology and its making, into a new discussion of the post-Holocaust moment. For Melvin Jules Bukiet and the authors of crackpot realism, we must, in White's words, work to "present a world in which we might choose to live" (68). Thus, the author must recognize the importance of the individual in the creation of this world: an individual who can recognize and critique ideology; an individual who can make his voice heard among the dissension and struggle to find a common ground; an individual who can look at and recognize the past, present, and future and while seeing repetition, maintain a desire to remain critically active and participatory in an effort to create a world where we will one day get it right.

Notes

1. Zygmunt Bauman, *Modernity and the Holocaust* (New York: Cornell University Press, 1989), 8.
2. Tadeusz Borowski, *This Way for the Gas, Ladies and Gentlemen*, trans. Barbara Vedder (New York: Penguin, 1976).
3. Victor E. Frankl, *Man's Search For Meaning*, 3rd ed. (New York: Simon, 1984), 108.
4. For example, Marshall Lee and Michael Steele, in "The Affective Approach in the Interdisciplinary Holocaust Classroom" in *Lessons and Legacies Volume II* (Illinois: Northwestern UP, 1998), 159-74, write, "Current postmodern literary theories, in particular the 'reader response' approach, according to which the reader brings no more than an immediate feeling about what he or she has just read to a discussion of the work, fail when faced with Holocaust literature" (160). While in and of itself a questionable statement and a faulty reading of postmodernist practices, a belief such as this is a critical commonplace for a large number of academics.
5. Martin Heidegger, "The Age of the World View," *boundary 2* 4, no.2 (1976): 341-55.
6. It is important to recognize that Martin Heidegger and his work have been commonly attacked as supporting the Nazi movement. I will not argue that Martin Heidegger was a member of the Nazi party or that his work can possibly be read as supporting this party. However, as many contemporary scholars have argued, Heidegger's work, especially his later work, can be read as an interrogation of those philosophies from which Nazism took so much power. In particular, one may choose to read William V. Spanos, "Heidegger, Nazism, and the Repressive Hypothesis: The American Appropriation of the Question," *boundary 2* 17, no.2 (1990): 199-280; or Dominick LaCapra, "Heidegger's Nazi Turn," in *Representing the Holocaust: History, Theory, Trauma* (Ithaca: Cornell University Press, 1994), 137-68. I read much of Heidegger's early work as an exploration of the dominant philosophies that brought about as well as emerged in the modernist moment; thus, much of his later work returned to such philosophies for the purpose of exposing the danger of such a belief system. While any discussion concerning the relationship between Martin Heidegger and his philosophy to that of Nazism is much greater than can be discussed in a footnote, I do not believe that a fuller treatment is necessary for the argument I am advancing in this essay.

7. For a discussion of the end of the postmodern moment and emerging literary and theoretical responses, see José López and Gary Potter, eds., *After Postmodernism: An Introduction to Critical Realism* (New York: Continuum, 2005); Neil Brooks and Josh Toth, eds., *The Mourning After: Attending the Wake of Postmodernism* (New York: Rodopi, 2007); or Robert L. McLaughlin, "Post-Postmodern Discontent: Contemporary Fiction and the Social World," *Symploke* 12, no.1-2 (2004): 53-68.
8. Melvin Jules Bukiet, *Signs and Wonders* (New York: Picador, 1999).
9. See Linda Hutcheon, *A Poetics of Postmodernism* (New York: Routledge, 1988) and Brian McHale, *Constructing Postmodernism* (New York: Routledge, 1992).
10. Thomas Kuhn, *The Structure of Scientific Revolutions* (Chicago: University of Chicago Press, 1962), 149.
11. Melvin Jules Bukiet, "Crackpot Realism: Fiction for the Forthcoming Millennium," *The Review of Contemporary Fiction* 16, no.1 (1996): 13-22; and Melvin Jules Bukiet, *After* (New York: St. Martin's, 1996). All further references to both this article and book will be noted in the body of the text.
12. Elie Wiesel, *Night* (New York: Hill, 1987).
13. Elie Wiesel, *All Rivers Run to the Sea* (New York: Schocken, 1995), 319-20.
14. Chantal Mouffe, "Radical Democracy: Modern or Postmodern," in *Universal Abandon: The Politics of Postmodernism*, ed. Andrew Ross (Minneapolis: University of Minnesota Press, 1988), 33.
15. Ibid.
16. Ibid., 44.
17. Curtis White, *Monstrous Possibility* (Illinois: Dalkey, 1998). All further references to this text will be noted in the body of the text.

The Second-Generation Holocaust Nonsurvivor: Third-Degree Metalepsis and Creative Block in Art Spiegelman's *Maus*

Michael Schuldiner

In the second chapter of *Maus II* (1991), Art Spiegelman, the son of Auschwitz survivor Vladek Spiegelman, is told by his psychologist that he, Art, and not his father who lived through Auschwitz, is the "REAL survivor."[1] It was the father who had experienced the terror that accompanied Hitler's invasion of Poland; he was moved from one ghetto to another, fled from shelter to shelter, was betrayed, caught, and forced to perform various types of labor at Auschwitz. Having survived Auschwitz until the closing days of the War, Vladek was put by the Nazis on a death march west to Dachau where he fell ill of typhus. He survived, however, and eventually made his way to Sweden and the free world. That he survived was due to resourcefulness—a talent for wheeling and dealing, the ability to quickly pick up various skills or pretend that he had, and to a certain extent an ability to deny himself. His son, Art, however, is having psychological difficulties, and these, says his psychologist, Paul Pavel, are the product of having grown up with a father who has been experiencing his own psychological problems as a result of having endured the Holocaust.

Pavel explains to Art that his father feels guilty for surviving—for having left so many behind, including Vladek's first son, Richieu, who was given poison by his aunt to avoid capture by the Nazis. Vladek copes with these feelings of guilt by distinguishing between those who have the talents to survive and were thereby virtually fated to survive, and those who do not have such talents and were fated to die. This theory—that some, like Vladek, had the skills and talents to survive while others did not—relieves Vladek of the guilt that comes of the sense that he did not do enough to help others survive (44). In his son Art, Vladek has created a "nonsurvivor type" with whom he can contrast himself, and who thereby serves to validate the distinction between "survivor and nonsurvivor" that Vladek has created in order to mitigate his feelings of guilt for having survived. Art was told bedtime stories of Auschwitz by his father.[2] Moreover, Art was belittled by his father whenever he helped him around the house: he was told by Vladek that he did not have the practical skills to survive an Auschwitz. As *Maus I* (1986) opens, Art is still—at age thirty—being treated as an irresponsible kid by his father who throws away Art's old coat because he thinks it's in an embarrassing state (Vladek instead gives Art a naugahyde windbreaker).[3] By being cast as a nonsurvivor type by his father and having attributed to him what are perceived to be the weaknesses of a nonsurvivor, Art becomes the victim of his father. At the same time, Art is a survivor in the sense that he survives his father's belittlement and efforts to cast Art in a position of childlike dependence.

The son, however, is not a passive recipient of his father's abuse. The portrait of his father that Art presents in *Maus*, as he full well realizes, is, in many respects, very unflattering. *Maus I* begins with the story of Vladek's early fling with the unfortunate Lucia Greenberg who, it is explained in no uncertain terms, is jilted by Vladek for Anja, Art's mother, who is not a very attractive woman but comes from a very wealthy family. Vladek explains that the more you got to know Anja, the more you came to love her. It is nonetheless clear that Vladek has behaved like a cad toward Lucia and married Art's mother for her money, regardless of how dedicated he becomes toward Anja afterward. Vladek certainly doesn't want the story of Lucia in Art's book. Art, in fact, promises not to put the story in his book (23). But of course he does.

Later, Art tells Mala (Vladek's second wife and herself a survivor) that he is worried that the portrait he is presenting of his father is that of the miserly old Jew who has hundreds of thousands of dollars in the bank but won't part with the cost of a handyman to put up the storm windows to keep himself warm (131-32). What worries Art is not that his father might be hurt by such a presentation, but that Jews in general might suffer from more popularization of the stereotype. It takes Pavel to explain to Art that regardless of his feelings toward his father, all young boys to some extent must admire their fathers, and that Art is feeling guilty for having proved his father wrong by becoming successful and having held his father up to ridicule in the first book (*Maus II* 44). Pavel is of course suggesting that Art should not feel guilty, and, in fact, Pavel's counseling seems to work. His patient goes on to present a particularly damning portrait of Vladek, in which Vladek is portrayed not only as a miser but also as a bigot.

It is not my intention here to discuss all of the problems that Art confronts as a "second generation nonsurvivor." The difficulties that Art experiences as the son of survivors have been discussed at length and with considerable insight by a number of critics.[4] Instead, I would like to discuss just one of Art's problems, the case of creative block that Art himself describes taking place in the second volume of *Maus*. Art's creative block has been discussed by only a few critics, and then only in passing.[5] The creative block accompanies and is related to the difficulties described above, but for the purposes of this paper the creative block will be discussed as a discrete condition. Indeed, the creative block becomes so severe that one of the drafts for this section was a very un-*Maus*-like six-frame narrative called "Creative Block" in which Spiegelman separates out the block that Art confronts.

Figure 1. *Complete Maus,* 177, draft 2.

The creative block was viewed by Spiegelman as warranting special attention. As the artist explains, his avowed purpose for writing the opening section of *Maus II*, chapter 2—one of the most well-known and often discussed sections of the *Maus* books—is his writer's block.[6] It is also in chapter 2, as well as in the preceding chapter, that some notable instances of metalepsis appear. In fact, as demonstrated in this paper, the literary device of metalepsis is employed by Spiegelman to both represent the problem and as a means of getting beyond the writer's block. Moreover, I discover here a new type or degree of metalepsis which only effectively appears in a medium where two sensory sources, such as words and pictures, combine. However, before discussing Art's creative block and the metaleptic event in *Maus,* it might be useful to say a few words about metalepsis.

In *Narrative Discourse*, Gerard Genette defines narrative metalepsis as the transition from one narrative level to another without the benefit of narration.[7] For example, when the narrator of a story tells the reader that the narrator's friend has been assassinated by a character in a book that he, the narrator, is reading, that is metalepsis: the two narrative planes—that in which the narrator reads his book and the narrative plane of the book in which the assassin appears—have been crossed by the assassin, according to the narrator. In effect, the assassin in the book being read by the narrator jumps out of that text, enters the narrator's plane of being, and kills the narrator's friend. For reasons that will become clear in a moment, I call this type of metalepsis, in which there is an unjustified movement from one narrative plane to another, second-degree metalepsis.

More recently, David Herman, employing the writings of Marie-Laure Ryan and the vocabulary of Alternative Possible World theory, has clarified another type of metalepsis, that in which a character from a story world is said by the narrator to relocate to the real world of the reader. Or, conversely, the reader is asked by the narrator to relocate to the world of the story.[8] For example, the narrator might explain that the assassin has been to the home of the reader and spared him his life; or the reader might be told that he, the reader, actually existed in the story some time long ago while asleep in his bed dreaming and didn't realize it. I call this type of metalepsis, in which the narrator intrudes or imposes on the reader, first-degree metalpsis. In both first- and second-degree instances, however, there is a certain violence done to the relationship between reader and narrator. Things are happening that the reader and narrator have tacitly agreed are not supposed to happen. The objective in both these types of metalepsis seems to be surrealism—they provide the reader with a sense of having been to a place that cannot exist, of having crossed borders that are fictional and therefore cannot be crossed. For these reasons, metalepsis is sometimes referred to as a "rupture" in the text, or "seepage" from one narrative level or Alternative Possible World to another. In the case of first-degree metalepsis, the rupture or seepage is between the world of the book and the life of the reader; in the case of second-degree metalepsis, the rupture is between levels of narration within a text.

It is in *Maus II*, chapter 2 that the reader is told in no uncertain terms that Art is having difficulty getting back to writing *Maus*. It is also worth noting that chapter 2 is laden with graphic metaphors for the creative block that Art is experiencing. At the very beginning of the chapter Art appears at his easel surrounded by a pile of dead, maskless bodies (everyone else in this section is wearing a mask). Art tells us that *Maus I* has already been published and it has been a critical and commercial success, but he is depressed and cannot write. The bodies remain with Art in the streets as he walks to the home of Pavel, his shrink, who deals with an array of problems that beleaguer Art (41, 43). As the session with Pavel proceeds, the reader learns that it is the corpses that stand in the way of Art's continuing his work on *Maus II*. Art fears that his work is in a manner desecrating the memory of the victims of the Holocaust. He finds himself lecturing to Pavel and quoting Beckett: "Samuel Beckett once said: 'Every word is like an unnecessary stain on silence and nothingness.'" After a moment, however, Art realizes that, "On the other hand, he SAID it." Pavel immediately recognizes that Art is on the verge of a breakthrough, and responds, "He was right. Maybe you can include it in your book" (45). While the knowledge that comes with Art's analysis of Beckett's words provides the courage to proceed, there are still several difficulties that Art confronts and that must be surmounted before he can continue to draw *Maus*. Art wants to know what it felt like to be in Auschwitz. Pavel responds by yelling "Boo" at Art, almost knocking him off his chair. "It felt like **that.** But ALWAYS," says Pavel. And lastly, Art needs to know what a tin shop at Auschwitz might have looked like. Pavel, who worked in a tool and die shop in Czechoslovakia, explains the implements that would have existed. Pavel is more successful treating some of Art's problems than he is with others, but one of the problems that is remedied is the particularly severe instance of writer's block that Art is confronting here in chapter 2. When Art is next seen by the reader, leaving Pavel's home through what appears to be the same streets he walked to get to Pavel's house, the bodies are no longer with Art, nor do they ever appear again (46).[9]

These maskless bodies—very clearly intended to be the bodies of Auschwitz from the narrative plane in which Vladek tells his story—are located by the graphic narrator in what Spiegelman call a "superpresent."[10] Their presence therefore could be thought of as an instance of metalepsis were it not so clear to the reader that they are probably meant to represent their presence in Art's unconscious. Metalepsis, it bears repeating, is by definition paradoxical. Of course, one can always make a kind of "sense" out of the pairing of even the most disparate images, but certain conventions within certain media allow explanations for some pairing to come more readily to the mind of the reader. Given the fact that we know Art has been trying to write about Auschwitz and that he is depressed, the bodies never really acquire that surreal edge that characterizes the appearance of a metaleptic event. The appearance of the bodies has more of the impact of a metaphor for Art's state of mind. And indeed, the fact that the bodies disappear when Art returns from the shrink suggests that the reader, in fact, is meant to view the bodies as representing the mental obstacles to Art's continuation of his writing—mental obstacles which, for all practical purposes, disappear.

But there is another instance of writer's block that is described in the first chapter of *Maus II*, and here Spiegelman does make use of metalepsis. The events of *Maus II,* chapter 1 are supposed to be taking place after the writing but prior to the publication of *Maus II*; and here in chapter 1 the reader is made aware of a first instance of writer's block which precedes the block that appears in chapter 2. This instance of writer's block is in a sense the beginning of that more severe experience of block in chapter 2, which is accompanied by depression. In the first chapter, the writer's block takes the form of an inability on Art's part to decide how his wife, Francoise, should be drawn. However, other, larger concerns lurk in the background. In particular there is the larger question of whether it is possible to do justice to the Holocaust in any type of medium, let alone the comic book—in effect the same concern that Art has to deal with in chapter 2 but which by that time has become more severe. What is interesting here is that the answer to the question of whether the comic is able to adequately represent the Holocaust is presented by metaleptic device. So too, the question and the answer to the question of how to draw Francoise is presented metaleptically. Moreover, the type of metalepsis used to present Art's difficulty drawing Francoise is a type that can only appear when two senses are addressed simultaneously, as is the case in the graphic novel where the verbal and visual combine or, sometimes, collide.

As *Maus II* opens, it becomes evident to the reader that Art has been having difficulty continuing with his father's story. Art has put off dealing with the question of how to visualize Auschwitz, that "reality" which, as he explains to Francoise, "was worse than my darkest dreams" (16). It is about 1986 or 1987 when the first pages of chapter 1 are drawn, and, conceptually, Art has only gotten as far as he did in 1972 when he published the three-page version of *Maus.* Both the three-page version of *Maus* and volume one of the two-volume book version of *Maus* end with Art's father arriving at Auschwitz. Moreover, by the time *Maus I* opens, the first volume has presumably been written and is awaiting publication, and Art is taking testimony from his father about his experience in Auschwitz. But Art has not yet even drawn the first page of *Maus II,* where his father's Auschwitz experience begins. He does not yet even know how to draw Francoise, the concern that opens chapter 1 of *Maus II*. Art is here in the first chapter experiencing creative block, even though its full severity is only revealed to the reader in the second chapter.

The reasons why Art is having problems drawing *Maus II* begin to unfold as he and Francois drive down from Vermont where they have been vacationing in the Catskills where his father has been staying for the summer. Mala, Vladek's second wife, has left him, and Vladek has asked Art and Francoise to stay with him. As the two drive along the countryside, Francoise detects that Art is depressed. "Depressed again?" she asks. Art replies that he is thinking about his book and how "presumptuous" it is of him to try to make sense of the Holocaust.

Art continues, “I feel so inadequate trying to reconstruct a reality that was worse than my darkest dreams. . . . And trying to do it as a comic strip! I guess I bit off more than I can chew. Maybe I ought to forget the whole thing” (16). Of course, Art does not “forget the whole thing.” Instead, the task before him appears daunting. He explains, “there’s so much I’ll never be able to understand or visualize. I mean, reality is too complex for comics . . . so much has to be left out or distorted.”

Figure 2. *Complete Maus,* 155.

Not only does Art feel guilty for not having experienced the camps as his parents had, which is one basis for his sense that he is incapable of representing the Holocaust, but he also feels that he is working in the wrong medium. The nature of the graphic novel, Art suggests, is such that it cannot adequately portray the Holocaust. Art blames himself and his medium.

What is especially significant here, however, is the dialogue that follows. Having heard Art’s complaints, Francoise replies, “Just keep it honest honey.” Art, referring back to the inadequacy of the comic in presenting reality and especially the reality of the Holocaust, responds, “See what I mean . . . in real life you’d never have let me talk this long without interrupting.” What the reader witnesses here is a not unusual instance of first-degree metalepsis. Art, the comic book character, is speaking as if he has inhabited both the world of the comic and our world. The character has to have inhabited a level of being or world other than that of the cartoon character to reasonably be able to tell Francoise that in real life she would never have let him talk that long without interrupting. We have a character, Art, who thinks he was real or is real, in addition to being a comic book character. He thinks he inhabits, or has inhabited, two different worlds. If the dilemma were that of a human who thought he could frequent a fictional world, we would identify him as delusional. Is a comic book character who thinks he inhabits the real world to be understood as any less delusional? Is the reader witness to a metaleptic event or a schizophrenic episode?

The schizophrenic episode can be thought of as non-text-based, first-degree metaleptic event. In the case of the schizophrenic episode the individual temporarily moves into a world that at least to some extent is of his own fabrication and does not exist. Similarly, in the case of first-degree metalepsis the character moves from the world of the book into our reality. But it seems also to be the case that, conversely, first-degree metalepsis is a way of presenting a schizophrenic episode. Given the fact that shortly after the metaleptic event Art is able to begin drawing and writing about Auschwitz, one might ask whether the reader is to assume that this instance of metalepsis or schizophrenia, which the author of the novel must to some extent participate in, has somehow remedied the creative block and depressed state that the author has been experiencing.

Art's problem, as he points out, is that he's feeling depressed, constrained by feelings of inadequacy as an artist and a human being who, compared to his survivor father, has led a relatively sheltered life. While his condition might demand some refurbishing of the psyche, there is nothing in the content of his delusion that is in any way of use to Art. That his wife might not have let him go on talking as long as he has if they were in an alternative reality that he thinks they once inhabited, tells Art nothing about his depressed state. However, the metaleptic leap that the mind makes as Art talks about being in two different worlds is in itself liberating. The sense of immobility that accompanies depression and prevents Art from continuing on with his presentation of Auschwitz is displaced by the exhileration of discovering in one's own mental activity how wonderful, after all, the mind's antics can be. Then, too, there must be the sense of accomplishment at having conveyed to the reader an impossible occurrence, and one that is also, quite simply, amusing. The crafting of a metaleptic event shortly after having admitted to the inadequacy of his medium and his background belies any inadequacy that might exist in either the craftsman or his medium. The author has presented an amusing event, one that is not supposed to be able to occur.

However, there is a second, and more significant, example of metalepsis that occurs at the very outset of *Maus II*, a metaleptical instance that requires two sensory sources such as words and pictures. As Art sees it, the problem that prevents him from starting *Maus II* is how to draw Francoise, his wife, who makes her first appearance at the very opening of *Maus II*, and who acts as surrogate shrink before fame and fortune permit Art the luxury of a professional psychologist. The scene opens with Art sitting underneath a tree in Vermont where they are vacationing, and in his sketchpad are several female animals, each dressed in Francoise's characteristic striped shirt and scarf.

Figure 3. *Complete Maus,* 150.

The options appear to have been to draw Francoise as moose, poodle, frog, mouse, or rabbit. She prefers the rabbit, but Art thinks the animal is too sweet and gentle for the French. Francoise insists then that she should be a mouse because she converted to Judaism. This minor dilemma that is presented by the verbal narrator, however, has already been decided by the graphic narrator. Francoise has already been drawn as a mouse, even as the character—via her verbal discourse—debates how she should be drawn. The graphic narrator has come to the rescue of the verbal narrator, without the verbal narrator knowing it.

The initial effect of this particular frame in which Francoise's identity is being discussed might be thought of as similar to that of a holographic representation. The picture changes, depending on how the available light hits the image, on which is imprinted two pictures, one on top of the other. So too, the meaning of the frame in which Francoise appears changes depending on whether the reader lets the words of the verbal narrator create an image inside the mind, or, instead, looks to the visual image that the graphic narrator has put on the page. If we focus on the words, as most noncomic book readers will do, Francoise's identity in *Maus* is still a matter of conjecture. If we view the picture, she is already a mouse. Yet the images can be imagined to coexist in the same space—one on top of the other, as it were.

What the reader meets with here is an instance of a new, third type of metalepsis that is actually different from the two types found in the traditional novel and effectively appears where sensory sources such as words and pictures are combined. The reader does not perceive a transgression from one narrative level to another by a character within the single narrative world of words; that is, the character does not jump out of a book being read by the narrator into the narrator's world (second-degree metalepsis). Nor is the reader made to feel that he has entered from the real world into the world of the novel, or that a character from the world of the novel has entered the world of humans (first-degree metalepsis). Instead, the reader moves back and forth between what are actually two sensory worlds—as opposed to narrative levels—within the novel itself: the verbal world of the author who wrote *Maus* and the visual world of the graphic artist who drew the book. In the world created by the author of the words—a world that is visualized only in the reader's mind—Francoise's animal identity has not yet been determined. In the world created by the graphic artist—the world that appears pictorially on the page and is taken in by the eye—Francoise is a mouse. Moreover, there is really no marker to terminate the reader's movement back and forth between the two competing image sources and interpretations of the panel. While it might appear to be the case that some closure exists when the words are read before the picture is interpreted—the picture would appear to answer the question posed by the words—if one reads the graphic first, as the more avid, younger comic book reader or the trained artist is likely to do, the words dismiss the intentions of the graphic artist. I call this type of metalepsis, which is based on an interminable movement back and forth from one sensory source to another within the same narrative level, third-degree metalepsis.

Moreover, one might suggest that there is still another type of metaleptic event that takes place as the reader distances himself and considers the thought processes that are occurring. The words and the picture inhabit the same frame—the same space and unit of time in a paradoxical way. Yet, the reader also moves from one narrative world to another, from the world of the verbal narrator to the world of the graphic narrator, back and forth dialectically as the reader's focus changes. That is, the mind moves metaleptically from acceptance of paradox to dialectical opposition. The paradox appears as one abstractly considers that the words and the picture are making diametrically opposed statements within the same frame. The dialectic becomes operative as one focuses on either the words or picture and begins imagining the scene painted by the words or identifying the significance of the picture.

But to return to the issue of writer's block: Art, by turning the question of how to draw Francoise into a dilemma, is, in one sense, simply avoiding the larger problem of how to draw Auschwitz. However, the alternation back and forth that the reader (and artist as reader) is required to perform, "traveling" between the picture created by the verbal artist and the picture drawn by the graphic artist, is itself representative of the type of dilemma that is symptomatic of creative block. The third-degree metalepsis in this case *is* the creative block experienced by the artist and made real for the reader as well as the reader-artist. But as in the metaleptic example discussed earlier—that is, Art's trip to his therapist—it is after this instance of metalepsis that the artist is able to move forward. Here, the metaleptic event provides the motivation to move forward with the discussion of the depression and feelings of inadequacy that he has been experiencing and which have not permitted him to take up paper and pen. Indeed, this instance of third-degree metalepsis virtually opens *Maus II*, and seems to have been necessary in order to even begin writing about the difficulties that he has had writing.

As noted earlier, Art's case of writer's block is due to a number of problems. There is more to the baggage that Art carries around than even the enormous weight of the Holocaust dead. There are the feelings of guilt that appear when *Maus I* is published. Art is made to feel that he has offended a number of people, Germans as well as Holocaust survivors. Art's offense, in the publication of *Maus I*, against the memory of his father is also a major obstacle, according to Art's psychologist, Pavel. Then, too, there is the concern that his own motives for writing *Maus* have been less than noble as he is besieged with offers to merchandize his book. Yet, Art gets over his writer's block, and in the process of showing the reader how he did it, he also shows the reader something about the presentation of the impossible.

There are of course obvious differences between first-generation Holocaust writers and second-generation accounts of what their parents experienced. The first generation is talking about itself, and in so doing presents the reader with an honest account of what they experienced that no reader has any right to expect. One thinks, for example, of Elie Wiesel's presentation of the relationship between himself and his father at Auschwitz. Wiesel admits to getting angry at his father for not avoiding being beaten, and that he began to count the advantages to be gained from his father's death, as others had in his situation. And even though he prays for the strength not to be happy in his father's death, Wiesel admits the reader to more of his internal world than he might have. In the case of Spiegelman's *Maus,* the sins witnessed to are not the confessed sins of the sinner; they are the sins as seen by his son, the spectator. Vladek never confesses to any wrongdoing, any act of unkindness in the camps that might have left another less capable of withstanding the harshness—the horror and torment—of Auschwitz. On the other hand, it is important to note that Vladek's miserliness, his bigotry, his survivalism at the expense of his son are all sins perceived by the less-than-objective (and something less than entirely sympathetic) narrator. To put it succinctly, the confessions of the first generation have been replaced by the inspections of the second generation.

It is in the matter of style that Spiegelman differs markedly from his predecessors. The key difference between Spiegelman and first-generation Holocaust writers such as Wiesel, Primo Levi, Tad Borowski, and others is of course the enormous artistic risks that Spiegelman takes in the very act of treating the Holocaust in a comic book, a risk of which Art Spiegelman is fully aware, and a task for which, at a certain point in the graphic novel, he confesses not being fully equipped. This risk taking extends to the creation of visual metaphors and to use of metalepsis.

Notes

1. Art Spiegelman, *Maus II, A Survivor's Tale: And Here My Troubles Began* (New York: Pantheon, 1991), 44. Hereafter, all references will be made parenthetically in the text.
2. In an earlier, three-page version of *Maus* that Spiegelman wrote, the reader discovers that Vladek told Art bedtime stories about his experiences during the Holocaust. (See "MAUS [the three-page version]," in Appendices to *The Complete* Maus, prod. Elizabeth Scarborough, Voyager, 1994, CD-ROM, 3, 12, 22.)
3. Art Spiegelman, *Maus, A Survivor's Tale* (New York: Pantheon, 1986), 69. Hereafter, all references will be made parenthetically in the text.
4. See Hamida Bosmajian, "The Orphaned voice in Art Spiegelman's *Maus* I and II," *Literature and Psychology* 44 no. 1-2 (1998): 1-22; Marianne Hirsch, "Family Pictures: *Maus*, Mourning, and Post-Memory," *Discourse* 15, no. 2 (1992-93): 1-27; Sophia Lehmann, "'And Here [Their] Troubles Began': the Legacy of the Holocaust in the Writing of Cynthia Ozick, Art Spiegelman, and Philip Roth," *Clio* 28 (1998): 29-52; Miles Orvell, "Writing Posthistorically: *Krazy Kat, Maus,* and the Contemporary Fiction Cartoon," *American Literary History* 4, no. 1 (1992): 110-28; and Stephen E. Tabachnick, "Of *Maus* and Memory: The Structure of Art Spiegelman's Graphic Novel of the Holocaust," *Word & Image* 9, no. 2 (1993): 154-62, to name just a few.
5. Nancy K. Miller, "Cartoons of the Self: Portrait of the Artist as a Young Murderer, Art Spiegelman's *Maus*," *M/E/A/N/I/N/G* 12 (1992): 45; Michael Rothberg, "'We Were Talking Jewish': Art Spiegelman's *Maus* as 'Holocaust' Production," *Contemporary Literature* 35 (1994): 674.
6. *Complete* Maus, 178, voice file.
7. Gerard Genette, *Narrative Discourse: an Essay in Method* (Ithaca: Cornell University Press, 1980, reprint 1985), 234-37.
8. David Herman, "Toward a Formal Description of Narrative Metalepsis," *Journal of Literary Semantics* 26, no. 2 (1997): 134-36.
9. In this same scene, Art also grows taller after having shrunk to the size of a child earlier (42). But this graphic development is a metaphor for other psychological problems that Art is experiencing, problems which continue to recur and is evidenced by Art shrinking again later (47).
10. *Complete* Maus, 178, voice file.

"Unfinished Business": Journeys to Eastern Europe in Thane Rosenbaum's *Second Hand Smoke* and Jonathan Safran Foer's *Everything Is Illuminated*

Jennifer M. Lemberg

The back covers of each of the two volumes of Art Spiegelman's *Maus* (1986, 1991) depict sets of superimposed maps: the first presents Poland during World War II as a background for a small map of Rego Park, Queens, while the second shows Birkenau surrounding an area in the Catskill mountains. As Nancy K. Miller writes in her careful analysis of these images, in the latter picture the body of Art's survivor father, Vladek, "connects the two territories—his head is in New York, his body in Poland."[1] She argues that the maps denote the "effects of these simultaneous geographies and temporalities" upon the character of Art, who, as a member of the second generation, struggles with the burden of his parents' Holocaust memory.[2] Indeed, the maps suggest that what Michael Rothberg calls the "maladies of time and space" that afflict Holocaust survivors can be transmitted to their children. The "unsettling of spatiotemporal boundaries" that for survivors result in the "coexistence of two temporalities," the present and the Holocaust past, is shown in these images to be part of the legacy of trauma.[3]

Spiegelman demonstrates that the identity of the second generation is formed by "mapping" the distances between past and present, between here and there. But as his artistic struggles in *Maus* make clear, this is no easy task. As "witnesses to memory," members of later generations exist in complex relation to Eastern European geographies they never knew.[4] They absorb strong ideas about the sites of their parents' suffering, but also inherit a lack, or what Ellen S. Fine has termed an "absent memory," of the event that is a constitutive feature of their identity.[5] Art's frustration at being unable to see for himself the places his father describes in his testimony, even as he is haunted by them, points to how the process of working through the effects of the Holocaust is imaginatively connected to space as well as time: as a character in Thane Rosenbaum's *Second Hand Smoke* (1999) asks, for example, "what Jew doesn't have some unfinished business with Poland?"[6]

Along with Rosenbaum's work, another recent Jewish American novel, Jonathan Safran Foer's highly popular *Everything Is Illuminated* (2002), suggests that "maladies of time and space" form an important trope in the literature of those who come after. Written by authors belonging to the second and third generations, these works consider travel undertaken by "memory tourists," or Jews searching for their roots.[7] Each depicts a young Jewish American man who travels to Eastern Europe in search of insight into a Holocaust past of which he has an excess or an absence of memory. But where Spiegelman in his autobiographical text self-consciously depicts his effort to recreate his father's vision of Poland, Rosenbaum and Foer imagine what happens as, many years later, those who come after see Eastern Europe with their own eyes. Without apologizing for the history of the area, they imply that viewing the region in its contemporary context helps later generations to mourn the losses of the Holocaust.

In their depiction of travel to Eastern Europe, both novels reflect a growing social trend. Efraim Sicher writes that "since around 1989, a 'recovery' has become possible of lost Jewish spaces . . . and they are being marketed on a tourist itinerary from Toledo to Prague, from Worms to Auschwitz."[8] Indeed, as new regions of Eastern Europe opened to tourists after the Cold War, groups such as Shtetlschleppers offered American Jews the opportunity to trace the "footprints" of their "ancestors" through shtetls, cities, and camps.[9] The appeal of such travel is widespread, as *The New York Times* reported in 2003 that each year more than 100,000 American and Israeli Jews visit Poland.[10] A phenomenon that took shape as survivors began to pass away, Jewish heritage travel, as it is called in the tourism industry, reaffirms the importance of the Holocaust to contemporary Jewish American identity.[11]

Second Hand Smoke and *Everything Is Illuminated* show the rewards and challenges of trying to follow in survivors' footsteps. In the former, Duncan Katz, the American-born child of survivors of Auschwitz and Bergen-Belsen, lives in the "prison" of his own mind, a result of the trauma transmitted to him by his parents and especially by his mother, Mila (whose name evokes the renowned street in the Polish Ghetto, memorialized in Leon Uris's *Mila 18*). After the revelation following Mila's death that she abandoned a child in Poland, Duncan goes there in search of Isaac, his half-brother. For Duncan, a trip to Poland threatens to lead him back in time directly to the camps, but with Isaac's aid, he will finally untangle the past from the present. In *Everything Is Illuminated*, a writer bearing the name of the text's author, Jonathan Safran Foer, goes to Ukraine to look for the town of Trachimbrod, where he hopes to find Augustine, a woman he believes to have hidden his grandfather from the Nazis. Jonathan is greeted by the "Heritage Touring" company, led by Alex, a young translator of limited abilities, and by Alex's cantankerous grandfather. The unlikely companions head into the countryside, but Trachimbrod has vanished, and they cannot find Augustine. Their journey facilitates Jonathan's imaginative engagement with Ukraine, however, and exposes the involvement of Alex's grandfather in the history of the region as an important source of family conflict.[12]

As they chronicle journeys that yield unexpected results, both novels also employ related narrative structures. They exhibit the impulse to bear witness, which Victoria Aarons identifies as a distinguishing characteristic of Jewish American fiction, and emphasize its importance as an experience capable of creating a "shared memory" among those who come after.[13] Each features a European counterpart to the American traveler whose existence challenges the notion that Eastern Europe is a place fixed forever in the Holocaust past. These men join their visitors in seeking ways to understand and describe Holocaust history: in *Second Hand Smoke*, Duncan and Isaac piece together their story long before the African American nurses who cared for Mila and know her history promise to impart it to them. In *Everything Is Illuminated,* Jonathan and Alex bear witness to testimonies offered by their elders, and exchange letters and writings in which they create a shared vision of the past. As a result, both works situate Eastern European spaces within an expanded framework of space and time, and broaden the context of Jewish American Holocaust memory.[14]

Additionally, the books use separate storylines to chronicle the past and the present and to test the boundaries of space and time altered by traumatic memory. In each text, two narratives haunt each other, seeming to draw closer as the travelers approach specific geographical points. At times, the "simultaneous geographies and temporalities" that trouble Art's character in *Maus* appear to be inescapable, especially in climactic scenes occurring at sites of destruction—Birkenau in *Second Hand Smoke* and the plaque where Trachimbrod once stood in *Everything Is Illuminated*—where the boundaries between space and time might be expected to be most fluid. Ultimately, the novels suggest that the connections forged among the brothers and friends keep those boundaries in place, not excluding the past from memory, but preventing it from becoming totally overwhelming or entirely absent.

These two recent works do not attempt to redeem Eastern Europe or even to suggest that anti-Semitism has faded in the years following the Holocaust; in fact, each points to disturbing attitudes toward Jews among the local populations.[15] Instead, they demonstrate the need to see Eastern Europe as it exists in the present, to detach it from a fixed point in time in order to facilitate mourning. Rothberg observes that contemporary representations of the Holocaust often combine the ideas of time and space, and explains that Mikhail Bakhtin's concept of a "chronotope," or, "literally, time-space," is useful in understanding the tendency to connect them.[16] As a tool for textual study focusing on the relationship between the two and giving equal attention to both, Rothberg writes, the idea of the chronotope helps to show how time and space are often conflated in Holocaust discourse. The most notable example may be found in Theodor Adorno's dictum regarding the uses of art "after Auschwitz," in which the concentration camp becomes not only a place on the map but also a point in time.[17] In the novels discussed here, the experience of visiting the sites is shown to plot new temporal coordinates onto those spaces, so that they are no longer located solely in the past.[18]

Because it permits a direct encounter with places associated with the blurred "spatiotemporal boundaries" of survivor memory, in these novels heritage travel allows later generations to define their own perspective, no matter how unwillingly they may do so at first. Eva Hoffman counsels that it is critical, for those who come after, "with utmost care and compassion, to use our vantage point outside the traumatic history itself in order to bring to it interpretations that may not be available to the victims," and stresses that the unique perspective of later generations can be developed only if we "depart from a sense of the past conveyed to us through . . . transferred knowledge."[19] By presenting protagonists who encounter the Eastern European landscape and its inhabitants not only as they exist in the traumatic memory of survivors, but also in the present, these books refashion the chronotope of Eastern Europe. They show that there may be no better way to find a critical point of departure than through a journey of return.

Second Hand Smoke forms the middle volume of what Rosenbaum calls his "post-Holocaust trilogy," composed also of *Elijah Visible* (1996) and *The Golems of Gotham* (2002).[20] The trilogy traces the effects of Holocaust memory on later generations, from the children of survivors struggling under their particular psychic burdens in the first book to a grandchild conjuring golems in the last. Andrew Furman notes that *Second Hand Smoke* is set in the "three central milieus of the Jewish diaspora: Miami Beach, New York, and contemporary Warsaw," and sees this as a widening of Rosenbaum's "geographic" and "social vision."[21] That Duncan's voyage to Poland is located at the center of the arc within the trilogy also indicates its importance to Rosenbaum's ideas about the multigenerational process of mourning the Holocaust.

As Furman writes, *Second Hand Smoke* is "primarily about rage."[22] Duncan is raised by a mother, Mila, who desires "not a son, but a comic-book superhero," and who wishes to see him become "a modern-day golem from Miami Beach who could defend any Jewish ghetto anywhere, anytime" (32, 36). Due to his mother's transference, for Duncan, as for Art in *Maus*, "all important aspects of the present take their identity from the past event."[23] After a childhood lacking in maternal affection and spent mastering violent sports, Duncan takes a job as a Nazi hunter for the U.S. government; obsessed with revenge, he sees enemies everywhere. In his study of cultural representations of Jewish masculinity, Warren Rosenberg maintains that "violence . . . constitutes a radical embodiment that makes one immediately present to oneself and thus creates the illusion of self integration," and as he responds to even the slightest provocation with an excess of aggression, Duncan comes to recognize himself through violence.[24] Yet, as time passes, he is fired from his job, his wife leaves him, and he is plagued by an anxious stomach, the results of an uncontrollable anger that rents his mental and physical existence.

Despite the warnings of those who know him that "no good can come" from his trip to Poland, finding Isaac will be the salve finally capable of healing Duncan's wounds (156). He tells his daughter, Milan, that he will be making a trip "home," but in undertaking the journey he prepares to arrive in a place where the horrors of the past threaten to overwhelm the present, as if he will be moving through time as well as space. The moment in which he crosses the border reveals how, for Duncan, Poland exists as a chronotope, a site where time and space are linked. As he waits at a checkpoint, Duncan thinks to himself, "Poland was Krypton; he was familiar with the paralyzing fragments of this imploded land—the accents, the nightmares, the abducted memories. But now before him was the thing itself, *terra unfirma*, the blackest hole in the Jewish galaxy" (180). His mind racing, Duncan thinks he is entering a "trap." When he cannot separate the shouting of the border guards who demand his passport from the "shrieking" of the dead, he has the first of what will be several breakdowns during his trip.

The novel's structure emphasizes the idea that to enter Poland is to seem to travel back in time. To use Rothberg's terms, here the "extreme" that characterized Holocaust experience threatens continually to intrude upon the "everyday" of post-Holocaust life.[25] Duncan's arrival precedes by just a few pages the story of Mila's departure many years before, so that these events seem to occur almost simultaneously. When the "lethargic and slovenly" border guards pull him from his car and treat him roughly, Duncan panics and drops a photograph of Milan, which then gets "stuck underneath the patrolman's boot" (195). Soon after, we discover that as she fled Poland Mila was forced by a group of bored, brutal soldiers to leave her only photo of Isaac behind. To Duncan, the men in Polish uniforms appear terrifyingly similar to those his mother would have encountered after the war, but the novel implies that in Poland it is easy to make this mistake. Arriving in Warsaw, Duncan finds that it is cluttered with signs and symptoms of its traumatic past, from the overgrown Jewish cemetery to the dwindling Jewish population. Finally, the narrator describes Poland as "a land where Pharoah's heart could never become unhardened, a country that had seen worse than mere plagues, where the seas were unpartable" (225). The reference has great resonance, as for the past century allusions to Biblical Egypt have been used to convey "a powerful and unchangeable image of Eastern Europe" in Jewish American literature.[26] While the novel shows Duncan's inability to distinguish one temporality from another to be part of his traumatic inheritance, again, it implies that to do so in Poland is especially difficult.

It is Isaac who will free Duncan from the "maladies of time and space" exacerbated by the visit to Poland. When he first meets his older sibling, Duncan is disappointed to find that Isaac looks just like their mother, and believes that he must have been a "dumpy, defenseless, four-eyed Jewish kid," picked on by the Poles (208). Indeed, Isaac fits the stereotype of Eastern European men in works by many post-Holocaust Jewish American male writers, who even as they were fascinated by *yiddishkeit* found its construction of masculinity insufficient in comparison to mainstream American cultural ideals.[27] However, Duncan underestimates Isaac's strength. Though his talent is belied by his soft physique, Isaac is a wildly popular yoga teacher, beloved by Poles throughout the city. While not formally religious, he wears a yarmulke and is dedicated to taking care of the Jewish cemetery. Most importantly, although Mila inscribed his arm with her concentration camp number before she left, and although he has grown up among the ruins of the Holocaust, Isaac has "achieved a transcendent peace, a spiritually safe place of his own making," something Duncan has been unable to do (167).

At odds with Isaac's ability to "let go" of the past, Duncan envisions a "return to Poland" that is "messianic."[28] He dreams of reclaiming Polish land so that the brothers can "take back their birthrights," as he says: "I'm talking Jewish vengeance. When we get through with this place, *aliyah* will take on a whole different meaning. Poland as the new Holy Land. Imagine . . . Warsaw, Kraków, and Lublin once again overrun with Jews" (211).[29] In their divergent attitudes toward everything from history to religion, Duncan and Isaac resemble the twin brothers in *Elijah Visible*'s "The Rabbi Double Faults" (1996), where Rabbi Vered, an Auschwitz survivor who appears in all of Rosenbaum's fiction, argues with a twin brother who left Poland before the war. These pairs draw from their Biblical predecessors—for example, Cain and Abel, Jacob and Esau—a structure identified by Rosenberg as important to contemporary male-authored Jewish American texts that imagine masculine struggle in the context of Jewish identity formation.[30] Finally, though, Isaac assists Duncan in reforming his point of view, while Duncan provides his elder brother with insight into their mother's character. The brothers slowly come to know each other, but their visit to Auschwitz-Birkenau, where Mila was interned, brings them even closer.

The visit to the camp near the end of the novel forces Duncan to distinguish between the past by which he is held hostage and the post-Holocaust present. Bypassing Auschwitz, now "more museum than death camp," he continues with Isaac on to Birkenau, where they find "a hard-core Holocaust vista, a raw combination of silence and the haunted memorabilia of what the prisoners themselves once saw," that ostensibly facilitates a more direct connection to the past (247). In a mixed metaphor that evokes a chronotope, Rosenbaum has said elsewhere that he won't "write about the years 1939-1945," a period he views "as holy ground."[31] Duncan therefore cannot follow directly in Mila's footsteps through Birkenau, but his mind and body collapse nonetheless as time loses all meaning there. Imprisoned by neo-Nazis, the brothers are forced to spend the night inside a barracks, and during this experience Duncan's thoughts rush from the horrors of the Holocaust past back to his troubled present, with little distinction between the two.[32] He finds his only comfort in Isaac's calm, meditative capacity to face their situation, his brother's tranquility a stronger defense against the psychic battle being waged by their captors than is his own preparedness for physical combat. And though we are left uncertain as to whether the episode was a product of the "trap" of Duncan's mind, afterward he is freed from the "time warp" in which he has been caught.

The novel ends with another journey of return, this time as Duncan arrives home in the United States. Travel has proved to be a necessary remedy to the angry, destructive life he had been leading. Duncan is reunited with his wife and daughter, and convinces Isaac to follow him to America, presumably to join a living Jewish family. The book closes as the two brothers say the mourner's kaddish over their mother's grave.[33] Mila's nurses join the brothers in prayer and agree to share what they know of her story. The mourning Duncan began in Poland is now fully underway, and he will dwell in his own temporality, able to live with his knowledge of the past. The rainstorm that pours down upon the mourners emphasizes this point, as Isaac's number is washed away and a bolt of lightening appears to "split the sky in two, separating this world from the other," that of the dead (303). This scene at a cemetery in Miami Beach, the novel proposes, is evidence that while Poland may still be hostile territory, for Duncan, much good has come from his visit there.

Before returning to America at the end of *Second Hand Smoke*, Duncan spends several months in Warsaw, attending synagogue and Isaac's yoga classes, where he finally learns to "breathe" freely. He comes to know the city, wandering its streets, sitting in its parks, pubs, and playgrounds. Attempting to find in the visages of its people some clue to the horrific past, he thinks to himself that "if not for the accident of Auschwitz and yet another detour in the Diaspora road map, he might have been born right here, in Warsaw, with these people as his neighbors" (284).[34] Similarly, in *Everything Is Illuminated*, Jonathan desires "to see Trachimbrod," the shtetl in Ukraine for which he is searching, "to see what it's like, how my grandfather grew up, where I would be now if weren't for the war."[35] While this kind of thinking will be difficult for them to sustain, at moments such as these the young men try to free their imaginations in order to envision Eastern Europe as not always already the site of the Holocaust.

Although Duncan will go as far as to sit in reflection in a church in Warsaw, as Alan L. Berger remarks, in *Second Hand Smoke* the project of remembering the Holocaust is an exclusively Jewish concern.[36] Things are different in *Everything Is Illuminated*, however, where the third-generation American character and his European counterpart embark on a shared project of mapping of the Holocaust's continuing effects. In his discussion of second-generation Holocaust works, Berger distinguishes between a "particularlist" versus a "universalist" approach. The former bears out ideas of "covenant and chosenness" in imagining *tikkun atzmi*, or a "(mending or repair) of the self," while the latter looks "to articulate universal lessons emerging from the Holocaust," and works toward *tikkun olam*, "the moral improvement or repair of the world."[37] We may draw from these ideas in order to explore the differences between the second and third generation texts discussed here. Where Rosenbaum focuses primarily on Jewish responses to the Holocaust among the second generation, Foer imagines how Holocaust memory may have a profound impact on the third generation of not only survivors but bystanders as well.

If in *Second Hand Smoke* Holocaust memory threatens the children of survivors with its proximity, here it affects the grandchildren of those who lived through the war in ways they are not able to recognize. In interviews, Foer has described going on a poorly planned trip to Ukraine in search of his family's history, during which "he found no one."[38] His failure is reflected in the novel, where there are many obstacles to uncovering the secrets of the past. However, facing these challenges is shown to build sympathy between Jonathan and his guides. Their inability to find what they are looking for increases their awareness of the devastation wrought by the Holocaust, an understanding of which they arrive at together.

Foer does not set out to redeem a country whose history is deeply implicated in the genocide of the Jews. Alex's macho posturing, the disgusted response of a waitress to Jonathan's request for vegetarian food, and even the attitude of Alex's grandfather toward "the Jew" with whom they are traveling are humorously presented as evidence of the "backwardness" of Ukraine. But lingering hostilities are treated more seriously as the group drives into the countryside, where they are clearly unwelcome. Traveling with a Jew and speaking a Russian-inflected dialect that identifies him as a resident of Odessa, Alex expects to be greeted with some suspicion. He begins to see that something deeper is at issue, however, when his requests for directions to the now nonexistent shtetl of Trachimbrod are met with anger and harsh instructions to "go away." Finally, he begins to grasp that the people do not welcome questions about the past: "it was seeming as if we were in the wrong country, or the wrong century, or as if Trachimbrod had disappeared, and so had the memory of it" (116). The area is established as a chronotope, here, as the landscape is imbued with a "'temporal' aspect."[39] The antagonism of the Ukrainian farmers makes the place seem unchanged; only their denials are new.

Lista, an elderly Jewish woman who at first claims to know nothing of Trachimbrod, then cries and tells Alex, "I have been waiting for you for so long," finally reveals the fate of the shtetl. "You are here. I am it," she says, in response to their queries (118). Her presence forms a stark contrast to her neighbors' refusals, for as her name implies, Lista lives as a record of the past. Her home is filled with the belongings of the residents of the town, salvaged after a massacre by the Nazis, and, isolated, ghostlike, she is at one point confused as to whether the war has ended. She leads the travelers to the now-empty field where Trachimbrod once stood, though as she tells them, it "ended fifty years ago" (154). If Lista "is it," and "it" has ended, she has essentially ceased to exist, swallowed up by her devotion to memory.

Amid these extreme instances of silence and remembrance, the young writer and his Ukrainian guide search for ways to understand and represent the traumatic past. Alex writes letters to Jonathan describing their journey and his growing concern for the Jewish history about which he is learning, while Jonathan creates an "imagined history" of Trachimbrod.[40] Their writing structures the book, with chapters alternating between the story of Trachimbrod (including the adventures of Jonathan's grandfather, Safran) and others detailing the journey taken in the present day. In arguing that later generations must guard against heavily proscribed views of the past, Hoffman advises that one way to achieve needed distance may be "to unfreeze our vision of the past from the point of historical trauma and start exploring again the multifarious life before . . . It may be time to return the Shoah, in our imaginations and collective consciousness, to the *longue durée* of previous and subsequent history."[41] Jonathan and Alex engage in in a related process in the narratives they create. Despite the farmers' denials and Lista's insistence that Trachimbrod has "ended," the town becomes part of a history that stretches back before the Holocaust and extends into the future as part of their shared memory.

Similar to Rosenbaum's novel, in *Everything Is Illuminated* the story of the past—in this case, Jonathan's history of the Trachimbroders—is carefully paced, so that the unfolding of past events coincides with others taking place in the present. Thus, we read about the wedding of Jonathan's grandfather to his first wife, as Jonathan imagines it to have been, almost simultaneously with the arrival of the travelers at the site where it might have occurred. With their overlapping geographies, the two narratives seem to follow each other very closely, and as readers we may delight in those moments which seem to bring us nearer to the past. But as one narrative approaches the day when the Trachimboders are murdered by the Nazis while the other takes us to the plaque that now stands in their place, the notion of this simultaneity is more difficult to bear, and it becomes excruciating to consider the difference in temporalities marked by this single point in space.

Lista leads the group to their destination, where they discover the plaque dedicated by Itzhak Shamir to the 1,204 townspeople who were killed. Their arrival at the field which is the former site of Trachimbrod elicits testimony first from Lista and later from Alex's grandfather, releasing the extreme into the everyday and raising questions as to how places seem to occupy particular moments in time. As Lista tells the story of being shot in the stomach while pregnant, then left for dead among the friends and relatives whose murder she witnessed, past and present threaten to collide. This scene is followed by one in which, back at their hotel the night before Jonathan is to leave, the group picks through the contents of a box from Lista's collection, called "In Case," and filled with the possessions of the dead. We discover that Alex's grandfather originated from a nearby town, and that when the Nazis arrived he gave up his best friend, a Jew, in order to save his own family. Just pages later, the history of Trachimbrod comes to an end, as in a devastating conclusion to the magical realist tale, a series of ellipses marks the silencing of the lively shtetl and we read of the massacre from which Jonathan's grandfather escapes.[42]

In the presence of the multiple stories of the past communicated by survivors, bystanders, monuments, and objects, Jonathan and Alex create a narrative of their own. Their shared experience is described in a chapter called "What We Saw When We Saw Trachimbrod *or* Falling in Love," and is shown to solidify a deepening bond between the two men, who lay down together beneath the stars, processing their reaction to the events around them (181). By the end, Alex has been drawn into the "testimonial chain" of Holocaust witness and discovered its impact on his family.[43] His grandfather's devastating act is presented as an explanation for the abusive behavior of Alex's father, who has inherited a legacy of trauma transmitted through silence and guilt. We learn that Alex has been hiding the fact that he is gay from his father, while trying desperately to protect his younger brother from the older man's drunken rages. As "everything is illuminated"—a phrase that is heavy with meaning, suggesting a mystical light emanating from Trachimbrod while its inhabitants make love, and the revelations that bring knowledge and change near the end of the novel—Jonathan and Alex must create a broader framework in which to fit their new knowledge of both past and present. They will no longer write to each other by the novel's end—Alex claims that he needs distance from everything related to the Holocaust, though his need for separation may be driven by the love he feels for Jonathan—but the two young men have nevertheless formed lasting memories of their own. In the changes wrought in Alex's life and in the story of Trachimbrod before, during, and after the Holocaust, the novel dislodges the notion of the countryside of Ukraine as a point forever fixed in the traumatic past. The effects of that past are indeed ongoing, but as part of a sweeping and dynamic story which brings memory into the present.

Analyzing the effectiveness of Holocaust monuments, James Young reminds us that it is not only what the markers at sites of destruction allow us to remember that is important, but that by visiting them, we create new memories and form new communities. As he writes, "remembering together becomes an event in itself that is to be shared and remembered."[44] Traveling through Eastern Europe, the protagonists of *Second Hand Smoke* and *Everything Is Illuminated* find an aftermath to which they must bear witness. To do so properly, they must create new stories in cooperation with those they find there. Each novel builds toward a conclusion in which a young American creates what Avishai Margalit calls new "communities of memory" with a figure he meets in Eastern Europe, through a shared viewing of sites of destruction.[45] While defining community differently, the novels foreground acts of telling and listening, as brother to brother, tourist and guide, the American and European men together bear witness to what came before and to what unfolds in the present.

Envisioning Holocaust memory as a project sustained by members of later generations, *Second Hand Smoke* and *Everything Is Illuminated* do not shrink from exposing it as a difficult undertaking. Their authors heed warnings against narratives that flatten historical memory, explore a range of perspectives on how time and space connect, and dramatize the process through which "shared memory" is formed. Introducing new temporal dimensions to existing ideas about Eastern Europe, they imagine how journeys there might help us to create new forms of Holocaust memory, capable of honoring the past while attending to the demands of the future.

Notes

1. Nancy K. Miller, "Cartoons of the Self: Portrait of the Artist as a Young Murderer—Art Spiegelman's *Maus*," in *Considering Maus: Approaches to Art Spiegelman's 'Survivor's Tale' of the Holocaust*, ed. Deborah Geis (Tuscaloosa: University of Alabama Press, 2003), 47.
2. Ibid.
3. Michael Rothberg, *Traumatic Realism: The Demands of Holocaust Representation* (Minneapolis: University of Minnesota Press, 2000), 165.
4. Lawrence Langer, *Holocaust Testimonies: The Ruins of Memory* (New Haven: Yale University Press, 1991), 39. Alan L. Berger uses Langer's phrase to characterize all "second-generation texts" in *Children of Job: American Second-Generation Witnesses to the Holocaust* (Albany: State University of New York Press, 1997), 20.
5. Ellen S. Fine, "The Absent Memory: The Act of Writing in Post-Holocaust French Literature," in *Writing and the Holocaust*, ed. Berel Lang (New York: Holmes & Meier, 1988), 44.
6. Thane Rosenbaum, *Second Hand Smoke* (New York: St. Martin's, Griffin, 1999), 134. Hereafter noted parenthetically in the text.
7. James E Young, *The Texture of Memory: Holocaust Memorials and Meaning* (New Haven: Yale University Press, 1993), 144.
8. Efraim Sicher, "The Future of the Past: Countermemory and Postmemory in Contemporary American Post-Holocaust Narratives," *History & Memory* 12, no. 2 (2001): 61.
9. "JewishGen: The Home of Jewish Genealogy," JewishGen. http://www.jewishgen.org/shtetlschleppers (May 17, 2003).
10. Peter S. Green, "Jewish Museum in Poland: More Than a Memorial," *The New York Times*, January 9, 2003.
11. Amy Hungerford, *The Holocaust of Texts: Genocide, Literature, and Personification* (Chicago: University of Chicago Press, 2003), 78.
12. Even as they explore its meanings, both texts mock the heritage tourism industry. The dubious qualifications of Alex and his grandfather as guides in *Everything Is Illuminated* humorously call into question the credentials of other such groups, while in *Second Hand Smoke* the narrator more somberly describes Jewish tourism in Poland as allowing "Poles who hated Jews . . . to cash in on the absence of Jewish life" (107).

13. Victoria Aarons, *A Measure of Memory: Storytelling and Identity in American Jewish Fiction* (Athens: University of Georgia Press, 1996), 5; Avishai Margalit, *The Ethics of Memory* (Cambridge: Harvard University Press, 2002), 51.
14. The structure of these novels further resembles other post-Holocaust texts. In their separate discussions of *Maus* and Anne Michaels's *Fugitive Pieces* (1998), Marianne Hirsch and Susan Gubar point to Klaus Theweleit's analysis of the Orpheus myth that, as Gubar writes, in war literature and elsewhere "implicitly places a dead woman in the crucial role of bringing into being male couples who replace her procreativity with their own higher creativity," as a useful critical model. Gubar suggests that *Fugitive Pieces* successfully "reinterprets traditionally male-dominated approaches to the Shoah," by associating "the crisis in aesthetics so often attributed to the catastrophe with a related crisis in masculinity." Similarly, the works discussed here reflect the myth but also rework it as they portray masculine aggression as an inadequate response to tragedy. Susan Gubar, "Empathic Identification in Anne Michaels's *Fugitive Pieces*: Masculinity and Poetry after Auschwitz," in *Gender and Cultural Memory*, ed. Marianne Hirsch and Valerie Smith, special issue, *Signs* 28, no. 1 (2002): 250-51; Marianne Hirsch, *Family Frames: Photography, Narrative, and Postmemory* (Cambridge: Harvard University Press, 1997), 34.
15. As this essay goes to print, several recent titles have directed public attention to the Holocaust and wartime history of Ukraine and other countries in the region, including Father Patrick Desbois's *The Holocaust by Bullets: A Priest's Journey to Uncover the Truth Behind the Murder of 1.5 Million Jews* (New York: Palgrave Macmillan, 2009), and Timothy Snyder's *Bloodlands: Europe Between Hitler and Stalin* (New York: Basic Books/Perseus Book Groups, 2010).
16. M. M. Bakhtin, *The Dialogic Imagination: Four Essays*, ed. Michael Holquist, trans. Caryl Emerson and Michael Holquist (Austin: University of Texas Press, 1981), 425.
17. Rothberg, 21.
18. In addition to considering issues of proximity and distance to Holocaust memory in *Maus*, Rothberg offers an analysis of the "interpenetration of everyday time and concentrationary time both during and after the war" in the work of Auschwitz survivor Charlotte Delbo (164). His discussion has informed my approach here.
19. Eva Hoffman, *After Such Knowledge: Memory, History, and the Legacy of the Holocaust* (New York: Perseus, Public Affairs, 2004), 196-97.
20. "Choking on Life," Thane Rosenbaum interviewed by Dinah Selzer, *JewishFamily.com.* http://www.jewishfamily.com/culture/books/choking_on_life.txt (May 17, 2003).
21. Andrew Furman, *Contemporary Jewish Writers and the Multicultural Dilemma: The Return of the Exiled* (Syracuse: Syracuse University Press, 2000), 79.
22. Ibid., 80.
23. Hungerford, 86.
24. Warren Rosenberg, *Legacy of Rage: Jewish Masculinity, Violence, and Culture* (Amherst: University of Massachusetts Press, 2001), 6.
25. Rothberg, 6.
26. Asher Z. Milbauer, "Eastern Europe in American-Jewish Writing," in *Handbook of American-Jewish Literature: An Analytical Guide to Topics, Themes, and Sources*, ed. Lewis Fried et al. (New York: Greenwood Press, 1988), 360. Milbauer looks at Jewish American texts in which the "land of the Pharaoh" refers mostly to Russia, but describes the phrase as often denoting Eastern Europe more generally.

27. Rosenberg, 154.
28. "Choking on Life."
29. Alan L. Berger cites this passage as evidence of Duncan's continuing rage and as one of the ways in which Rosenbaum provides various "outlines of a possible post-Holocaust redemption." Support for this interpretation comes from Rosenbaum's statement, in an interview, that "retribution makes sense," though "it can still be deadly." Alan L. Berger, "Mourning, Rage, and Redemption: Representing the Holocaust: The Work of Thane Rosenbaum," *Studies in American Jewish Literature* 19 (2000): 11; "Choking on Life."
30. Rosenberg, 44.
31. Thane Rosenbaum, "Art and Atrocity in a Post-9/11 World," in *Jewish American and Holocaust Literature*, ed. Alan L. Berger and Gloria L. Cronin (Albany: State University of New York Press, 2004), 125.
32. Berger ("Mourning, Rage, and Redemption," 12) points out the similarities between Duncan's breakdown in this scene and the collapse of Adam Posner in *Elijah Visible*'s "Cattle Car Complex," during which Adam becomes convinced that a broken-down elevator is in fact a cattle car transporting him to the camps.
33. Kathleen Brogan observes that the idea of "secondary burial," used in anthropology to describe "a funerary ritual in which the dead are exhumed and reburied," provides a useful model for considering the structure of ethnic American literature. Brogan writes that "final burial shifts power from the dead to the living, and . . . while effecting a separation of the dead and the living, nevertheless integrates the dead (as newly accessible spirits) into the ongoing life of the community." Read in this context, the final scenes of *Second Hand Smoke* might represent Mila's "reburial," a solemn corrective to her funeral near the beginning of the book, which, as Furman (78) observes, "descends into chaos and farce." Where Duncan needs to be "unburied," as Isaac says, Mila must be laid to rest. Thanks go to Christa Baiada for bringing Brogan's text to my attention. Kathleen Brogan, *Cultural Hauntings: Ghosts and Ethnicity in Recent American Literature* (Charlottesville: University Press of Virginia, 1998), 67.
34. The notion of Polish and Jewish "neighbors" was complicated by the publication of Jan T. Gross's book of that title in 2001. The book describes the massacre of 1,600 Jews by their Gentile neighbors in the town of Jedwabne, Poland, in 1941, and has sparked continuing debates about Polish-Jewish relations.
35. Jonathan Safran Foer, *Everything Is Illuminated* (New York: Houghton Mifflin, 2002), 59. Hereafter noted parenthetically in the text.
36. Berger, "Mourning, Rage, and Redemption," 12.
37. Berger, *Children of Job*, 4. Berger categorizes Rosenbaum's *Elijah Visible* as falling in the former category.
38. Joyce Wadler, "Seeking Grandfather's Savior, and Life's Purpose," *The New York Times Online*. http://www.nytimes.com/2002/04/24/nyregion/public-lives-seeking grandfather-s-savior-and-life-s-purpose.html (March 17, 2003).
39. Sawomir Kapralski, "Battlefields of Memory: Landscape and Identity in Polish-Jewish Relations," *History & Memory* 13, no. 2 (2002): 36.
40. Wadler.
41. Hoffman, 198. This view has been adopted by many Holocaust educators. For example, the Museum of Jewish Heritage—A Living Memorial to the Holocaust, which opened in New York City in 1997, states on its website that "The mission of the Mu-

seum is to educate people of all ages and backgrounds about the broad tapestry of Jewish life in the 20th and 21st centuries—before, during, and after the Holocaust." http://www.mjhnyc.org.

42. Readers of this essay who are familiar with the film of *Everything Is Illuminated* (Warner Bros., 2005) will recognize significant differences between the plot and structure of the movie and that of the book. Besides eliminating the imagined history of Trachimbrod, among other changes the film portrays Alex's grandfather as a Jew who escapes being killed and then goes on to hide his religious identity. This shift significantly alters the nature of Alex's connection to the Holocaust.
43. Dori Laub, "Bearing Witness or the Vicissitudes of Listening," in *Testimony: Crises of Witnessing in Literature, Psychoanalysis, and History*, ed. Shoshana Felman and Dori Laub (New York: Routledge, 1992), 71. Interestingly, Jonathan asks Alex to stop translating as Lista continues with her tale, as if it is too much for him to bear. In some ways, therefore, Alex comes to possess a deeper factual knowledge than Jonathan of the history of the area.
44. Young, 7.
45. Margalit, 69.

Part 2

Folklore, Fantasy, and the Metanarrative

The Escapist: Fantasy, Folklore, and the Pleasures of the Comic Book in Recent Jewish American Holocaust Fiction

Lee Behlman

Jewish American writers addressing the Holocaust in recent fiction have encountered a daunting set of moral and aesthetic difficulties. Among these are the seemingly unbridgeable historical divide between a relatively comfortable American Jewish present and the dark European past and the inadequacy of any attempt, fictive or not, to capture the scope and intensity of such a massive collective experience. Recent fiction by young writers shows that these difficulties have become exacerbated by time. With this widening cultural and historical gap, and the loss of many witnesses to the Holocaust, has come a loss in direct access to the experience of the Holocaust and its effects. One major response to the problem of representation by young American writers has been the use of fantasy, folklore, and magical-realist devices.[1] The first section of this essay describes how in their first books two of these writers, Nathan Englander and Jonathan Safran Foer, make creative use of these devices in order to both thematize and manage the issue of their own distance from the Holocaust. A second section discusses how Michael Chabon's *The Amazing Adventures of Kavalier & Clay* (2000) not only makes use of fantasy but also produces a more direct argument about its value and relevance for contemporary Holocaust-themed fiction. *Kavalier & Clay* offers a notably bold and provocative assessment of the problem of representing the Holocaust. Though the novel fits squarely within a tradition of realistic narrative—specifically, the Jewish American immigrant novel tradition that combines blunt social critique with a narrative describing a young man's economic struggle and advancement—at the same time, it thoughtfully explores the power and possibilities of a particular form of nonrealist art: the superhero comic book. With superhero comic books, Chabon presents a form of fantasy that resolutely avoids the real, for it seeks to resolve history either by overcoming it through neat, miraculous reversals or by escaping its terms completely.

Lawrence Langer has ably described the moral and aesthetic difficulties all writers have faced in addressing the Holocaust in fiction: "When the Holocaust is the theme, history imposes limitations on the supposed flexibility of artistic license. We are confronted by the perplexing challenge of the reversal of normal creative procedure: instead of Holocaust fictions liberating the facts and expanding the range of their implications, Holocaust facts enclose the fictions, drawing the reader into an ever-narrower area of association."[2] Holocaust fiction is restricted aesthetically, in this formulation, by the moral privilege that must be accorded to historical fact. "Literature," Langer goes on to write, "generalizes human experience, while the events of atrocity we call the Holocaust insist on their singularity."[3] Sue Vice has warned of a further problem that accrues to much of Holocaust fiction: by its very nature, she notes, much of mainstream fiction seeks resolution, and with resolution may come sentimentality and a false redemption.[4] As an alternative, Vice calls for a kind of fiction that, like much documentary testimony, "is riven with a more fitting linguistic and narrative self-doubt" (5-6). This fiction will be harsher and more ugly on the surface, and will include "crude narration, irony, black humour, appropriation, sensationalism, even characters who mouth anti-semitic slogans" (9). This anti-aesthetic of "disruption and unease" would ostensibly disturb the easy comforts of typical realist fiction and its readers (160). Vice associates her model with Bakhtinian dialogism, but in her hands Bakhtin's always provisional, rather loose set of descriptive terms becomes a more rigidly enforced set of aesthetic precepts, characteristic of various modernist and postmodern formalisms, perhaps most appositely the "shock" theater tactics of Artaud and Brecht.

Although Vice could better define the limitations of her own aesthetic model, it still provides a very helpful guide to understanding recent trends in American fiction on the Holocaust, particularly works by young Jewish American writers. Some of the most striking work by these writers does indeed privilege "disruption and unease" and features endings that avoid easy closure. What is particularly important about these recent works' practice of "dis-ease" is their use of Ashkenazi Jewish folklore and the fantastic in conjunction with details of the brute reality of genocide. The reader's sense of shock or surprise in these works derives from the apparent clash between the familiar characters, conventions, and storylines of Yiddish folklore and the dreadful events that would destroy the culture that produced them.

Yiddish folklore, in this juxtaposition, does not simply play the part of conventional narrative that is torn apart by the incursion of the darker, anarchic force of Holocaust reality; the folkloric storytelling in these works, much like the general tradition of Yiddish folklore, is not, in Vice's terms, problematically "seamless . . . [and merely] aesthetically pleasing" (160). Instead, it maintains its own disruptive, dark comic powers and existential profundity, resources that Kafka and Isaac Bashevis Singer famously drew upon in fashioning their own fictions. But it does stand as a relatively innocent force, a source of humor and inspiration and a reminder of what has been destroyed.

All of this is evident in Nathan Englander's short story "The Tumblers," from his breakthrough 1999 collection *For the Relief of Unbearable Urges*.[5] Here, Englander subjects the Fools of Chelm, those classic clueless characters of Yiddish folklore and literature, to the depredations of Nazi occupation and genocide.[6] The people of Chelm are placed in a ghetto and subjected to an increasing set of restrictions, culminating in their being forced into boxcars and sent off to be murdered. In an unlikely turn of events, a small group of Chelmites, the Mahmirim, enter a boxcar containing a Romanian circus troupe and manage to survive by performing as circus "tumblers" with the rest of the group. Throughout the story, the Mahmirim continue to misinterpret reality the way the people of Chelm do in the classic stories, but the reality they miss is now of course horrific; they understand the loss of the other Jews to be a great trick, "the magic of disappearing Jews" (42-43). In the final scene of the story, the tumblers appear in a German circus and are laughed at by the audience for being "as clumsy as Jews" (54).

Although Mahmirim are left miraculously alive at the end, the reader is left with no illusions about the the deathly reality that surrounds them, one which they still fail to grasp: "But there were no snipers, as there are for hands that reach out of the ghettos; no dogs, as for hands that reach out from the cracks in boxcar floors; no angels waiting, as they always do, for hands that reach out from chimneys into ash-clouded skies" (55). The facticity of the Holocaust is juxtaposed throughout this story with the "benighted" innocence of the tumblers, until, through the narrator's voice, it intrudes to close out not just this story, but the shtetl culture that would produce this storytelling tradition.

In his precocious first novel, *Everything Is Illuminated* (2002),[7] Jonathan Safran Foer includes an ongoing work of fiction by one of its characters, the eponymously named Jonathan Safran Foer. This story tells the eighteenth- and early-nineteenth-century history of Trachimbrod, a fictionalized version of the real-life Ukrainian shtetl Trochenbrod that would be completely obliterated in the Holocaust. Despite its connections to this veristic history, the character Jonathan's Trachimbrod narrative features a host of magical-realist devices, including a baby mysteriously born from a river, a synagogue that moves on wheels, and at one point, a sighting of the shtetl by a future astronaut on the moon. This framed story is offset by the contemporary letters of Jonathan's Ukrainian pen pal, Alex; Alex himself is writing a novel (from which we also view a set of chapters) based on a "real-life" visit Jonathan has made to the Ukraine in search of remnants of Trachimbrod and the woman who saved his grandfather from the Holocaust. The accuracy of Alex's novelistic account of Jonathan's visit is put into serious question in several of Alex's letters.[8] The novel foregrounds, through a set of untrustworthy narrators, the impossibility of any unmediated, wholly accurate access to the past, while at the same time the novel's conclusion leaves no doubt as to the disastrous, very real effects of the Holocaust on both Alex's and Jonathan's families. Jonathan's ultimately fruitless search for Trachimbrod and his father's savior has an unexpected result at the end. Alex's grandfather, a generally sympathetic character, is provoked by this search for evidence of the past to reveal something he has kept hidden for more than fifty years: his responsibility for the death of his best friend, a Jewish man, at the hands of the Nazis. And the grandfather's telling of this story, too, is mediated by Alex. In Foer's novel, the magical realist and folklore-based material is a self-conscious device for imagining the past, one which also announces the gap between itself and the past as it was experienced. It is this experience that is ultimately privileged but never quite accessed directly in the novel.

In their use of folklore, fantasy, and magical-realist devices, Englander and Foer both address the problem that Lawrence Langer describes—that "Holocaust facts enclose the fictions"—by making fictions that announce their fictiveness, and that intimately surround historical experience but do not present that experience directly. Instead, they suggest its shape through, in the case of both writers, ironic contrasts between folkloric Jews and the real Jews whose culture produced their stories, and in the case of Foer alone, through a set of voices that always distance and mediate experience. These writers set up jarring contrasts between the folkloric and fantastical Jewish worlds they describe and the world of historical experience that they surround or are juxtaposed with. A significant effect of these juxtapositions is an uneasy sort of humor, as in the general cluelessness of the people of Englander's Chelm about their predicament, or in Foer's division of a city between its Jewish Quarter and its "Human Three-Quarters."[9] In both cases, the humor is based to a strong degree on what the folkloric, fantastic Jewish world does not know, in its comparative innocence.

To be sure, the use of fabulistic techniques in Holocaust-themed fiction is not a recent development, nor is it specific to American authors—writers as various as David Grossman, Cynthia Ozick, Philip Roth, and even Primo Levi have used such approaches in their Holocaust-themed writing.[10] What stands out about the recent fictions under discussion here is the degree to which they emphasize the now-vast temporal and cultural distance between late twentieth- and twenty-first-century America and the Holocaust, as well as the gap between our time and the American experience of the Holocaust for previous generations. While distance has always been a prevalent theme for writers addressing the aftermath, it has newfound importance given the loss of tangible linkages to the past. A signal example of these emphases on generational difference and loss is Art Spiegelman's *Maus I* (1986) and *Maus II* (1991). As several critics and Spiegelman himself have noted, this two-part graphic novel is centrally concerned with the transmission of the Holocaust survivor's story to his son, and the impossibility of gaining any access to the past, except through a medium that announces its own contrived, provisional nature.[11] In this case, the medium is the panel-by-panel, progressive narrative form of the comic book.

Near the end of *Everything Is Illuminated,* Alex, the fledgling Ukrainian writer, composes a letter in his own inimitable, thesaurusized English, in which tells his friend Jonathan about a precious fantasy:

> *If we are to be such nomads with the truth, why do we not make the story more premium than life? It seems to me that we are making the story even inferior. We often make ourselves appear as though we are foolish people, and we make our voyage, which was an ennobled voyage, appear very normal and second rate. We could give your grandfather two arms, and could make him high-fidelity. . . . It could be perfect and beautiful and funny, and usefully said, as you say. . . . I do not think there are any limits to how excellent we could make life seem.*[12]

Alex fantasizes about eluding the terms of his own history and healing the physical and emotional wounds of both his and Jonathan's families. The new fiction that could result might well be fantastical itself, with a miraculous set of happy reversals and revisions of the past. Alex expresses this wish for an escape from an uncomfortable reality, if only for a few moments, near the end of the story, and his perspective is not clearly endorsed by a narrative that more typically uses fantasy to give shape to ugly truths.

While in *Everything Is Illuminated* this wish to escape through fiction appears only briefly and as a subterranean desire, it is very much the main subject of Michael Chabon's Pulitzer Prize-winning novel, *The Amazing Adventures of Kavalier & Clay* (2000).[13] Through its sweeping narrative about two young Jewish comic-book artists making their careers in New York during the "Golden Age" comics era of the late 1930s and 1940s,[14] *Kavalier & Clay* explores the use of fantasy, not as a means of giving shape to the documentary facticity of the Holocaust, nor as a set of stage properties surrounding the real, but as a potentially valid means of escape from the past. Chabon's novel explores a major moral and aesthetic issue which is only partially addressed in the Holocaust fictions I have discussed thus far: the fact that fantasy itself, no matter how disruptive and unsentimental it may be, nevertheless may give pleasure to an artist and an audience, and that pleasure may be a distraction from the past. What's more, and this is where Chabon is most surprising, his novel guardedly presents the idea that that distraction is itself a valid response. *Kavalier & Clay* is an extended meditation, with comic books as its central subject, on the value of fantasy as a deflective resource rather than a reflective one.[15]

Escapism is a prominent characteristic of American popular art forms, and this quality, when it is found in Hollywood entertainment, episodic television, or mass-market fiction, is often dismissed by critics as essentially shallow or trivial. Without denying the trashiness of much American popular culture, Chabon issues an aesthetic and ultimately moral defense of escapism as it is found in one of America's only original art forms (along with jazz music), superhero comic books. Through its exploration of comic books, the novel is remarkable for its intimate exploration of the pleasure and value of fantasy for both creator and reader. Chabon's intent in exploring superhero comics is not to issue a postmodern critique of realism, nor a populist assault on "elites" and their art, but to show, in a phenomenological way, how fantasy feels, and how it may assuage pain. With this comforting gesture may come the admittedly problematic, quintessentially American phenomenon of forgetting.

Kavalier & Clay announces from its beginning a fracture between the distanced American experience of the Holocaust and the events of the Holocaust themselves. In what is in many respects a classic Jewish immigrant narrative, Josef Kavalier, a teenage art student from Prague, travels to America and makes his way in this new world at the side of his American cousin and partner in comics, Sam Clay (formerly Klayman) of Brooklyn. The novel begins almost immediately with the meeting of these two characters and then flashes back in a series of episodes to Josef's early life in Prague, where we learn of his secular, upper-middle-class Jewish family's increasing difficulties under the Nazi regime in the late 1930s, and of his eventual, lonely escape to America. As an adolescent, Josef had learned the skills of escape artistry under the guidance of Kornblum, an *ausbrecher* (or escape artist) of Eastern European origin, and Josef comes to use these skills in his escape from Prague. The rest of the novel takes place in America and follows Josef and Sam's career as they invent and further develop their character, "The Escapist," a superhero who, like Houdini, can escape from any restraint and, like Captain America and the original Human Torch, can fight whole divisions of Nazi soldiers single-handedly. The comic book itself becomes the key means of imaginative escape for Josef, who works constantly to effect the physical escape of his brother, Thomas, from occupied Prague to America.

The recent history of comic books—particularly the longer-form graphic novels produced by such artists as Will Eisner, Daniel Clowes, and Chris Ware—has demonstrated the vast storytelling potential of the form beyond the limitations of the superhero genre in pamphlet or magazine form. Many critics and serious comic-book artists alike seek to draw aesthetic distinctions between such recent work and the sixty-year history of stories about men and women in tights. Art Spiegelman has both acknowledged and forestalled the connotations of triviality often associated with both artists and fans of superhero comics by popularizing an alternate term, *comix*, which stands for a co-mix of images and words.[16] Yet in *Kavalier & Clay*, Chabon embraces the superhero comic book in its earliest incarnation, with its crude drawing style, monotone dialogue, and unlikely plots, as a rough but vivid form.[17] Unlike Clowes and Ware, who in some ways embrace the form but also tend to put ironic quotes around their referencing of superheroes,[18] Chabon's work is notable for its enthusiastic endorsement of superhero comics. In a bravura section beginning on page 74, Chabon's narrator describes the early history and aesthetics of comic books with a kind of learned enthusiasm not unlike that found in Melville's discussion of whale facts and statistics in the "cetology" chapters of *Moby-Dick*. Chabon's narrator does such things as compare the relative artistic merits of superhero comics covers and their inside material, and in doing so he can also be quite critical, with the wonkish air of any enthusiast, about the limitations of the form:

> In 1939 the American comic book, like the beavers and cockroaches of prehistory, was larger and, in its cumbersome way, more splendid than its modern descendant. . . . [Yet] as with all mongrel art forms and pidgin languages, there was, in the beginning, a necessary, highly fertile period of genetic and grammatical confusion. . . . The men tended to stand around in wrinkleless suits that looked stamped from stovepipe tin and in hats that appeared to weigh more than the automobiles, ill at ease, big-chinned, punching one another in their check-mark noses. . . . Consequently, the comic book, almost immediately upon its invention, or soon thereafter, began to languish, lacking purpose or distinction. There was nothing here one could not find done better, or cheaper, somewhere else (and on the radio one could have it for free).
>
> Then, in June 1938, Superman appeared.[19]

Inspired by the extraordinary success of the Man of Steel, Siegel and Schuster's crude but portentous invention, Sam (with Josef in tow as his artist) proposes a new superhero comics line for Sheldon Anapol's Empire Novelties Company. Anapol agrees to let them produce a sample issue, which leaves them in the position of having to come up with a hero to build their comic book around over a single weekend. In a witty scene that follows, complete with in-jokes about later comic-book inventions, we witness Sam and Josef struggle to come up with a new comic-book hero, and we are told that many such conversations are simultaneously blooming in New York in the post-Superman year of 1939. Sam argues that the problem involved in creating a new superhero is not centrally about what powers he will have, but about his motivation.

> "This is not the question," he said. "If he's like a cat or a spider or a fucking wolverine, if he's huge, if he's tiny, if he can shoot flames or ice or death rays or Vat 69, if he turns into fire or water or stone or India rubber. He could be a Martian, he could be a ghost, he could be a god or a demon or a wizard or monster. Okay? It doesn't *matter*, because right now, see, at this very moment, we have a bandwagon rolling, I'm telling you. Every little skinny guy like me in New York who believes there's life on Alpha Centauri and got the shit kicked out of him in school and can smell a dollar is out there right this minute trying to jump into it, walking around with a pencil in his shirt pocket, saying, "He's like a falcon, no, he's like a tornado, no, he's like a goddamned wiener dog. Okay? . . . The question is *why*." (94)

Over the next forty-eight hours, Sam and Josef toil with a group of young fellow artists to create a set of superheroes for a new series called Masked Man Comics, and among the heroes will be their main creation, the Escapist, a figure who combines the *ausbrecher* talents of Houdini with the dark, secret history of the Shadow, along with the prodigious but limited physical strength of the early Superman. In the time before America enters the Second World War, the Escapist fights the Nazis on the cover of the first issue, putting the kibosh on Hitler himself. But Chabon does not just describe Sam and Josef's cocreation of the character; he inserts a full chapter (123-34) in which the origin tale of the Escapist is told as a short story, in prose that manages to combine sophisticated narrative and descriptive material with the gee-whiz dialogue of Sam Klay's comic book. The comic-book story, then, is transmuted in the narrator's hands into a kind of literary hybrid. It becomes a purely textual short story that includes a level of physical detail and even psychological sophistication that would never appear in a comic book of this era; yet it is also clearly a comic-book story, with all the trappings of its fantasy world: a lame boy who can suddenly walk, secret evil societies, men from the East with arcane knowledge. With this "origin" tale, as well as that of a later character Sam and Josef create—the mousy-librarian-turned-superheroine "Luna Moth" (267-74)—Chabon gives life to the pulpy energy, excitement, and crude imaginative power of superhero comics without a trace of condescension.[20]

In telling the story of the development of Sam and Josef's creative career, Chabon sets them within a larger story of the development of "Golden Age" superhero comics, a story populated largely by Jewish men. Most of Sam and Josef's fellow artists are New York Jews, and real-life Jewish comic creators such as Jack Kirby, Joe Simon, and Siegel and Schuster are referenced.[21] Perhaps the most important influence on the novel's conception of Jewish comic-book artists in this period is the life and autobiographical works of Will Eisner, an innovative early comic artist and, more recently, theorist and inventor of the graphic novel form.[22] The connection between Jewish artists and their comic-book creations is frequently alluded to in the novel, as when Sam says, "What, they're all Jewish, superheroes. Superman, you don't think he's Jewish? Coming over from the old country, changing his name like that. Clark Kent, only a Jew would pick a name like that for himself" (585).

In some respects, *Kavalier & Clay* aims to be a novel of social realism, capturing the working environments of late depression-era New York, but despite its attempts at a hard-edged depiction, the novel more often slips into a sentimental view of this period and setting.[23] For much of the middle section of the novel, Chabon describes in loving detail different New York milieus, including the lower-middle-class home of Sam's mother in Flatbush, Brooklyn and the Greenwich Village intellectual set of Josef's girlfriend, Rosa Saks Luxemborg. But the main emphasis is on the workplace, Sheldon Anapol's "Empire," where the Jewish comic-book artists are usually underpaid and overworked, under their

Jewish boss. In its representation of the rough world of commerce of the time, Chabon doesn't approach the gruff realism of Saul Bellow's Chicago in *The Adventures of Augie March* (1953). For example, in an unlikely development, Sam and Joe manage to leverage from their employer a percentage of profits on certain Escapist-related products (including the Escapist radio show); this during a period in which comic artists were almost always cut out of a share of the profits that accrued from their creations.[24]

It is understandable that Sam and Josef's New York lives are told in a somewhat broad and even sentimental manner, for these two characters must carry a great symbolic weight in *Kavalier & Clay*. They represent the divided experience that is the story of Jewish American life at this time and in our time, for they are both American and Other, native born and refugee, newly formed and unsettlingly old. Josef stands, in many respects, for a particular Jewish American notion of the dark but romantic Mitteleuropean past, with his serious intellectual bearing, his background of suffering and stoicism, and his masculine and slightly mysterious aura; Sam, on the other hand, is the short, clever, fast, funny, and ambitious New York Jew, a man who "Like all of his friends . . . considered it a compliment when somebody called him a wiseass" (4). Neither character conforms perfectly to these archetypal roles—for example, Sam's closeted homosexuality adds considerable complexity to his portrayal—but instead, like Dickens' greatest creations, each is both a finely delineated, idiosyncratic human figure and a caricature or type.

In Sam and Josef's story, Chabon represents a familiar Jewish American conception of America as the place of Jewish creativity and hope, the place to escape to, and of Europe as the place of Jewish history and death, the place to escape from. The Jewish story, in this telling, seems at first to end in the Holocaust but is, at least to an extent, revived in America, and this is nowhere so evident as in Chabon's use of the Golem legend. In the early chapters of the novel, Chabon describes how Josef's escape is made possible by the rediscovery of the body of Rabbi Loew's famous Golem of Prague. This giant immobile figure, formed from the clay of the River Moldau, has long been kept hidden in an unmarked, sealed-off room in an apartment house near the *Alneuschul* (the Old-New Synagogue), but it is eventually retrieved by Josef and Kornblum (his *ausbrecher* tutor) and becomes the means for Josef's escape out of Europe. Josef and Kornblum disguise the Golem as a "dead *goyische* giant" (52), secret Josef away in its casket, and send it eastward, out of Nazi-controlled territory and into Lithuania. Once he escapes from the confines of the Golem's casket, Josef manages to sojourn halfway around the world through the Soviet Union and Japan, and finally to America and (physical) salvation.

The Golem in this story represents both the dead hope of Jewish life in Europe and the ever-living promise of Jewish creativity, which can be transferred to the new world. It is a predecessor, then, as an artifact of Jewish fantasy, to the new Jewish fantasy creation, the comic-book hero. Chabon makes this connection between Golems and comic books clear early in the novel, when Josef sketches a Golem in his first effort at representing a superhero; upon seeing it, his future boss, Sheldon Anapol, is confused and exclaims, "Is that the *Golem*? . . . My new Superman is the Golem?" (86). The connection is made even more explicit late in the novel, in a fascinating passage:

> The shaping of a Golem, to [Josef], was a gesture of hope, offered against hope, in a time of desperation. It was the expression of a yearning that a few magic words and an artful hand might produce something—one poor, dumb, powerful thing—exempt from the crushing strictures, from the ills, cruelties, and inevitable failures of the greater Creation. It was the voicing of a vain wish, when you get down to it, to escape. To slip, like the Escapist, free of the entangling chain of reality and the straitjacket of physical laws. (582)

The Golem represents the dream of escape, which in this passage involves a flight from both the physical bondage of the Nazis and the imaginative bondage that may limit the expression of any artist. As such, the Golem is commensurate with comic-book superheroes and with comic books themselves as artifacts of escapist Jewish creativity in the fecund commercial world of American pop culture.

We arrive, through the figure of the Golem, at comic books as the central signifier and vehicle for the fantastic of *Kavalier & Clay*, and with it the central issue of this essay, which is the question how young Jewish American writers understand the nature and efficacy of fantasy in the context of the Holocaust. Comic books, in Chabon's hands, represent a form of Jewish fantasy markedly different from Englander's Chelm legends and Foer's magical-realist shtetl, Trachimbrod: while these two authors indirectly give shape to the reality of the Holocaust through these fantastical devices, Chabon uses comic books as a recourse or alternative to shaping that reality. The Escapist, like America itself, is always set in contrast to the Holocaust experiences of Josef, and is never used as vehicle for the depiction of those experiences, indirect or otherwise.

Through their deliberately broad, even crude vocabulary, the Escapist storylines and layouts provide an opportunity for Josef to mobilize anti-Nazi sentiment in the period before America would enter the war, and to provide for himself a dose of short-lived imaginative revenge. Josef furiously wants to believe that if he and Sam "could not move Americans to anger against Hitler, then Joe's existence, the mysterious freedom that had been granted to him and denied to so many others, had no meaning," and yet he is also aware that his persuasive powers will always be limited, for "the Escapist was an impossible champion, ludicrous and above all *imaginary*, fighting a war that could never be won" (172-73, 168). While the Escapist fulfills the fantasy of protecting the persecuted (much like Rabbi Loew's Golem patrolling the streets of Prague) and even goes further to visit active retribution upon Hitler and his cronies, still, the effectiveness and the satisfactions of such a creative consolation are seriously curtailed by an awareness of what is actually happening in Europe. Josef also realizes the fact that superhero comics may promote dangerous fantasies of the kind of violent revenge that fuel the Nazi assault on Jews.[25] Chabon thus acknowledges through Josef's experiences the problem of the extreme incommensurateness between fantasy and reality, most intensely in the scene where Josef discovers that, despite his great efforts to save his brother, Thomas, the boy has been killed along with a ship full of other Jewish refugee children by a German U-Boat.

Yet near the end of the novel, Chabon does make some efforts to reconcile the American impulse to escape through fantasy with the memory of the European Jewish past and of the Holocaust itself. He seeks to achieve this reconciliation by bringing the Golem, and its memory of the lost, pre-Holocaust Jewish European past, into the present, so that it no longer just prefigures American comic books but becomes their subject. After finding out about Thomas's death, Josef leaves to become a U.S. serviceman and cuts off contact from Sam and his pregnant girlfriend, but years later, he returns to their lives, and reveals that he has been spending time secretly writing a 2,256-page comic book based loosely on the Golem legend. It is both a superhero story and a Golem story, a "long and hallucinatory tale of a wayward, unnatural child, Josef Golem, that sacrificed itself to save and redeem the little lamplit world whose safety had been entrusted to it" (577). For Josef, it seems that this new, breakthrough work is "helping to heal him" (577) of his wounds, not by erasing his memory of the pre-American Jewish past, but by recasting them in comic-book form, and having European Jewish fantasy mingle with the American variety. In a similar gesture at acknowledging the "pastness" of the European Jewish past and yet seeking to recall it into memory, Chabon has the long-lost casket of the Golem reappear in Josef's life at the very end of the novel. Whereas before the Golem was fully formed but nearly weightless, now it is but a heap of dust; yet it is heavy now, perhaps with the souls of the lost European Jews.[26]

But despite Chabon's efforts in applying a kind of thematic reconciliation to match the characters' scenes of reconciliation at the end of the novel,[27] the reincursions of the Golem into the conclusion of the novel seem a sudden and therefore somewhat clumsy and unconvincing narrative device, particularly for a writer who is usually so consummately in command of his plot. This device seeks to place the burden of the Jewish European past—the burden of the Holocaust itself—into an American narrative, and therefore to give more heft and relevance to the superhero comic-book dream of escape, but it's not clear that the concept of escapism itself can properly assume such a weight. What is assumed, in any case, is not the memory of the past, nor the direct experience of the Holocaust, but an idea of it, one that is, in Chabon's account, necessarily abstracted by American distance. James E. Young discusses this phenomenon in the context of distinguishing U.S. Holocaust memorials from their European counterparts:

> Where European memorials located *in situ* often suggest themselves rhetorically as the extension of the events they would commemorate, those in

> America must gesture abstractly to a past removed in time and space. If memorials in Germany and Poland composed of camp ruins invite visitors to mistake them for the events they represent, those in America inevitably call attention to the great distance between themselves and the destruction. . . . In this sense, American memorials seem not to be anchored in history so much as in the ideals that generated them in the first place.[28]

According to Young's description, American engagements with the Holocaust never gain full purchase on its history because they tend to turn facts into abstracted "ideals," a practice characteristic of American distance (as well as a Protestant-influenced messianic optimism). Chabon's novel exposes this impulse to abstract the Holocaust from a Jewish American present as it describes the consolations to be gained from a straightforwardly fantastic (though temporary) set of reversals and escapes from history. The novel is most effective in defending fantasy not as a device that gives shape to the real but as one that is inevitably and yet productively distant from it. As the narrator says of Josef in the novel's strongest defense of escapism,

> Having lost his mother, father, brother, and grandfather, the friends and foes of his youth, his beloved teacher Bernard Kornblum, his city, his history—his home—the usual charge leveled against comic books, that they offered *merely an easy escape from reality*, seemed to Joe actually to be a powerful argument in itself. He had escaped, in his life, from ropes, chains, boxes, bags, and crates, from handcuffs and shackles, from countries and regimes. . . . The escape from reality was, he felt—especially right after the war—a worthy challenge. (575)

By noting that escapism is "especially" worthy for survivors immediately after the war, Chabon is careful to mark out escapism's limitations, but the fact remains that even in the short term, escapism is a turn away from history. It is a safe refuge from the memory of the Nazi genocide and not a sufficient means of representing it directly—something that, to its credit, the novel never attempts. Though Englander and Foer use fantastic elements of Jewish folklore as a vehicle for memorial, Chabon shows, through his meditation on the thoroughly Jewish American medium of early superhero comics, how fantasy may also act as an interruption to memory, a holding action against the damages of the past.

Notes

1. For a jaundiced treatment of magical-realist devices as part of what the author sees as a pervasive mawkishness in works by Foer, Chabon, and other writers of "Brooklyn Books of Wonder," see Melvin Jules Bukiet, "Wonder Bread," *The American Scholar* 76, no. 4 (2007): 22-35.
2. Lawrence Langer, *Admitting the Holocaust* (New York: Oxford University Press, 1995), 75.
3. Ibid., 77.

4. Sue Vice, *Holocaust Fiction* (London: Routledge, 2000), 9. Hereafter cited parenthetically. Later in *Holocaust Fiction*, Vice locates such problematic redemptive gestures in William Styron's *Sophie's Choice* and D. M. Thomas's *The White Hotel* (with its final chapter set in the afterlife).
5. Nathan Englander, *For the Relief of Unbearable Urges* (New York: Knopf, 1999). Hereafter cited parenthetically. For a more recent and equally striking use of Yiddish folklore in a work of Holocaust fiction, see Steve Stern's novella *The North of God* (New York: Melville House, 2008).
6. The two major literary reworkers of the Chelm legend in Yiddish fiction include Sholem Alecheim and, Isaac Bashevis Singer. Barbara R. Gitenstein emphasizes the universal quality of the humor in Singer's Chelm stories in her short article, "Fools and Sages: Humor in *The Fools of Chelm and Their History*," *Studies in Jewish American Literature* 1 (1981): 107-11. Dan Miron reviews the history of shtetl life as it appears primarily in Yiddish literature in *The Image of the Shtetl* (Syracuse, NY: Syracuse University Press, 2000), esp. 1-48.
7. Jonathan Safran Foer, *Everything Is Illuminated* (Boston: Houghton Mifflin, 2002).
8. See, for example, Foer, *Everything Is Illuminated*: "I also invented things that I thought would appease you, funny things and sad things. I am certain that you will inform me when I have traveled too far" (54); and, "I made certain to involve every detail, and I also invented several new details, so that Grandfather would understand the story more" (62).
9. Foer, *Everything Is Illuminated*, 10.
10. David Grossman, *See Under: Love*, trans. Betsy Rosenberg (New York: Farrar, Straus and Giroux, 1989) and Cynthia Ozick, *The Messiah of Stockholm* (New York: Knopf, 1987) both acknowledge the literary influence of Bruno Schulz, the fabulistic Jewish-Polish writer of the 1930s. Schulz's famous lost work, *The Messiah* is referenced in both novels, and Schulz himself also makes incursions: in *The Messiah of Stockholm*, two characters claim to be his long-lost child, and in the "Bruno" section of *See Under: Love* (87-184), Schulz miraculously survives the Second World War and lives on, transformed, as a salmon. Philip Roth's *The Ghost Writer* (New York: Farrar, Straus and Giroux, 1979) features a famous extended fantasy about the later life of Anne Frank; see also the stoichiometric fiction of Levi's "Lead" and "Mercury" chapters in *The Periodic Table*, trans. Raymond Rosenthal (New York: Schocken, 1984), 86-111.
11. As James E. Young notes, "What distinguishes many of these artists from their parents' generation of survivors is their single-minded knack for representing just this sense of vicariousness, for measuring the distance between history-as-it-happened and their own postmemory of it." James E. Young, "The Holocaust as Vicarious Past: Art Spiegelman's *Maus* and the Afterimages of History," *Critical Inquiry* 24, no. 3 (1998): 670.
12. Foer, *Everything Is Illuminated*, 179-80.
13. For an overview of Chabon's career through *Kavalier & Clay*, see Lee Behlman, "Mi chael Chabon," *Holocaust Literature*, ed. S. Lillian Kremer (New York: Routledge, 2003), 224-30.
14. For more on the Golden Age, see Mike Benton, *Superhero Comics of the Golden Age* (Dallas: Taylor Publishing, 1992); Ron Goulart, *The Great Comic Book Artists*, vols. 1 and 2 (New York: St. Martin's, 1986); and Ron Goulart, *Great History of Comic Books* (Chicago: Contemporary Books, 1986). All three texts are listed among the sources in Chabon's author's note in *Kavalier & Clay* (586).

15. Since the 2004 publication of an earlier version of this essay in the journal *Shofar*, several critics have further explored the novel's representation of the Holocaust and its use of comic-book motifs and other modes of fantasy. Marc Singer, in "Embodiments of the Real: The Counter-Linguistic Turn in the Comic-Book Novel," *Critique* 49, no. 3 (2008): 273-89, discusses the linguistic strategies used to adapt comic-book narratives into the novel; Alan L. Berger, in "Michael Chabon's *The Amazing Adventures of Kavalier & Clay*: The Return of the Golem," *Studies in American Jewish Literature* 29 (2010): 80-89, further discusses Chabon's use of the Golem as a figure of imaginative escape; Hillary Chute, in "Ragtime, *Kavalier & Clay*, and the Framing of Comics," *Modern Fiction Studies* 54, no. 2 (2008): 268-301, addresses the narrativation of history in the novel, and in doing so argues that Chabon presents a more extensive critique of escapism than I am proposing; and D. G. Myers, in "Michael Chabon's Imaginary Jews," *Sewanee Review* 116, no. 4 (2008): 572-88, derides Chabon's use of Yiddish folklore and language throughout his fiction, part of a relentless and unseemly attack on Chabon and his self-description as a diasporic Jew.
16. See Spiegelman's 1995 interview with Gary Groth, *The Comics Journal* 180 (1995): 56, in which he criticizes the "bombastic" speech typical of Marvel superhero comics. The critic Edward A. Shannon, in "'It's No More to Speak': Genre, the Insufficiency of Language, and the Improbability of Definition in Art Spiegelman's *Maus*," *Mid-Atlantic Almanack* 4 (1995), has noted that the very term "comic book" can be an obstacle for artists seeking to make new use of the form: "somehow," Shannon writes, comic artists "must address their readers' perceptions, which are reinforced by the very name of the form" (5-6). Will Eisner also uses an alternate term, "sequential art," to define the form. See Will Eisner, *Comics & Sequential Art*, rev. ed. (New York: Poorhouse Press, 1994).
17. For an intelligent appraisal of the revival of critical interest in superhero comic books as an art form, see Brian Doherty's early review of *Kavalier & Clay*, "Comics Tragedy," *Reason* 33, no. 1 (2001): 48-55.
18. See, for example, the scene early in Chris Ware's *Jimmy Corrigan, The Smartest Kid on Earth* (New York: Pantheon, 2000), where a decidedly unheroic, George Reeves-type "Super-Man" actor sleeps with Jimmy's mother. See also Clowes's use of panels from the "Yellow Streak" superhero story in *David Boring*, a device that surreally parallels and comments on the larger narrative; Dan Clowes, *David Boring* (New York: Pantheon, 2000), 13-14, 35, 45, 54, 64, 73-74, 83, 95, 98, 115.
19. Michael Chabon, *The Amazing Adventures of Kavalier & Clay* (New York: Random House, 2000), 74-77. Hereafter cited parenthetically within the text.
20. For an example of Chabon's unique mix of "literary" description with comic book-like visual details and dialogue, consider the following extract from the Luna Moth origin tale, wherein the nascent superheroine surprises a set of thieves and displays her new costume. Note the mix of extended descriptions with the sort of dialogue that could fit comfortably within word balloons, as well as the narrator's evident affection for what he is describing:

    "It's a bat!" says a thief.

    "It's a bird!" says another.

    "It's a *lady*!" says the third, no fool, starting to run for the door.

    The lady turns, eyes flashing. The garment she has imagined for herself is iridescent green, part Merry Widow, part Norman Bel Geddes, tricked out with fins and vanes and laced, with evident complexity, up her front. Her lower parts, in their tight green underpants, are barely covered by the merest suggestion of a skirt, her nine miles of leg are enmeshed in black fishnet, and the heels on her ankle boots are stingingly high. . . .

"That's right, little mouse," she cries to the man headed for the door. "Run!" (275)

21. For a broad survey of Jewish American comic artists from Al Capp to the present, see Helena Frenkil Schlam, "Contemporary Scribes: Jewish American Cartoonists," *Shofar* 20, no. 1 (2001): 94-112. A recent special issue of *Shofar* (*Jewish Comics*, 29, no. 2 [2011]) also discusses the history of comics and Jews in America.
22. Eisner's first graphic novel was his 1978 work, *A Contract with God* (New York: DC Comics, 2000), a semi-autobiographical story about life in a 1930s Bronx tenement. Eisner's novella about the early days of comics, *The Dreamer* (New York: DC Comics, 1986), appears to be an important influence on the view of the field in *Kavalier & Clay*. It features characters such as "Jack King," a barely disguised version of the comic artist Jack "King" Kirby. Chabon refers in his Author's Note to interviews he conducted for the novel with, among others, Eisner, Stan Lee, and Gil Kane (creator of Batman) (637).
23. Consider, for example, the use of New York landmarks as romantic vistas in Sam's love scenes with Tracy Bacon, set variously in the Empire State Building and at the famous Trylon from the 1939 World's Fair.
24. For details on these negotiations, see 275-88.
25. Chabon writes, "Now it occurred to Joe to wonder if all they had been doing, all along, was indulging their own worst impulses and assuring the creation of another generation of men who revered only strength and domination" (286).
26. Chabon writes, "It was strange, Joe thought, that the box should weigh so much more, now, than it had when the Golem was still intact. He wondered if other dirt, extra dirt, had come to be added to the original load, but this seemed unlikely. Then he remembered how Kornblum, that night, had quoted some paradoxical wisdom about golems, something in Hebrew to the effect that it was the Golem's unnatural soul that had given it weight; unburdened of it, the earthen Golem was light as air" (611).
27. That is, Josef reunites with his girlfriend, Rosa, and begins to establish a relationship with his long-lost son, while Sam leaves for a presumably happier life in California.
28. James E. Young, "The U.S. Holocaust Memorial Museum: Memory and the Politics of Identity," in *The Jew in the Text: Modernity and the Construction of Identity*, ed. Linda Nochlin and Tamar Garb (London: Thames and Hudson, 1995), 293.

A Tale Told About Idiots: The Chelm Story and Holocaust Representation

Alexis Wilson

> Lo, and behold, the whole world is like Chelm.
> —from Yiddish folklore

In his short story, "The Tumblers," Nathan Englander[1] unites two seemingly incompatible genres: a Chelm story and a Holocaust story. Chelm—from Yiddish folklore in Eastern Europe—is a mythical town of fools, about which many comic stories and jokes have been told. Similar to England's Gotham, Italy's Cuneo, and Germany's Schildburg, Chelm is a fictional city inhabited by the simpletons of the Jewish world. What happens, then, when the Holocaust invades this legendary town of Chelm? The answer is a wedding of the unimaginable to the imaginary, a process that allows the telling of a phenomenon that is difficult, if not nearly impossible, to represent. By merging history with folklore, Englander creates a unique vantage point for registering responses to the unfathomable.

There are several different creation myths regarding Chelm. In Sholem Aleichem's account of its origins, the angel responsible for distributing souls all over the earth accidentally runs into a tree and spills the entire bag of fools into the city of Chelm. In another version, the angel is carrying a bagful of foolish souls back to heaven for repair when she gets lost in a storm and spills the bag into Chelm. In yet another version, God simply says, "Let there be Chelm," and there is Chelm.[2] Although Chelm was the name of an actual city forty miles east of Lublin, Poland, there is no apparent connection between the real city and the archetypal home of the half-witted—though endearing— fools. Nevertheless, Chelm has survived as one of the most famous cities in Jewish history. Chelmites such as Motke Fool, Dopey Lekisch, Feivel Bonehead, Gronam Ox, and Schlemiel make up just some of the community's inhabitants, who—as one can tell by their names—are continually doing foolish things or having foolish things done to them.

Typically, Chelm is a self-contained, timeless, alternate universe—by and large untouched by the "real world." Chelmites, themselves, are unable to distinguish illusion from reality. A popular tale of the town illustrates this well: When a citizen of Chelm asks his rabbi, "Which is more important, the sun or the moon?" the rabbi responds, "What a silly question! The moon of course! It shines at night when we really need it. Who needs the sun to shine when it is already broad daylight?"[3] Such logic is the norm in Chelm. According to Ruth Wisse, "Stories of Chelm . . . usually follow a single pattern—when a problem must be solved, the Chelmites come up with a formula that is theoretically correct, but practically absurd."[4]

In another such tale, a farmer offers a ride to a peddler from Chelm who is carrying a heavy bundle on his shoulder. The peddler gets into the wagon and sits beside the farmer, but he keeps his bundle on his shoulders. "Why don't you put your bundle down?" asks the farmer. "It's nice enough your horse is *shlepping* me," responds the peddler. "Do I have to add my bundle to his burden?"[5] On the one hand, Chelmites are unable to penetrate beyond the surface of appearances; on the other hand, however, in many cases, Chelm logic allows them to do things that would, in reality, be impossible. In Sholem Aleichem's "A Tale of Chelm,"[6] for example, Rabbi David—the wisest man in all of Chelm—comes up with an ingenious solution to help the poor. He declares that, from now on, every poor man will eat cream and every rich man will drink sour milk, instead of the other way around. As, from now on, cream will be called sour milk, and sour milk will be called cream. Anticipating poststructuralist thought, Chelmites—"reader[s] of sublime simplicity"[7]—play with the instability of words, as well as draw attention to the possibilities and the limits of language. This is shown, as well, in another part of Aleichem's story, when the rabbi is sent by his wife to buy a chicken from a farmer. When the farmer brags about his chickens because of how fat they are, the man decides he might as well just buy fat since that is better than chicken. When he is told that the fat he wants to buy is like oil, he decides to just buy oil. Finally, he is told that the oil is as pure as water, and he comes home with a jar of water instead of a chicken. Although it seems foolish to us, this is the wisest man in all of Chelm.

In Chelm, it is intellectualism that is often ridiculed for its suspected foolishness and innocence. In a philosophical debate between two wise men, one man asks the other, "If you're so wise, then tell me why is it that when a slice of buttered bread falls to the ground, it's bound to fall on the buttered side?" The other sage, who is a "bit of a scientist," decides to have an experiment to disprove this theory. When he butters a slice of bread and drops it to the ground, it lands with the buttered side up. "There you are! Where is your theory now?" The other sage just laughs, "You think you're smart! You buttered the bread on the wrong side!"[8]

In Jewish tradition, however, such philosophical debates are not unique to the fictional world of Chelm. Rabbinic debate in the Talmud—the endless repository of the oral law—can often be as comical and amusing as Chelm logic. In the Talmud, matters abstract and completely unrealistic are treated in the same manner as ordinary, everyday concerns. If a subject is worth mentioning, it is worth debating. For example, as Adin Steinsaltz tells it,

> The Talmud contains an extremely complicated discussion of a mouse that brings bread crumbs into a house cleaned of *hametz* for Passover. The sages launch into an analysis of the mouse, the number of crumbs in the house before and after his entrance, the possibility that a rat might enter after the mouse, and other potential developments. This discourse on rodents takes up almost an entire page of the Talmud and is rich in interesting theories and basic evidence, all aimed at solving the problem of the crumbs deposited by the mouse.[9]

As the core of Jewish oral tradition, as well as the center of Eastern European Jewish life, the Talmud is, perhaps, the true inspiration of Chelm stories and jokes. In an intensely intellectual world, humor such as the Chelm legend added levity to the seriousness of the Eastern European Jews' difficult lives. Wisse explains, "In the same way that the Hasidic movement protested against the arid intellectualism of Talmudic scholasticism, these Chelm jokes ridicule sophistry, or sterility of thought, which is dissociated from practical experience."[10] What we would consider wise is, to a Chelmite, foolish.

In Chelm, roles are often reversed between the wise and the foolish—children are the wisest of all in Chelm. Indeed, the Chelm genre is most often employed in children's stories. Isaac Bashevis Singer—a writer of such narratives—argues that because of their innocence, "children are the best readers of . . . literature."[11] If Singer is correct that true wisdom lies in childlike innocence, then could true wisdom lie in the Chelmite's understanding of the world? Chelm, quite possibly, may be full of scholars instead of fools. The ideal trait of a Talmudic scholar is someone who is constantly asking questions and seeking wisdom, and it is in the act of seeking that they exemplify what a scholar is. Chelmites, who are "forever meeting to solve the great issues of the day,"[12] certainly fit these criteria.

Moreover, despite their foolishness, citizens of this fictional town have traditionally succeeded in making their world just—even if it seems superficial to the reader. Their vision of justice becomes more important than reality. In one popular legend, a few Chelmites decide to venture into the "outside world" in search of "justice." Knowing that the citizens of the town have a reputation for gullibility, two scoundrels decide to sell the Chelmites a "barrelful of justice," which turns out to be a barrelful of rotten fish. "Aye! The justice of the world smells bad!"[13] The justice of the outside world—the rotten barrel—is disappointing to the Chelmites, and they decide that they prefer their own version of justice. What happens, then, when the Holocaust invades this fictional universe? Can the Chelm logic and the Chelm idea of justice hold up?

In Englander's short story, "The Tumblers," the citizens of Chelm have divided themselves into two groups: the students of Mekyl, and the students of the Mahmir Rebbe, the Mahmirim. Similar to the split between the school of Hillel and the school of Shammai, the Mekyls are very lenient in their interpretation of the law, while the Mahmirim are very literal and extremely strict. Indeed, in Hebrew, *mekyl* literally means lenient, and *mahmir* is strict. When a decree is made for all inhabitants of Chelm to board a train and take only their "essential items," the Mekyls interpret this to mean everything that one would need to stock an unfurnished summer home, while the Mahmirim exclude everything except their long underwear. The Mahmirim even shave their heads so as to avoid any "excess adornment" that might get them confused with a Mekyl. In a comic twist, the Mahmirim accidentally board a Gentile train of circus performers, instead of the ones presumably bound for the death camps. Because of their "bland and colorless attire—and so skinny too," the "shaved-headed fools" are mistaken for acrobats. Mendel, a recent convert to the Mahmirim, saves their lives by learning of their mistaken identity and of the final destination of the other trains. Based on what Mendel tells him, the Mahmir Rebbe decides, "We must tumble," and the Mahmirim are able to disguise themselves by performing a tumbling routine. Ironically, their performance is so terrible, the audience thinks they are Gentiles performing Jews. "More of the Jewish ballet," someone yells. The story ends with their successful performance, and the Mahmirim from Chelm are saved.

The outcome of the Mahmirim's experience on the train, as well as the supposed outcome of the Mekyls on the death trains, is both believable and unbelievable, both imaginable and unimaginable at the same time. The story of "The Tumblers" becomes suspended somewhere between psychological conceivability and disbelief, and Englander uses the language of magic to emphasize this paradox. Something beyond belief appears to have happened, but how exactly it has happened is inexplicable—not only to the reader, but to the characters in the story as well. Describing the fate of the death trains, one of the circus performers observes that "those who witness it faint dead away, overcome by the grand scale of the illusion. For a moment the magician stands, a field of Jews at his feet, then nothing. . . . The train sits empty. The magician stands alone on the platform. Nothing remains but the traditional puff of smoke. This trick he performs, puff after puff, twenty-four hours a day." One of the other performers even tries to imitate this "magic trick" with animals, but realizes "that it would never match the magnitude of a trainload of Jews" (40). In another feat of magic, the Mahmirim are transformed into acrobats. For Englander, this possibility is no more overwhelming in the question of its conceivability than the former. Englander chooses, however, to construct the possibility that did not happen. The reality of the death train—in its "magnitude"—cannot be repeated in fiction, not even through magic.

The Chelm story, though, offers a new world, a new logic, and a new possibility for representing the unimaginable. Just as Englander can create this Chelm story as a possibility, the Chelmites can project their own desires onto reality. The city of Chelm, itself, works as a metaphor for fiction. It is a self-contained universe where words can construct new identities and new possibilities. During the great "sour cream shortage," for example, Mendel's grandfather "single-handedly [saved] the Feast of Weeks from complete and total ruin" by renaming water sour cream. In a very postmodern way, language is the building block of all constructions in Chelm—constructions which can just as easily be deconstructed and reconstructed. Just as in a fictional creation, anything that the Chelmites—or Nathan Englander—can imagine can be possible. By denuding words of their meaning, the Chelmites are able to create their own world. Every problem can be solved with a simple substitution of names: sour milk can become cream, a death train can be a circus train, and Jews can pass as Gentile acrobats passing as Jews.

This phenomenon of substitutions constitutes the very essence of "The Tumblers" as well as many Chelm stories and jokes, and the Chelmites use this play of words to work towards their advantage. Indeed, we are told at the beginning of the story that because "there were so many good things lacking and so many bad in abundance," the people in the ghetto of Chelm "renamed almost all that they had: they called their aches 'mother's milk,' and darkness became 'freedom'; filth they referred to as 'hope'—and felt for a while, looking at each other's hands and faces and soot-blackened clothes, fortunate" (28). It is in this aspect of the Chelm legend that the deconstructive impulse is most evident. By drawing attention to the instability of names, or signifiers, the Chelm substitutions expose the performative nature of language. "Essential items," for example, can mean everything one needs to stock an unfurnished summer home, or it might mean nothing but the underwear one is wearing. Such exaggerated disparities in the interpretation of just two words make the tension between the Mekyls and the Mahmirim seem ridiculous at first. The Mahmirim, we are told, are even so concerned about the possibility of breaking Jewish law, they will fast for three days instead of one—just in case there has been a mistake made in calculating the lunar calendar. Such severe and drastic divides in *halachic* (legal) interpretation are not at all unique to Chelm. In traditional Talmudic culture, it is not uncommon for there to be pages and pages of discussion over the interpretation of one word, or a debate over whether to interpret a biblical command at its literal or its figural meaning. In Englander's story, the divide—while at first seeming to make no crucial difference—turns out to be the difference between life and death.

And just as one word can perform different functions, even the identity of a person can masquerade as something other than itself. When the Mahmirim—"these clowns without makeup"—look like they have just come from a concentration camp in their "bland and colorless attire—and so skinny too," the "shaved-headed fools" are mistaken for and able to pass as acrobats (37-38). Ironically, when they are performing as acrobats, they look more like Jews.

Though the audience thinks they are Gentiles performing Jews, they are really Jews performing as Gentile acrobats, and this performance is the thing that is able to divert attention from them. The shifting instability of identity rests not only on the performers though, but also on the members of the audience who can perform the role of a magician. One voice—"a maker of magic to be sure"—exclaims, "Look . . . They are as clumsy as Jews" (54).

Such uncertainty over one's identity, and the identity of others, is a common part of Chelm folklore. Things are continually mistaken for things other than themselves. In another popular Chelm legend, a rabbi and his student are spending the night at an inn. In order to catch his train, the student asks a servant to wake him up early in the morning. As instructed, the servant wakes up the student who proceeds to get dressed in the dark so as not to wake the rabbi. In doing so, though, the student accidentally puts on the rabbi's gabardine. As he boards his train, he is dumbfounded when he catches a glimpse of himself in the mirror. "What an idiot that servant is! I asked him to wake me, but instead he woke up the rabbi!"[14] Chelmites not only take metaphors literally, but everything they see is taken at face value. Thus, in Englander's narrative, the death trains appear to be magical because they can't see or understand what happens on them. People magically disappear, and the magic of the trains, as well, is described as a performance. One witness, puzzled by what he has seen, explains, "They go away full—packed so tightly that babies are stuffed in over the heads of the passengers when there's no room for another fullgrown—and come back empty, as if never before used." The trainload of Jews being transformed into a trainload of circus performers is yet another one of the "unmatched feats of magic being performed with the trains" (39).

Like so many Chelmites before them, the Mahmirim are able to reverse an oppressive situation. Mendel thinks to himself, "[It was] no more unbelievable than the reality from which they'd escaped, no more unfathomable than the magic of disappearing Jews. If the good people of Chelm could believe that water was sour cream . . . then why not pass as acrobats and tumble across the earth until they found a place where they were welcome?" (42-43). And why not? The illusion is certainly more appealing than the reality. In a recent children's book, Eric A. Kimmel writes about another version of the Chelm creation myth: "According to that version, the jar the angel dropped was *not* the one containing foolish souls at all, but the one filled with wise souls. That is how the people of Chelm came to be so wise that nobody else understands them. Everybody regards them as fools. But are they really? No one can say, for no one knows which version of the story is true."[15] Israel Knox, too, asks "May it not be that the irony lies in calling the denizens of Helm simpletons? May it not be that there is a kinship between the irony implicit in branding the inhabitants of Helm as simpletons and the irony of Socrates in assenting that he is the wisest of men, but only so because he knows how little he knows, in contrast to the vast majority of men who take their ignorance to be sagacity?"[16] Is Englander also suggesting that the Mahmirim from Chelm are truly wise in choosing to live in a world of delusions and that they came from the "jar of wise souls" rather than the "jar of fools"? After all, the very elements that comprise the traditional Chelm story—substitutions, performances, mistaken identities—are what save the lives of the Mahmirim, at least in the story.

At the same time, Englander has added a new dimension to the Chelm story. When the Holocaust invades the fictional town of Chelm, the town's innocence and simplicity come to an end. The opening lines of the story tell us how they had previously remained untouched: "Who would have thought that a war of such proportions would bother to turn its fury against the fools of Chelm? Never before, not by smallpox or tax collectors, was the city intruded upon by the troubles of the outside world" (27). Englander's story deviates from the traditional Chelm story when the self-enclosed world comes into contact with the Holocaust. Although there is the occasional individual passing through, Chelmites rarely have any interaction with the outside world, and when they do, it is never a pleasant experience, as in the story of the barrelful of justice. On the whole, Chelm is an isolated universe. One of Singer's Chelm stories—"Schlemiel Went to Warsaw"—aptly illustrates the self-containment of the town. In it, Schlemiel decides that he wants to go see the "outside world," but, he gets turned around and ends up back in Chelm. He is convinced, however, that he has discovered that there are two Chelms, and he has reached the second one. "Why shouldn't the second one be exactly like the first?" he asks. In the end, Schlemiel decides to stay at "Chelm Two" until the other Schlemiel comes back. He sings to himself, "Those who leave Chelm end up in Chelm. Those who remain in Chelm are certainly in Chelm. All roads lead to Chelm. All the world is one big Chelm."[17] However, unlike Singer's self-enclosed world, Englander's Chelmites are forced to leave Chelm.

Though "The Tumblers" may well be a Chelm story, it is no longer a children's story, and it is no longer redemptive in the sense that a problem is solved, an injustice is reversed, and a comical solution is offered. Rather than end with a punch line, this Chelm story ends in a serious—even dubious—tone as Mendel assumes that their identity has been revealed:

> Mendel . . . stepped forward, moving downstage, the spotlight harsh and unforgiving against his skin. He reached out past the footlights into the dark, his hands cracked and bloodless, gnarled and intrusive. Mendel turned his palms upward, benighted. But there were no snipers, as there are for hands that reach out of the ghettos; no dogs, as for hands that reach out from the cracks in boxcar floors; no angels waiting, as they always do, for hands that reach out from chimneys into ash-clouded skies." (54-55)

Englander's story shifts from a comical fantasy to a reminder of the horrific reality, while at the same time maintaining that the version he told is the one that happened.

The same year that Englander's story was published, another story about a "magical train" also appeared. In Radu Mihaileanu's film, *Train de vie* (Train of Life),[18] a small Jewish village in France learns that the Nazis are coming for their town, and they must decide what they are going to do. Shlomo, the village idiot, comes up with a plan to save their lives. A few of the townspeople will masquerade as Nazis, and they will deport the other villagers—the "prisoners"—before the Germans even arrive. Although there are many close calls on the way, the "train of life" escapes the Nazis and makes it to freedom. In the last five minutes of the movie, however, Shlomo tells us, "That is the true story of my shtetl . . . well, almost true." The camera zooms out from just his face to show him in a concentration camp, and he sings an eerie song about his shtetl: "Shtetl, shtetl, shtetle, don't forget my shtetle . . . don't let me forget their eyes, that's what keeps me alive, their sublime folly in strife . . . train of life." What started out as lightheartedness and comedy, like "The Tumblers," concludes with a darker tone. The "sublime folly" of the villagers, while just a fantasy, is nonetheless Shlomo's means of mental survival.

Throughout Jewish history, humor has been a mechanism of survival during difficult circumstances, and the Chelm joke is a major part of this tradition. Indeed, such stories originated while Eastern European Jews were living in poverty in the shtetls, surrounded by anti-Semitism. The humorous logic of the Chemites allows them to turn an oppressive situation into whatever they desire it to be. Englander and Mihaileanu look at the Holocaust through this lens, but while Mihaeileanu explicitly comes out and says that this is just a fantasy—it has all been in Shlomo's imagination—Englander concedes that the fantasy did occur, although subtly reminding us of the reality. In neither story are we given a happy ending, though, as always guaranteed in a Chelm story or joke.

One must also not forget the Mekyls from Chelm who are no longer mentioned after the boarding of the trains. Englander's appropriation of the Chelm trope very appropriately dramatizes the dilemma of writing about the Holocaust here. Michael Andre Bernstein articulates this dilemma as being the negotiation between the responsibility to write about it, and the realization of "the incommensurability between the experience to be represented and the means of representation, the unattainability of any fitting decorum to mediate between the author's words and the world of the Shoah."[19] The problem of writing about the Holocaust—or anything for that matter—is the risk of doing violence to the subject—the violence coming from the *différance* between language and what it is attempting to describe. Since words are not the things they name, the signified is never going to be fully present in the text—there will only be a trace. Englander is poignantly aware of the limits of language—of fiction—in choosing not to describe the "final destinations of those nuisance-causing trains" (39). Any description would immediately be an effacement of the events. Though we know the destination of the train the Mekyls board, Englander does not attempt to describe it—words would finally fail in the Chelm world.

In this way, Englander reveals not only how common logic fails in understanding something such as the Holocaust, but also how the fictional Chelm logic has limits and ultimately fails as well. When discussing the Chelmites substitution of words, Mendel explains, "It was only death that they could not rename, for they had nothing to put in its place. This is when they became sad and felt their hunger and when some began to lose their faith in God" (28); "This is the curse that had befallen them. Always one less word" (38). While other words have fluidity and life to them, death cannot pretend to be anything other than what it really is. It is a name for something that is not there—a void, "signifying nothing." The "possible world" that Englander has imagined becomes a metaphor—in the deManian sense—about its own impossibility. Englander's Chelm is clearly a new generation of Chelmites sharply divided from the "simple times" of previous generations. Englander, essentially, puts an end to the mythical Chelm.

Chelm represents the ideal, fantasy image of the shtetl. No pogroms ever come to Chelm and no Gentiles are seen in Chelm; in addition, no one ever leaves Chelm, as seen with Schlemiel in Singer's story. It is a simple world, full of simpletons—though this, of course, is not completely accurate. Dan Miron explains that representations of the shtetl have always been unhistorical since the beginning of modern Yiddish literature. Indeed, the image of the shtetl as a "pure, unalloyed, and undiluted Jewish world"—an image that has become the norm—was given to us by the fathers of modern Yiddish literature (e.g., Aleichem, Abramovitsch, Peretz, and Agnon) in order for them to satirize it.[20] Englander's re-creation demystifies the romanticized, unhistorical shtetl by reinscribing it as Holocaust literature.

Rather than following in the footsteps of successful Jewish American writers like Saul Bellow and Philip Roth, Englander, in this story, places himself in the literary lineage of these Yiddish writers. In doing so, though, he also exposes a disconnection from this Yiddish culture. Not only did the Holocaust interrupt and put an end to an entire culture, but it also truncated a fictional world. Chelmites, the innocent victims of all the injustices in the world, embody a sort of tragic loss. Like an Eden, Chelm moves from innocence to knowledge, from life to death, and the Holocaust is the breaking point in this story.

Along with many others, Englander seems to be part of a new generation of American Jewish writers who are turning to their Eastern European roots for subject matter, in contrast to the previous generation who focused more on American urban settings. In a similar fusion of fiction, history, and humor, Jonathan Safran Foer re-creates shtetl life in his novel, *Everything Is Illuminated* (2002). Foer's protagonist—coincidentally named Jonathan Safran Foer—travels to the Ukraine to find the woman who may have saved his recently deceased grandfather from the Nazis. Foer (the protagonist) is, concurrently, writing a fictional history about his grandfather's village—Trachimbrod. Though he makes no mention of Chelm, Trachimbrod clearly echoes the legendary town. In one scene for example,

> Almost all of the shtetl's three hundred-odd citizens had gathered to debate that about which they knew nothing. The less a citizen knew, the more adamantly he or she argued. There was nothing new in this. A month before there had been the question of whether it might send a better message to the children to plug, finally, the bagel's hole. Two month's before there had been the cruel and comic debate over the question of typesetting, and before that the question of Polish identity, which moved many to tears, and many to laughter, and all to more questions.[21]

Foer blends Chelmlike imaginings of his grandfather's village with epistolary accounts of the trip to the Ukraine, but the novel's fact and fiction come to the same fate in the end. Like Englander, Foer ends his novel with the death of "Chelm." When the character Foer arrives in the Ukraine, he learns that the entire village was killed and all that remains is a monument: "This monument stands in memory of the 1,204 Trachimbroders killed at the hands of German fascism on March 18, 1942."[22] Englander's Chelm, similarly, comes to an end when it is invaded by the outside world.

Foer seems to be following in Englander's footsteps by using the Holocaust as a link to reclaiming the shtetl. Rather than a nostalgic reflection though, when placed next to the Holocaust, the fantasy shtetl is made to seem absurd. In doing so, however, it also places an emphasis on the absurdity in the Holocaust. The substitution of water for sour cream, or a circus train for a death train, is more believable compared to thousands of people disappearing on trains everyday. One might think that turning a Holocaust story into folklore would be trivializing it—to make it mythical and fantastical. Englander, however, performs a significant act by using the Chelm legend. Because we are so far removed from the Eastern European world, Englander, in what David Roskies might call a "creative betrayal,"[23] fuses together two parts of Jewish history to create something new for today. Though the world from which it came may have vanished, Englander recreates Chelm for the world in which we live.

Notes

1. Nathan Englander, *For the Relief of Unbearable Urges* (New York: Vintage, 1999), 27-55. All subsequent references to the book will be made parenthetically within the text.
2. See Arnold Perl, *The World of Sholem Aleichem*, directed by Don Richardson, produced by Henry T. Weinstein (Ashville, NC: Ivy Video, 1996); Isaac Bashevis Singer, *The Fools of Chelm and their History* (New York: FSG, 1973); and Solomon Simon, *The Wise Men of Helm and their Merry Tales* (New York: Behrman House, 1945).
3. Henry D. Spalding, ed., *Encyclopedia of Jewish Humor* (New York: Jonathan David Publishers, 1973), 122.
4. Ruth R. Wisse, *The Schlemiel as Modern Hero* (Chicago: University of Chicago Press, 1971), 10.
5. Leo Rosten, *The Joys of Yiddish* (New York: McGraw Hill, 1968), 85.

6. See Perl, *The World of Sholem Aleichem.*
7. Paul deMan, *Allegories of Reading: Figural Language in Rousseau, Nietzche, Rilke, and Proust* (New Haven: Yale University Press, 1979), 9. DeMan uses this term to refer to the character Edith Bunker, from the 1970s sitcom *All in the Family*, in an example he gives "from the sub-literature of the mass media" about the tension between grammar and rhetoric. "Asked by his wife whether he wants to have his bowling shoes laced over or laced under, Archie Bunker answers with a question: 'What's the difference?' Being a reader of sublime simplicity, his wife replies by patiently explaining the difference between lacing over and lacing under, whatever this may be, but provokes only ire." It even sounds like something that could come out of Chelm. More could be said about the deconstructive impulse in Chelm logic.
8. Nathan Ausubel, "Pure Science," in *A Treasury of Jewish Folklore* (New York: Crown Publishers, 1948), 337.
9. Adin Steinsaltz. *The Essential Talmud* (Basic Books, 1976), 235.
10. Wisse, 11.
11. Isaac Bashevis Singer, "Are Children the Ultimate Literary Critics?" in *Stories for Children* (New York: FSG, 1985), 332-37.
12. Sanford Pinsker, *The Schlemiel as Metaphor* (Illinois: Southern Illinois University Press, 1991), 16.
13. Israel Knox, "The Wise Men of Helm," *Judaism* 29, no.2 (1980): 190-91.
14. Nathan Ausubel, "The Mistake," in *A Treasury of Jewish Folklore* (New York: Crown Publishers, 1948), 326.
15. Eric A. Kimmel, "The Jar of Fools," in *The Jar of Fools: Eight Hanukkah Stories from Chelm*, illust. by Mordecai Gerstein (New York: Scholastic, 2001), 1-4.
16. Knox, 186.
17. Isaac Bashevis Singer, "When Schlemiel Went to Warsaw," in *Stories for Children* (New York: FSG, 1985), 3-7.
18. *Train de Vie,* VHS, directed by Radu Mihaileanu (Hollywood, CA: Paramount, 2000).
19. Michael Andre Bernstein, "Narrating the Shoah," in *Foregone Conclusions: Against Apocalyptic History* (Berkeley: University of California Press, 1994), 43.
20. Dan Miron, *The Image of the Shtetl* (Syracuse: Syracuse University Press, 2000).
21. Jonathan Safran Foer, *Everything Is Illuminated* (New York: Houghton Mifflin, 2002), 12.
22. Ibid., 149.
23. David Roskies, *A Bridge of Longing: The Lost Art of Yiddish Storytelling* (Cambridge: Harvard University Press, 1995).

Laughter and Trembling: The Short Fiction of Steve Stern and Nathan Englander

Monica Osborne

In an essay called "After the Law," Steve Stern recounts an old Hasidic tale[1] regarding the forest, the fire, and a prayer:

> The Baal Shem Tov, when he has a problem, goes to the forest, lights a fire, says a prayer, and finds wisdom. The next generation has forgotten the prayer, but they can still go to the forest and light the fire; the generation after that has forgotten the prayer and can't make a fire, but they can still go to the forest. But the following generation is unable to find the forest, light the fire, or remember the prayer, though at least they know the story—and that must suffice. Then along come the children of the children of the immigrants, so divorced from tradition and community that they can't even recall the story.[2]

Referring to his own childhood and early adult years, marked by little more than the most marginal trappings of Jewish culture and thought, Stern asserts the dangers of inhabiting a storyless space—of being so forward looking that we forget how to gaze back onto past narratives—and chooses instead to search for the stories of earlier generations as a means to gain ownership of the stories as well as access to the memories that inspired them. Consequently, the fiction of Stern draws so forcefully from the memories of the turn-of-the-century Jewish immigrant experience, that it is often difficult to remember that its impetus was indeed Stern's own accidental discovery of the Pinch, a shtetl-like community of Orthodox Jews living on North Main Street in his hometown of Memphis, Tennessee. Stern describes the jarring experience of bending around the corner of Poplar

Avenue and North Main Street, and feeling as though he had fallen "through the fabric of time" as he stumbled into what magically appeared to be a "blighted old ghetto" neighborhood, a street that seemed inhabited by ghosts that would later colonize his most successful fiction.[3] It was a community that was not quite of this world, but almost eerily unaware of, or apathetic to, its status as a community of outsiders. For here was seemingly a microcosm of lost Eastern European Jewry, an immigrant society consumed with articulating through word and deed the gestures of a phantom world.

It was, perhaps, particularly ironic that such a community—devoted to making the past reappear—thrived in the Southern city of Memphis, a "city remarkable for erasing its own past."[4] Ghosts they were not, however, and Stern found that their "antics made for diverting stories." Indeed, Stern's stories—much like those of Nathan Englander, whose work will be discussed later in this essay—resonate with the collision of Old and New Worlds as modern secularism and Jewish religious tradition come crashing into each other, leaving shards of narrative that magically recreate the Old World and Jewish American immigrant shtetls blatantly infused with a bizarre but comical mixture of sexuality, mysticism, Yiddishisms, religious zealotry, and Old World folklore. They are humorous in a way that is almost fanatical as seeming polarities are forced to merge in a reckless effort to recapture a lost Jewish art and tradition. In the title story of Stern's short-story collection *The Wedding Jester* (1999),[5] Saul Bozoff accompanies his mother to a wedding at the Concord Hotel in the Catskills—a place that Saul holds in magical regard, but perhaps only because it is the place "where magic died."[6] He grudgingly attends the wedding, his mind occupied instead by the fact that his fiction—he happens to be a Jewish American fiction writer—has earned him only a very small audience in what "he considered 'the ghetto'" (161). Ironically, Stern describes Saul's fiction as "full of exotic Jewish legends translated to contemporary settings . . . well-received among a generation that was already half legend itself. . . . Among his peers, [however,] Saul Bozoff had no currency at all" (161). Much like Irving Howe in the late 1970s, Saul believes that the kind of literature he writes—Jewish American fiction—is part of a dying breed of literature that, like the Catskills, is past its heyday and now more of a cultural artifact than a vibrant indicator of a flourishing culture. Saul was in his early forties when he was "seduced" by the notion of people's "heritage" (162)—heritages of Baptist preachers, folklorists, "blind blues singers with half a dozen wives," and a pawnbroker who sold the young Elvis Presley his first guitar—a seduction that led him to interview the people whose stories captivated him. Saul's captivation with the cultural baggage of other people slowly creates within him a desire to discover his own heritage—a phenomenon not unlike Stern's own preoccupation with retrieving cultural tradition through the mode of storytelling.

Like many of Stern's characters, Saul Bozoff experiences a prolonged period of discontentment, harboring an overwhelming premonition that he has somehow missed out on experiencing something that is rightly his. Saul mourns for the loss of the Jewish culture he never really had; he covets the capacity of other people to realize their shared heritage, and for a time he exists by internalizing the stories of others, feeding on the depth of their experience and cultural awareness in an almost perverse manner. Saul's obsession with gathering the stories of other people reflects Stern's emphasis on the process of recovering an effervescent cultural past from the tethers of an assimilated culture. Stern often employs a muse in his stories—whether in the shape of an old hermit man or a beautiful immigrant woman—to assist his writer characters in reclaiming and reshaping the stories and memories that precede them, often by generations. Janet Handler Burstein notes that whether the writer "falls in love with his muse or simply leaves her a glass of fresh milk, his work begins to 'remember the world' . . . only when it recovers the past."[7] Stern's mission to recover the past produces an imaginative recollection that is transplanted from a world the writer never knew, but one that now becomes "home to his imagination."[8] The problem, however, is that Stern's characters often find themselves completely dependent on the muse—once the muse disappears or is temporarily hidden, the excavation into the past is halted, the writer left grasping at shards of cultural memories, no longer able to reconstruct the lost world.

By chance, the storytelling pawnbroker mentions to Saul a "transplanted Old World community on North Main Street," and Saul takes a pilgrimage to this community, where he finds crumbling buildings and utter desolation, but also a vision: "immigrants . . . pumping their sewing machines like swarming hornets in the tenement lofts, braiding Yiddish curses into their yellow challah bread" (162). And so, like many of Stern's main characters Saul "takes up residence among the dead" and transcribes their ghostly experiences into stories, much like Stern himself. While humorous images and magical instances abound in Stern's fiction, a more nuanced analysis of his stories reveal the author's fascination with the lure of death and the horror of an existence over which the shadow of death hovers.[9] Even Saul's fascination with the Catskills, the place where both magic and Jewish culture were once alive, is contingent on it being a place haunted by the dead and frequented only by the members of a dying epoch.

Having grown up in a place and era that had escaped the immigrant hold, Saul covets the memories that growing up in the Lower East Side would have afforded him, including yearly summer visits to the Catskills, and so his fiction writing is an attempt to recapture the stories of his parents and grandparents. But while Saul is exhilarated by the fantasy of arriving at the Catskills and stepping back in time and back into the hub of Jewish memory, what he finds instead is a "tacky terminus to the dream of a golden America, [a] Jewish wasteland" that seemed to have nothing to do with him (169). Even death, it seems, is disappointing—a theme found in many of Stern's other stories. Well past its 1950s heyday as a conspicuous gathering of Jewish families and the launching pad for many Jewish comedians and musicians, the Catskills community has gone stale with age and the scattering of Jewish distinctiveness. With an almost lurid pride,

Saul proclaims that "this is the place where magic died" (185), perhaps considering that he himself had not been bar mitzvahed; "his Jewishness, like his connection to his mother's family, was several times removed" (189). He is an "artificial Jew," the Jew who does not even know the story any more, despite the fact that it nonetheless seems to haunt him. But it is this place—a place where Jews had grown deep roots—that reminds Stern's character of the intrinsic knowledge he has always possessed, the weight of being a Jew.

Though the endings of Stern's stories are often either ambiguous or effectively surprising, his metaphors for and depictions of the contemporary Jew's struggle to locate his or her identity in some form of collective framework is always lucid. In a hilarious twist of fate, the marriage ceremony attended by Saul and his mother reveals that the bride has been possessed by a dybbuk, "who like [Saul is] stuck between this world and another" (194). Saul Bozoff is not a new character for Stern, who introduced us to the writer character in "The Ghost and Saul Bozoff," one of the stories in *Lazar Malkin Enters Heaven* (1986), nor is the suggestion that Saul himself is not fully anchored to the realm of the living and the weight of mortality. "I wouldn't mind coming to a place like this when I'm dead," said the Saul Bozoff of the earlier story. "Rumor has it . . . that you already are," responds another character.[10] In "The Wedding Jester," the dybbuk inhabits the bride's body, but speaks with the voice of a famous Borscht Belt comedian, cracking inappropriate jokes and contorting the bride's body into inhuman forms. Saul, having dabbled a bit in Kabbalah, (and it must be said, feeling guilty for having stood on the balcony of his hotel room the night before, wishing desperately for the return of the Borscht Belt comedians and musicians to the Catskills) takes matters into his own hands, and tries to exorcise the dybbuk—a bizarre attempt to metaphorically seize for his own creative energies the literal ghost of a fading Jewish era and to in effect control its vanishing trajectory. He finally frees the bride's body from the dybbuk, who, as a symbol of Jewish life and nostalgia, takes hold of whoever it can in an effort to ensure that its legacy will survive. What Saul does not realize, however, is that by grappling with the dybbuk—that is, by grappling with the legacy of the Catskills Jewish community—he struggles with his own legacy and learns to identify himself within the structure of a collective Jewish history. He becomes flesh on the bones of a skeleton of Jewish history and nostalgia.

As the dybbuk takes up residence in his body, Saul leaves the Catskills with exactly what he came for—an internalization of the memories of his parents and grandparents. But it is an internalization of a memory that is still oddly suspended between two worlds—a dilemma that is very real for Stern himself—an eternal dividedness that "edges darkly an otherwise comic story with an otherwise characteristically antic ending."[11] Like the flying rabbi in Stern's "A Tale of a Kite," also from *The Wedding Jester*, drifting away against "dark clouds swollen with history rolling in from the east" (20), the memories of a forgotten Jewish past always seem to feel just out of reach for Stern—an elusiveness, however, that also ensures that this seeker of a vibrant and personal Jewish heritage will continue to search for the remnants of a Jewish mode of being that is always already part of him. Much like the significance of studying Torah is located in the act or process of studying and seeking, rather than in the knowledge one hopes to gain from the scholarly pursuit, Stern's stories reflect the possibility that part of what it means to be Jewish is to long for what is in a sense already yours, to watch for it as diligently as one awaits Moshiach, but in the knowledge that it comes only when it is no longer necessary. By this I mean to say that while the trappings of Jewish culture may be difficult for contemporary American Jews—the sons and daughters of the assimilated American Jews of the Roth-Bellow-Malamud literary era—to distinguish, the Jewish identity is one that is must always remain in question, interrogated constantly. To be Jewish, perhaps, is simply to ask what it means to be Jewish.

To be Jewish, and particularly to be a Jewish writer, is very much about being human—about embracing and articulating often competing identities and ideologies, about inhabiting overlapping worlds and looking always to the future while never relinquishing the need to gaze back on the past in an effort to revive it, to fuse a legacy of loss and grief with one of hopefulness and tenacity. To be Jewish is to be intricately tied to humanity's most precious components: desire and longing, home and exile, sorrow and its tears, as well as laughter. Laughter in particular is a profoundly human trait inasmuch as we regard the comic spirit as "a living thing."[12] Humor, the comic, and laughter—they do not exist outside of the human realm; they are distinctly human attributes. At the same time, however, the impulse to laugh—to be moved by a comical gesture—is rooted in a human's capacity to distance him or herself from feeling: "laughter has no greater foe than emotion."[13] Laughter often appears to replace, or shield us from, deeper emotional responses; its roots are both tied to and severed from human emotion. And Jews, it seems, have been laughing since the beginning of time. One needs only to remember the laughter of the biblical matriarch Sarah, upon being told that her aging, withered body would give birth to a son, that her womb would ostensibly cultivate the beginning of nations. Sarah—reluctant to allow herself to buy into her husband Abraham's dreams for a future of sons and daughters, though the very fact that she laughs suggests her need to distance herself emotionally from a promise that might become, like so many others, as barren as the desert that she and her husband inhabit.

Likewise, Stern's fiction—with its tragic comics, colorful misfits, fallen angels, neurotic writers, and unlikely muses—falls into step with centuries of Jewish laughter and storytelling, tapping into the complexity of humanity while simultaneously forcing us to consider the impetus for our laughter, and from what we distance ourselves as we engage in laughter. But like the nature of laughter, his stories are equivocal, belonging "neither altogether to art nor altogether to life," but to something suspended between the two, and indicative of what it means to be human, to be Jewish, to long indefinitely.[14] In "The Sin of Elijah," for example, Stern uses Elijah the Tishbite, "former prophet of the Northern Kingdom of Israel, translated to Paradise in a chariot of flame while yet alive," to upset the boundaries between life and death, as well as heavenly and earthly pleasures (*Wedding Jester,* 81). Weary of living the heavenly life, and bored with attending endless circumcisions, performing mitzvot, and wandering around in various disguises, perpetually in search of a righteous act to perform, Elijah looks to the past—his earthly past—and begins to take an unheavenly pleasure in the erotic escapades of Feyvush and Gitl Fefr of the Lower East Side of New York.

Stern cleverly upends ideas of the sacred and the profane as the couple's sexual ecstasy is ultimately so intense that it transports them, like Elijah (who was taken to heaven because he was so thoroughly righteous on earth), to eternal bliss. But perpetual Paradise is not all it is cracked up to be, as Feyvush and Gitl discover that the price they have paid for such happiness is the loss of the capacity to experience sexual pleasure. Torn between the pleasures of earth and of the world to come, what ensues is trouble in Paradise and the couple's frantic quest to return to the physical realm for the remainder of their lives. Time's perimeters disintegrate as the past, present, and future become unrecognizable, and as the couple reaches their earthly past only to discover that all of the Jews of the Lower East Side's immigrant community have moved to Westchester and the Upper West Side and been replaced by other immigrants, returning only to Delancey Street on Sundays for delicatessen. Like many of Stern's fictional characters, his stories renegotiate the cultural, social, and religious boundaries, and Stern's fascination with the Old World ascertains that we are indeed well past the era dominated by the Roths and Bellows who sought to shed themselves of their immigrant skin. But it also suggests a new, perhaps more nuanced, longing on the part of Jewish American writers to reconstruct the stories of their grandparents.

While Stern's fiction is filled to capacity with the magical realism of flying rabbis, mysterious muses who appear by night to finish a struggling author's manuscript, brides whose bodies are inhabited by dybbuks, erotic demon lovers who live inside mirrors, and angels who have lost their way, Nathan Englander's short stories are situated more precisely in the everyday experiences of real life. Published in the same year as Stern's *The Wedding Jester*, the stories contained in Englander's *For the Relief of Unbearable Urges* (1999), though often comical, are much less whimsical than Stern's, and typically lack the jovial lightheartedness that characterizes many of Stern's stories. There are numerous moments in which we laugh, but it is a laughter that is not as proficient at covering up deeper emotional responses—a laughter under which horror resides, and never completely surfaces in the ways we expect it to. When we laugh at various points in Englander's stories, it is a laughter that is simultaneously "a token of an infinite grandeur and an infinite misery," the unique collision of tremendous human responses.[15] Often grounded in larger historical and cultural narratives of loss and longing, Englander's humor is usually more heartbreaking than humorous. His characters are deeply aware of the difficulty of being both human and Jewish. In

"The Wig," for example, Ruchama, a Hasidic woman whose wig-making skills free the women of her community who are "trapped in their modesty," longs for the freedom and sensuality of long cascading curls of her own instead of the shaved and wig-covered head of an observant Hasidic woman.[16] She allows herself to explore her own vanity and imagine a life more sexually and emotionally satisfying, despite her religion's intolerance of such thoughts. And in the collection's title story, Dov Binyamin, shunned physically and emotionally by his wife, is given special permission by his rabbi to visit a prostitute, to relieve those urges that seem unbearable. Tentative and fearful of such a typically forbidden encounter with a woman, Dov struggles with what his conscience tells him is acceptable and what the rabbi has given him permission to do. In what seems to be a cruel clash of the sacred and profane, the story ends with an image of Dov, in the bathroom, "on fire inside," though not consumed by what is apparently a venereal disease—the grim reality of his special dispensation (191).

Though Englander is hesitant to call his stories Jewish stories, they resonate with the influences of Saul Bellow, I. B. Singer, Bernard Malamud, and even Isaac Babel, as well as many Jewish folkloric tales. Bellow has insightfully noted that stories are Jewish when "laughter and trembling are so curiously mingled that it is not easy to determine the relations between the two," and Englander's fiction falls steadily within the boundaries of such a definition.[17] It is also worth pointing out that Bellow's pairing of laughter and trembling in the context of what constitutes Jewish literature is particularly provocative because it alludes to Søren Kierkegaard's *Fear and Trembling* (1843), which is ostensibly a definitive work about the "teleological suspension of the ethical," or the postponement of the ethical or moral law for the sake of a supreme law.[18] By replacing Kierkegaard's "fear" with "laughter," Bellow calls further, if subtly, into question the feasibility of distinctions between the ethical and the moral, the spiritual and the temporal, the fear and the laughter of both victims and persecutors, implicitly compelling us to revisit and reexamine the places where they meet, where they are not so inseparable.

Indeed, what if laughter, fear, and trembling are not so discrete? Charles Baudelaire of course saw laughter and tears as "equally the children of woe," the laugh often merely a "sign of just as great a misery" as tears in one's eyes. "The Sage laughs not save in fear and trembling," quotes Baudelaire from an ambiguous source.[19] With his subtle reconnection of superficially disparate impulses, Bellow merely tapped the grainy surface of centuries of philosophic inquiry into the relation between fear (and other emotional responses including trembling, misery, and terror) and laughter. But rereading these arguments through the lens of Jewish fiction—in fact, through Jewish and biblical history—deepens the notion of laughter as the "expression of a double, or contradictory, feeling" and gives it a profoundly serious dimension.[20] The implication of this dynamic is the possibility that laughter exists as a space more adequately attuned to the complexity of human longings and fears. It is, again in a Bergsonian sense, distinctively human, arguably more so than the straightforward emotional response of sadness or fear. Laughter separates humans from the material realm, but it also separates them from the world of animals. Consider a man whose closest and constant companion is his dog, a fiercely devoted animal. It is not unthinkable that an outsider might witness something that appears to be sadness in the look and gait of the dog, who lays about and refuses to eat, should the man leave the animal alone for an extended period of time. Nor in another instance would it be out of the ordinary to witness something in the animal's demeanor that suggests it is fearful of something, perhaps even that it experiences terror in some form. But laughter is impossible unless it bursts from the lips of a human being, like a secret tip from the divine, directing us to the place where we are most human.

But if laughter is the supreme human function, or the rawest and rarest of distinctly human responses, then the next question concerns what it also means to be human. Maurice Blanchot once suggested that Judaism is an "essential modality" of all that is human.[21] Judaism—or, more generally, Jewish thought—is at it its roots concerned primarily with championing ethical behavior; central to Jewish thinking is a system of ethics that places all human life at the top of the list of priorities. By some form of deductive reasoning, then, one might say that to be human in the most nonperfunctory way is to be ethical, or at the very least, to concern oneself with what it means to be ethical. Bellow's delicate connection of Jewish literature to a classic work of ethical explorations—and his apparent dismantling of Kierkegaard's "fear and trembling" in honor of a slightly reconfigured pairing—links them in such a way to suggest the unique place of Jewish literature when it comes to discussions of the ethical. For who better to speak, even via fiction, of the ethical than Jewish writers whose legacy includes a memory or singular awareness of the Holocaust, the decisive collapse of ethical responsibility?

The place of laughter in the work of Stern and Englander, not to mention numerous other Jewish writers, is not simply a coincidence, nor is it purely the authors' attempt to transform the brutal pangs of longing into an entertaining story. Laughter, in literature and beyond, opens up new possibilities for ethical discourse; the act of laughing forces us into an ethical space. Consider again the ancient example of Abraham and Sarah, a story in which all Jewish literature and thought have roots. Sarah's laughter is not the laughter of madness—not the diabolical laughter of Hamlet—but a laughter that is a Bergsonian appeal to intelligence.[22] That she chooses to laugh in response to the idea that she will bear a child late in life reveals precisely that she does not suffer from madness, nor from disbelief, though the Judeo-Christian tradition has historically interpreted her response as evidence of her disbelief, her lack of faith, in contrast to her husband Abraham's unwavering faith (which is perhaps more indicative of the possibility that Abraham suffers from a madness that would allow him nearly to kill his son, Isaac). Rather, her response indicates a more nuanced awareness of life's disappointments, and a sharp cognizance of the crucial nature of questioning. Her laughter in this moment—burned forever onto the spirit of the promised child, Isaac, whose name means laughter, or one who laughs—is a dark foreshadowing of what will ultimately be Abraham's failure to respond appropriately to issues of an ethical nature. For Abraham, when told by God to sacrifice his son Isaac, moves mechanically through the motions of preparing to slaughter his son. He asks no questions, nor does he laugh. Perhaps Abraham should have laughed at God's command as heartily as Sarah laughed at the revelation she received. Perhaps the true test was in actuality whether Abraham could laugh, whether he could symbolically open up a larger space for a discussion of the ethical, for a conversation about whether killing his son was really what God desired. Sarah's response is ultimately the more Jewish response—the impulse to laugh that is indicative of an ability to continually spin ideas around, exploring and probing them in order to determine what lies beneath and to discover what it means to enact ethical behavior. This is not to say that fear or trembling cannot accompany such laughter—quite the contrary. Fear and trembling have a place within certain kinds of laughter, and Bellow's recognition of this continues to reaffirm the relevance of Jewish and American Jewish writing not just in the literary or aesthetic sense but in the ethical realm as well.

In merging laughter and trembling, two of Englander's stories in particular force the reader into the space of the ethical without trepidation. The stories are set in the very real contexts of Stalinism and Nazism, but the power of their dark humor derives specifically from the "magnitude of the pain that [they] ultimately assure us is unreal"—unreal, however, only in the fictional realm.[23] We know it is fiction, and therefore while presumably complicit in the willing suspension of disbelief, we are emotionally removed. But it is a disbelief that is undercut by historical evidence—the fact that although we are lured into a fictional encounter through the reading of the story, we are inevitably reminded of the harsher, perhaps ineffable nature of what it meant to experience the threats of Nazism and Stalinism firsthand. The first story, which may also be Englander's best story, is "The Twenty-seventh Man," a tale about a Stalinist purge of Jewish writers; the second is "The Tumblers."

In this second story, when the town of Chelm is invaded by Nazis and the townsfolk are transported out of the town, they discover that they share a train with a group of entertainers and resolve to impersonate acrobats in order to save themselves. Here Englander subjects the Fools of Chelm—classic characters of Yiddish literature and folklore—to the devastation of genocide. They are poor performers, and a pathetic bunch, but they manage to get away with it for a time. "They are as clumsy as Jews," a member of the audience, a Nazi official, shouts in ironical admiration. One of the unlikely performers moves forward, his arms extending upward, as if reaching past the faces of the audience. The story concludes, abruptly, with this sentence: "But there were no snipers, as there are for hands that reach out of the ghettos; no dogs, as for hands that reach out from the cracks in boxcar floors; no angels waiting, as they always do, for hands that reach out from chimneys into ash-clouded skies" (55). While it alludes to the ultimate horror of the little narrative within the terror of the grand,[24] it is merely a performance, literally and figuratively, of the degradation of Jews during the Holocaust. But, eerily, it is a performance that not even these Jews of Chelm understand even as they perform it. They continue to misinterpret reality much like the inhabitants of Chelm do in Yiddish folklore. When one of their own children is shot before boarding the train to leave the town, with the exception of one character they refuse to look back at the sound, having "learned the lessons of Sodom" (35). Even more horrific is their misinterpretation of the disappearance of so many other Jews as a great trick: "the magic of disappearing Jews" (42).

While Stern's use of repeated instances of the fantastical and of the magically revived Eastern European shtetl communities subtly reminds us of the lost world of European Jewry, Englander's stories convey the horror of such loss in a starker, more profound way. We laugh at the antics of the Jews of Chelm, but only with the laughter of one who is beside himself. His juxtaposition of traditional Jewish folklore and the gruesome veracity of the Holocaust and other experiences of Jewish persecution can be startling—a disturbing convergence of Jewish tradition and the horrors that would hasten its destruction. His stories, though they often end on a tragic or bewildering note, resist concrete endings, as if to remind us of the instability and uncertainty of the future. Such open-ended "closures" also confound our instinctive tendency to, as readers, bring a story to close and allow it to end with its themes, lessons, and insights. "The Tumblers" ends ambiguously. We don't get to know literally the fate of the would-be acrobats. We don't get to watch as they are forced to face the reality of the atrocity, to reinterpret—reenact, as it were—their own bleak realities, the dark realities of so many others. Englander's characters, as drawn to them as we inevitably are, are fictional. Their own ambiguous endings force us to consider more fully the horrors of reality.

Lawrence Langer claims that when the "Holocaust is the theme, history imposes limitations on the supposed flexibility of artistic license. We are confronted by the perplexing challenge of the reversal of normal creative procedure: instead of Holocaust fictions liberating the facts and expanding the range of their implications, Holocaust facts enclose the fictions, drawing the reader into an ever-narrower area of association."[25] Englander's story, though enclosed by our own knowledge of the Holocaust, opens up new possibilities for examining its harshest realities. And despite Wendy Shalit's controversial claim that Englander, among other new Jewish writers, does not understand the Orthodox world he describes, his stories of men and women within Orthodoxy depict what it means to be truly human in a way that transcends the letter of the law and oversteps the boundaries of Orthodox limitations.[26] Like Stern, Englander does not strive to create literal depictions of Jewish religious communities. His stories sidestep didactic lessons about Jewish ritual in favor of more complicated—dare I say authentic?—though often caricatured portraits of the human need to belong to a larger trajectory, a desire that is particularly present in the most recent fiction by young American Jewish writers such as Stern and Englander.

Englander's fiction, like Stern's, is a literature of return from the exile of assimilation and mourning. Their paths are disparate in many ways, but are similarly bent on reconnecting with what is familiar to them through stirrings of dreams and the memories of their grandparents. Their use of magic or terror, and sometimes a combination of both, perhaps in the shape of laughter, however, speaks to the fact that these third-generation American Jewish writers are distinct from their parents and grandparents. Much like Charles Luger, of Englander's "The Gilgul of Park Avenue," a WASPy man who receives a sudden epiphany that he is Jewish, and who in the story's final scene struggles to "stand without judgment . . . to be wholly seen" as a Jew (137), third-generation writers such as Englander and Stern understand their status as evolving Jews as simply two more critical parts of the very intricate mosaic of collective Jewish experience. In 1977, Irving Howe famously forecasted the end of Jewish American literature in light of what he saw as the depletion of cultural resources from which to draw. More recently, others have noted that the only Jewish literature that will survive is the literature that is immersed in Judaism. But if I had to place my own wager on the Jewish literary form that will survive, I would say without reservation that it will be the literature that depicts ambivalence—stories that explore what it means to be torn, or to be suspended between worlds, to be fragmented. To be Jewish is also to struggle, not necessarily externally, but always internally, and so Jewish fiction must reflect this. It must reflect the painful paradox of longing for what one already has, but which seems simultaneously to be just out of reach; indeed, it becomes an imperative to long. One of the last chapters of the biblical book of Deuteronomy expresses this paradox:

> For the commandment that I command you this day: it is not too extraordinary for you, it is not too far away! It is not in the heavens, (for you) to say: Who will go up for us to the heavens and get it for us and have us hear it, that we may observe it? And it is not across the sea, (for you) to say: Who will cross for us, across the sea, and get it for us and have us hear it, that we may observe it?[27]

Understood by most biblical scholars as a late addition to the larger text of Deuteronomy, the verses' insistence that the "commandment"—that is, Jewish law, culture, and tradition—is not beyond the capacity of knowing is oddly prescient. The message to Stern's Saul Bozoff might be: you don't have to return to the Catskills to internalize what it means to be Jewish because you already know. But if Jewish literature will survive, its characters must also laugh, must force us both to laugh and tremble in order to arrive at the place where the literary and ethical converge.

Notes

1. This is a tale of which many Jewish writers are fond, particularly those Jewish writers who have a direct connection to the Holocaust, and for whom the telling of the story of the Holocaust is critical. Elie Wiesel, for example, uses it as an epigraph to his novel, *The Time of the Uprooted* (New York: Knopf, 2005).
2. Steve Stern, "After the Law," *Tikkun*, November-December, 1997, 48.
3. Ibid., 47.
4. Ibid., 48.
5. Although I make numerous brief references to Stern's various stories in this collection, I have chosen to concentrate primarily on "The Wedding Jester," one of the longer stories of the collection, and one that seems particularly relevant to the purpose of this essay.
6. Steve Stern, *The Wedding Jester* (St. Paul: Graywolf Press, 1999), 185. Hereafter cited parenthetically.
7. Janet Handler Burstein, *Telling the Little Secrets: American Jewish Writing Since the 1980s* (Madison: University of Wisconsin Press, 2006), 103.
8. Ibid.,104.
9. Even the titles of some of Stern's collections reveal a fascination with the idea of death, and the possibility of transgressing its impermeable border through the art of fiction: e.g., *Isaac and the Undertaker's Daughter* (Fayetteville, AR: Lost Roads Publishers, 1983) and *Lazar Malkin Enters Heaven* (New York: Viking, 1986).
10. Steve Stern, *Lazar Malkin Enters Heaven* (Syracuse: Syracuse University Press, 1995), 185.
11. Burstein, 105.
12. Henri Bergson, "Laughter," in *Comedy: Meaning and Form*, ed. Robert. W. Corrigan (Milwaukee: University of Wisconsin Press, 1981), 328. In his famous "Laughter," Bergson cautions his readers against attempting to imprison the "comic spirit" in any one definition. His insistence that we "regard it, above all, as a living thing" speaks to its significance as a signifier of all things human (328). I am also struck by the similarities of Bergson's description of laughter, or the comic spirit—as growing, expanding, evolving, and capable of illuminating the more abstract concepts of humanity—to the ways in which we define the Torah (evolving, illuminating, dynamic, and indicative of what it means to be human).
13. Ibid., 329.
14. Ibid., 332.
15. Charles Baudelaire, "On the Essence of Laughter, and in General, on the Comic in the Plastic Arts," in *Comedy: Meaning and Form*, ed. Robert. W. Corrigan (Milwaukee: University of Wisconsin Press, 1981), 316.
16. Nathan Englander, *For the Relief of Unbearable Urges* (New York: Vintage, 1999), 87. Hereafter cited parenthetically.
17. Saul Bellow, Introduction, *Great Jewish Short Stories,* (New York: Dell, 1963), 12.
18. Søren Kierkegaard, *Fear and Trembling*, trans. Alastair Hannay (London: Penguin, 1985), 64. In *Fear and Trembling* Kierkegaard explores Genesis 22, where Abraham is commanded by God to sacrifice his son Isaac, whom he loves. The paradox that Kierkegaard examines is the insistence that God must be obeyed, and the tacit understanding that murder is immoral. Although the Mosaic law had not yet been offered at this point in biblical history, the point is that it still violates what our conscience understands as the ethical, as what Emmanuel Levinas would later define as our "in-

finite responsibility to the Other." In Kierkegaard's analysis of Genesis 22, the ethical is consequently suspended for the sake of a higher goal (*telos*).

19. Baudelaire, 313 and 312.
20. Ibid., 150.
21. Maurice Blanchot, *The Blanchot Reader*, ed. Michael Holland (Oxford: Blackwell, 1995), 249.
22. Bergson states that the appeal of laughter is "to intelligence, pure and simple," but it is an intelligence that must "always remain in touch with other intelligences"—a social gesture that requires a response also motivated by intelligence and, I would argue, the ethical in many instances.
23. Jonathan Greenberg, "Nathaniel West and the Mystery of Feeling," *Modern Fiction Studies* 52, no. 3 (2006): 9.
24. I should note that I am thinking very generally about Jean-Francois Lyotard here, and his notorious discussion of grand narratives in *The Postmodern Condition* (Minneapolis: University of Minnesota Press, 1984).
25. Lawrence Langer, *Admitting the Holocaust* (New York: Oxford University Press, 1995), 75.
26. In the *New York Times Book Review*, January 30, 2005, Wendy Shalit launched a verbal assault on writers including Nathan Englander, Tova Mirvis, and Tova Reich, among others. Shalit takes offense at the ways in which such writers, whom she claims are estranged from Orthodox tradition, depict Orthodox and Ultra-Orthodox Jewish communities. She contends that their depictions are ridiculous and unflattering, and that the writers of such depictions are outsiders who have no right to speak about a lifestyle to which they do not adhere. Clearly, Shalit misses the more crucial and authentic depiction of human, even Jewish, emotional and spiritual complexity to be found in the work of writers such as Englander. Tova Mirvis responded in an essay in *The Forward*, February 4, 2005, calling Shalit a latter-day Leopold Wapter, the judge in Philip Roth's *The Ghost Writer* (New York: Farrar, Straus, and Giroux, 1979). Shalit responded to Mirvis's article in an essay published in *Jewish World Review*, February 15, 2005.
27. Deuteronomy 30:11-14. I am quoting from Everett Fox's translation of the first five books of the Hebrew Bible—*The Five Books of Moses* (New York: Schocken, 1995)—because it maintains the original rhythm and lyricism of the Hebrew. Fox's translation is also based on an earlier translation done by Franz Rozenzweig and Martin Buber.

Metafictional Witnessing in Jonathan Safran Foer's *Everything Is Illuminated*

Tracy Floreani

Jonathan Safran Foer's 2003 novel, *Everything Is Illuminated* inherently critiques the possibilities for writing the trauma of the Holocaust. This critique comes through in the very flaws of the complicated, metafictional narrative. As critics of the novel have complained, it verges on becoming "a kind of aesthetic trap, reducing the form of the novel to a bag of readily available tricks." Another declares the Holocaust "*too* big a subject for [Foer's] undeveloped talent."[1] On the contrary, Foer's use of a self-aware, metafictional approach goes beyond a set of aesthetic "tricks" to expose the writing process as a combining of memory, imagination, and language to create and dispense some form of knowledge—a process engaged in by all parties involved. In what seems like a potentially flawed post-Holocaust narrative we come to see how writing complicates the ability to know and, consequently, reveals the limits of fully excavating, and serving as witness of, the past.

The novel opens with the voice of the charmingly ungrammatical Ukrainian teenager Alex. The author's fictionalized alter ego Jonathan, a young Jewish American novelist, arrives in Ukraine in search of the woman who "saved [his grandfather from] the Nazis,"[2] and is placed with Alex as interpreter, and Alex's overtly anti-Semitic grandfather as low-budget driver and tour guide. The comedic narrative consists of epistolary components and descriptions of the tour through Ukraine, as told by Alex, interwoven with pieces of a fictional, magical realist novel that Jonathan is writing about his grandfather's shtetl, dating back to the eighteenth century, in which he imaginatively retrieves the community and family history disrupted by pogroms and the Holocaust. We learn throughout these narratives that the pieces of manuscript are exchanged through the mail after the events of the trip, and, while we never see his letters commenting on Alex's writing, we infer Jonathan's various reactions embedded within Alex's responses. Through their mutual critiques, the processes of writing, storytelling, and memory are laid bare as matters of willful construction.

Yet, as Marion Spies points out, we never actually see the end result of their writing collaborations: "We . . . are asked to construct the final narrative; this is only possible by going back and forth in the text, choosing from equally convincing variants, something that, of course, is never wholly successful. One could describe this as the writer's (and the reader's) imaginative way of dealing with the neuroscientist's question of the accuracy of memory." Similarly, Melvin Jules Bukiet writes, "Memory is the mantra of all the institutions that reckon with the Holocaust, but memory is an inaccurate term. For anyone who wasn't there, on either side of the barbed wire, Jew or German, thinking about the Holocaust is really an act of imagination. All we know is how little we know."[3] The narrative, then, is constructed not only by the characters and the author, but also by the reader. What some readers might find a frustrating reading experience actually mirrors the frustrations of the author in putting together a cogent set of histories.

The novel's climax hinges on—as does this essay's analysis—an emotional scene in the chapter titled "Illumination," in which Alex must translate from Ukrainian to English what his grandfather witnessed and how he reacted during the Nazi occupation. In translating what his grandfather says, Alex must process the story as he hears it for the first time, while Jonathan, to whom the truth matters most, remains a passive witness. As Alex notes, the acts of hearing and translating the story entirely shift his sense of identity: "When I listened to him, I did not listen to Grandfather, but to someone else, someone I had never encountered before, but whom I knew better than Grandfather. And the person who was listening to this person was not me but someone else, someone I had never been before but whom I knew better than myself" (245). Much of the theory of "witnessing" in Holocaust studies comes to bear here, in ways that have yet to be applied to the novel. In fact, the verb "to witness" appears repeatedly in Alex's narrative, because he uses it nonidiomatically in place of the verb "to see"; however, once the plot has unfolded completely, the use of the word "witness" takes on double meaning, both literal and theoretical, as it is repeated increasingly throughout the scene of finding the heroic woman they call Augustine and her revealing of the remains of the shtetl Trachimbrod. In the end, all of the characters have revealed or participated in some level of witnessing of events related to the Shoah, and the three men's lives are changed thereafter.

When they first meet, Alex asks the elderly woman ten times whether or not she has "witnessed" any of the people in the photo that Jonathan has brought with him to identify her; later, as they circle the same rural area looking for the lost village, he frustratedly declares, "We have already witnessed this place" (117); as it grows dark, they lose Augustine in the dusk, and he repeats twice, "It is almost impossible to witness her" (183). What he does not realize in his literal observations is that the ability to "witness" the shtetl will only come in figurative and indirect ways. The village no longer exists for Jonathan to see. The inability to "witness" Augustine (who has come to embody the whole village) lies in the fact that the young men must instead witness what Grandfather will soon tell them. In this sense, some form of knowledge about the village's disappearance has been in the car with them all along.

Crucial to the theme of witnessing is the motif of photographs. Within the plot, they drive action or trigger memory, but they also serve to reinforce the notion of the visual as the base component of witnessing and as a means of accessing family history. In her work on Art Speigelman's *Maus* and its relation to photography theory, Marianne Hirsch writes, "It is precisely the indexical nature of the photo, its status as relic, or trace, or fetish—its 'direct' connection with the material presence of the photographed person—that intensifies its status as harbinger of death and, at the same time and concomitantly, its capacity to signify life."[4] The same is true of the photographs within Foer's narrative, with its emphasis on the photos that drive the narrative but also the hundreds that paper the wall of Augustine's house, simultaneously commemorating lives and reminding us of the deaths or displacement of the village's Jewish inhabitants. Hirsch also notes that family photos related directly or indirectly to the Holocaust "connect . . . the past and the present, . . . because these family photographs are documents both of memory (the survivor's) and of what I would like to call post-memory (that of the child of the survivor whose life is dominated by memories of what preceded his/her birth)."[5] The photograph of Augustine and, later, the found photo of Grandfather as a young man with his young family and his good friend Herschel, serve this same function, visually and psychologically driving the "post-memory" experiences of Alex and Jonathan.

The letters, multiple fictional and nonfiction narratives, and awkward translations that compose the novel, while complicated, are not the only source of Jonathan's confused attempt to understand the events that occurred in his own grandfather's life. Part of the confusion lies in the inability to know if the beautiful old woman they find is really Augustine. All three men suspect not, yet all are willing to believe that she is Augustine because, psychologically and emotionally, they need her to be. Investing her with an almost mythical quality, Alex writes, "She was so beautiful, like someone who you will never meet, but always dream of meeting, like someone who is too good for you" (149). After spending quite a bit of time with her, he comments, "And then I remembered that I did not know this woman's name. I perservered to think of her as Augustine, because, like Grandfather, I could not stop desiring that she was Augustine" (154). (Later we learn that her name is actually Lista.) Also frustrating to Jonathan's recovery of knowledge is Alex's grandfather's inability—even as a witness to the events decades before—to provide an actual destination or a memory that provides some sort of desired closure for Jonathan in the limited space of his trip. Alex ominously notes that they could have stopped after simply finding the geographical site of the village: "We could have stopped it there. We could have viewed Trachimbrod, returned to the car, and followed Augustine back to her house. The hero would have been able to say that he was in Trachimbrod, he could have even said that he met Augustine, and grandfather and I would have been able to say that we had completed our mission" (184-85). While the experience of making a pilgrimage to the village might be enough, the ideal would be to uncover memories of the triumph of escape and survival of Jonathan's grandfather, of hearing this at last from the woman who enabled the continuation of his family. However, the two remaining witnesses can only provide memories of horrifying trauma, of repressed guilt, in the old man's case, and material witnessing of the existence of one hundred people who may or may not have had firsthand relationships with Jonathan's grandfather. Alex realizes this, in retrospect: "It was a situation without winning. The possibilities were none, between what was possible and what we wanted" (242).

That last form of witnessing, the now-familiar preservation of material culture representing the victims of the Holocaust, appears in the form of the boxes and crates of photographs, clothes, menorahs, and random household objects from the shtetl that fill "Augustine's" house. As the men stand in awe of the archival facility that her house has become, she notes that "the ground is still filled with rings, and money, and pictures, and Jewish things. I was only able to find a few of them, but they fill the earth" (152). In fact, because she now has someone who wants to find the village after all these years, the character who comes to be called Augustine is the only one who comes close to achieving closure, which is articulated in her relieved utterance at the strangers' arrival: "I have been waiting for you for so long" (118). Their arrival releases her from the burden of sole knowledge of the shtetl's existence—she is no longer the only witness. One wonders why Augustine stays in her obviously lonely, isolated home after she has made her testimony and received an offer from Grandfather to return with them to Odessa. But when she asks, mystified and sincere, "Is the war over?" (193), we realize that she cannot remove herself from a perpetual state of witnessing the past, and she must remain within an almost mythical role. Jonathan understands that the saved objects serve as "Evidence. Documentation. Testimony" (192). Like Lista, he saves objects invested with the sacred, most importantly the bags of dirt he hauls home from the Trachimbrod site. While he recognizes better than Alex does that these objects *are* Trachimbrod, and that he takes away a piece of the village in the box full of mementoes marked "in case," many of the objects are certain to belong to families other than his own (102).

Perhaps Jonathan seeks to retrieve family memory in the "wrong" way, as interpreted by critic Aliki Varvogli: "the trauma of the Holocaust resides in Europe, and he feels he must get there to find it. In this, Jonathan is typical rather than unique: he conceives of his family's wartime past in terms of actual geographical space, rather than imagining it in terms of psychological trauma, or memories handed down through generations."[6] However, because Jonathan's grandmother will not talk about the past, he is left with no choice but to reside in the symbolic. In fact, he acknowledges early in the quest that, realistically, they probably will not find the mythical Augustine, and implies that the quest itself matters most. When he does find something relevant, the convergence of place, material witnessing, and memory disturb his typically controlled mode of containing knowledge: writing in his diary. It turns out that Lista does know who Jonathan's grandfather Safran was (though knows nothing about his escape), and a few of her many photos include Safran and his first wife. Alex narrates: "I gave the hero each picture as she gave it to me, and he could only with difficulty hold it in his hands that were doing so much shaking. It appeared that a part of him wanted to write everything, every word of what occurred, into his diary. And a part of him refused to write even one word" (154). Conversely, when they are searching for the village and finding nothing, Jonathan finds much to write about the quest itself: "The less we saw, the more he wrote" (115). Here again we see the novel's metafictional structure highlighting how writing is used simultaneously as a way to impose knowledge where it is not, and as a very limited means of processing the uncontextualized pieces of history with which one is confronted.

While some of the atrocities associated with Trachimbrod's fate are revealed at the geographic site, Grandfather's own participation in the events comes out once the three travelers have returned to their hotel. Though Grandfather's family had actually lived in the neighboring village of Kolki, a photo of Grandfather and his friend Herschel appears while the travelers lightheartedly explore the box of mementoes from Trachimbrod that "Augustine" has given Jonathan. Triggered by the sight of this photo, Grandfather describes what happened when the Nazis came to the village and how he had to give up Herschel as a Jew in order to save his own family; Alex stops translating for Jonathan. He admits, "You cannot know how it felt to have to hear these things and then repeat them, because when I repeated them, I felt like I was making them new again" (185-86). However, the translation actually stops at Jonathan's request. Though the story has nothing to do directly with Jonathan's ancestral village, he cannot bear to hear it. Once Grandfather begins, though, he cannot stop his own words and recounts the until-now repressed story of a mass execution in a paragraph that runs for about five pages, with words becoming increasingly conflated and jumbled as he grows more emotional: "I didwhatIdid" and "I am I and Iamresponsible" (251). The American tourist disappears from the scene completely as Alex gets absorbed in the act of rewitnessing. Jonathan gets the full translation only after the fact, after returning to the U.S., apparently, as it is recounted in the last manuscript segment Alex has sent to him.

In their work on survivor narratives, Michael Bernard-Donals and Richard Glejzer distinguish between witnessing—the firsthand view of an event—and the recounting of that event after the fact, the testimony. Important to them, too, is the intervening space between the two acts. For example, in one videotaped account, they analyze the details of a man's testimony, reading "a point between witness and testimony that can be seen as a moment of trauma, a moment in which the historical real and the memory of it as demanded by the imperative to testify to it disintegrate and present for both the witness and the interviewer . . . a break," which "in Cathy Caruth's words . . . 'is grasped only in the very inaccessibility of its occurrence.'"[7] I would argue that this is the very thing that happens to Alex's grandfather. That he was apparently gentile seems not to have mattered, as he expresses with simultaneous shame and defensiveness, "It happened to everybody, do not make any mistakes. Just because I was not a Jew, it does not mean that it did not happen to me." Understandably, he resists accessing the moment of trauma, and when he does finally testify, the "ghosts" behind his eyelids are released (246).

One might assume that this admission is causally related to his suicide at the end of the novel, because he experiences some version of survivor guilt. While the act of testimony does become traumatic for Grandfather because he helped to perpetrate that which he witnessed, there is often power in testifying to atrocity, in naming it and exposing it to catharsis or to justice. Elie Wiesel says of writing as witnessing, "Not to transmit an experience is to betray it; this is what Jewish tradition teaches us."[8] In a sense, then, Grandfather's testimony or confession is an undoing of the very betrayal in which he engaged. Further, Alex's writing of the story enables him not to "betray" what he has witnessed—a testimony of betrayal itself. This advances the effect of Grandfather's story as a tribute to Herschel and an act of reconciliation with all Jews, which is symbolized for Grandfather by his desire to defend Jonathan later in the story and to continue the quest for Augustine even after the young tourist has returned to the U.S. Alex seems to realize his own role in all this when he says in a letter to Jonathan, "*With writing, we have second chances*"—however imperfect that writing may be (144). Indeed, the suicide note addressed to Jonathan (translated by Alex) at the end of the novel indicates that Grandfather goes to his death not because he cannot live with the unearthed memory, but because his testimony has begun a process of making things right throughout his own dysfunctional family: "I would give everything for them to live without violence. Peace. That is all that I would ever want for them. Not money and not even love. It is still possible. I know that now, and it is the cause of so much happiness in me. They must begin again. They must cut all the strings, yes? . . . [Alex] has started it, and now I must finish it" (275). Here, then, we see that that the "break" between witnessing and testimony has led to catharsis and relatively progressive change for the family that has inherited a legacy of violence.

Throughout the novel, each segment of Alex's manuscript is eventually followed by an implied letter that reveals Jonathan's critiques; however, the scene of Grandfather's translated testimony and his suicide note have no follow-up. Menachem Feuer argues, "Through the use of characters that are grandchildren of survivors and perpetrators, and by contrasting two entirely different approaches to memory, one tragic and the other comic, Foer brings out the quandary of post-Holocaust reconciliation." In this lack of a final critique of Alex's writing Feuer infers "Jonathan's ultimate refusal of friendship and reconciliation" and that the author Foer is positing an argument that "Holocaust representation . . . should resist not only comedy but also full reconciliation."[9] This notion is reinforced through Jonathan's declaration that he no longer likes humor because he has come to see it as "a way of shrinking from the world" (Foer 154). The opposite is true for Alex, however. Comedy serves as an integral part of his relationships, as he parenthetically writes to his Grandfather at a difficult point in the narrative, "That is also why I try so inflexibly to be a funny person. Everything is to protect you. I exist in case you need to be protected" (227). Christoph Ribbat sees the ebbing of comedy in the novel's second half less as a matter of politicized commentary than a matter of how plot evolves thematically within the genre of travel narrative, and his ideas do seem to account for a rather more natural sense of character evolution in terms of the classic picaresque. He writes, "The mission of [the company] 'Heritage Touring' was to guide American Jews on emotional journeys into the stories of their past. On this specific trip, however, the tour guides encounter their *own* heritage. And at this point the farce ends, the comedy implodes."[10]

Feuer notes, too, the dependence of the friendship and recovery of memory upon the act of writing. While he doesn't delve into the complicated metafictional structure of the novel, he does note how "friendship is not sought after through normal channels; it is arrived at, or thwarted, through the trickery of writing."[11] At times, though, Jonathan's silences within the epistolary segments read not entirely as a refusal of friendship. In fact, their writing projects seem to coalesce as the narratives become more emotionally complicated, and Alex comes to see that their communication and relationship exist more powerfully within their exchanged narratives than in the letters themselves. At one point, in a section that uses italics to signal Alex speaking directly to Jonathan from within the manuscript Alex is writing, he asks that they no longer comment on each other's writing in terms of writerly quality, because what they have written means something more than critiques of accuracy or aesthetics can attest to: "*let us not praise or reproach. Let us not judge at all. We are outside of that already. We are talking now, Jonathan, together; and not apart. We are with each other; working on the same story, and I am certain that you can also feel it*" (214). We also learn in the last pages of the novel that their communications finally end not because of "Jonathan's ultimate refusal of friendship and reconciliation,"[12] but because Alex needs to cut off all previous ties and start a completely new life after expelling his abusive father from the family.

While the quest is Jonathan's, it becomes an inadvertent one for Alex, as well. As the narrative unfolds, he actually evolves in the ways of a classic protagonist more so than Jonathan does: he moves from youthful arrogance and lies to a more mature humility as he confronts his own family history and takes on the responsibility of rescuing his little brother from their abusive home. Jonathan's silence within the narrative—and especially at the end of the novel—keeps readers from knowing whether or not he has gotten anything emotionally useful from the trip to Ukraine, apart from the creative impulse for the magical realist novel he is writing. Vargogli notes, "Though Alex is the main narrator, he announces from the start that Jonathan is the 'hero' of his narrative, and it is significant that the American traveler is depicted indirectly, through Alex's impressions of him, and through his own fictional story of Trachimbrod. With his decision to create an American hero who is only glimpsed through other narratives, Foer has found a formal analogy for the issues of identity that his book explores."[13] Varvogli implies that this fragmented, impressionistic identity is also an inherently Jewish identity, one that, as noted earlier, is not unique to Jonathan; it is the product of disrupted and diasporic community histories.

A more inadvertent outcome of the trip and the writing process is the undoing of Alex's anti-Semitism. While Jonathan's lack of response to Alex's narrative might read as a denial of friendship, his friendship in the interim has served to challenge Alex's notions about Jews. In fact, Alex admits to never having met a Jew before becoming Jonathan's translator, yet he has clearly absorbed anti-Semitic thinking from Grandfather, as evidenced in the early part of the story when he says things like, "I had the opinion that Jewish people were having shit between their brains. This is because all I knew of Jewish people was that they paid Father very much currency in order to make vacations *from* American *to* Ukraine. But then I met Jonathan Safran Foer, and I will tell you, he is not having shit between his brains" (3). In addition to such comments in the early stages of the journey, he focuses many of his descriptions of Jonathan on what he perceives as uncooperative or neurotic characteristics: his dislike of Grandfather's dog, his vegetarianism, his asking for translations at inconvenient times. Most disturbing, he admits to surprise at Jonathan's appearance because he has always assumed that all Jews of all generations look like the archival photos of emaciated and uniformed concentration camp survivors (32). Yet, the events of the journey, the truth of his grandfather's guilt over Herschel's death, his on-going engagement with Jonathan's writing, and his own newfound interest in writing about Jonathan all chip away the anti-Semitic bravado that mirrors his grandfather's obvious guilt-originated version. In the latter half of the novel, we see in Alex's letters to Jonathan repeated requests for forgiveness, though we do not know exactly for what.

Alex's character development does not exist free of the metafictional structure of the story. As Feuer notes, Alex's comments on Jonathan's novel excerpts "indicate that Alex is reading the text in a self-reflexive manner, and that in so doing, he questions his own values and beliefs."[14] We see this most forcefully when he must transcribe the story of Herschel's death: "Here it is almost too forbidding to continue. I have written to this point many times, and corrected the parts you would have me correct, and made more funnies, and more inventions, and written as if I were you writing this, but every time I try to persevere, my hand shakes so that I can no longer hold my pen. Do it for me. Please. It is now yours" (226). Alex's unwillingness to commit to paper this testimony speaks of the difficulty of moving from the process of perception to that of documentation, as explained in witnessing theory: "in the gap between the traumatic experience—and its forgetting—that constitutes witness, and the creation of a narrative that may be said to move a victim forward that constitutes testimony, there exists the underside of knowledge, what troubles knowledge and insists upon disrupting its language."[15]

Jonathan's triumph comes at the end of the novel, then, because of the creative ways in which he forces himself to use troubled language to reimagine a knowable past. As noted earlier, Feuer sees Jonathan's silences toward the end of the novel as a condemnation of friendship and reconciliation in the third generation of Holocaust survivors; instead, I see the latter pages of Jonathan's novel, the fictionalized story of the romances of his grandfather Safran, as a refusal to be silent. However, this creation does not spring entirely from Jonathan's mind. In the box of mementos "Augustine" gives him (which is later stolen on a train), he finds an old volume titled *The Book of Past Occurrences*, which we learn has been a source of the magical realist story segments we have been reading all along. Where knowledge of historical fact and the absence of usable memory leave a void, Jonathan creates a usable past from this text and inserts his own family history within—one that contains mostly pages and pages of delight, and then a few of the tragedy. According to Martha J. Cutter, within writing as witnessing is the important element of "emplotment—the placement of historical events within narrative trajectories—[which] can lead to innovative versions of past stories that correct the mistakes of historical erasure and generate new histories."[16] In his own imaginative emplotment of Trachimbrod's history Jonathan does not ignore the suffering of Safran, the character based on his grandfather as a young man; the tragedy of the Nazi invasion must be included in the narrative (but it is a rather small portion of the overall story) because it is the liminal frontier between the unknown Ukrainian past and the Jewish American family in which Jonathan grew up. But in taking this hazy Ukrainian past all the way back to the eighteenth century, to the beginnings of a dynamic Jewish community, he triumphs in refusing to let the entire narrative of his family be reduced to just a Holocaust story. Rachel Leah Jablon asserts that to witness through writing is akin to enacting a symbolic form of *shivah* that helps to repair a sense of community. Jonathan's story does restore community, even as it accounts for its loss.[17]

One could argue that, within literature and popular media, the farther we get from the Holocaust, the stronger the tendency to romanticize it or use it as a creative device based only nominally within history. Some may certainly accuse Foer of the same, of using the Holocaust as a device for a clever and overly complicated book, but revealing little new about the events themselves. Author Thane Rosenbaum discusses writing "post-Holocaust" fiction as one that should focus not on the experience itself or the camps, which seems inherently unethical for Jewish writers of later generations, but about the "aftermath": "the barbed-wire is only metaphorical, representing the way in which the mind can become a prison when it is forced into the servitude of memory."[18] It seems fitting to view Foer's novel within this "post-Holocaust" genre, as he takes on the troubling legacy of the generation once-removed from the survivors. The basic storyline of Jonathan Safran Foer's trip is clearly based on autobiography. However, while writing a straightforward memoir might lead an author down a more solipsistic path, the intentionally unheroic, bumbling diarist caricature of Foer demonstrates his very awareness of such a tendency. One might imagine the original book going a much different direction, yet the messy, metafictional result reveals an unwillingness to tread the romanticized road of the personal-disaster-tourism memoir. The fragmented narrative of an attempt at witnessing reveals even further the "presence of absence" felt by the generation preceding Foer's own.[19] Rosenbaum's differentiation of Holocaust versus post-Holocaust fiction certainly counters the assertions of critics who see this as a failed Holocaust narrative, because such criticism misses the point: the novel is a post-Holocaust story, and the event itself is indeed too big for the memory of the protagonist. Like Rosenbaum, Foer attempts to "make emotional, psychological, and spiritual sense out of the infinite hole left in the world after Auschwitz."[20] By doing so through metafiction that confuses and troubles the reader as much as the characters, Foer reveals how very difficult such a task remains.

Notes

1. Siddartha Deb, review of *Everything Is Illuminated*, "Novel of the Week," *New Statesman*, July 1, 2002, 55; Brooke Allen, review of *Everything Is Illuminated*, "Books & Critics," *Atlantic Monthly*, April 2002, 141-42.
2. Jonathan Safran Foer, *Everything Is Illuminated*, (New York: Perennial, 2002), 59. Hereafter cited parenthetically in the text.
3. Marion Spies, "Recent Directions in Holocaust Writing," *Religion and the Arts* 8, no. 2 (2004): 258; Melvin Jules Bukiet, Introduction, *Nothing Makes You Free: Writings by Descendents of Jewish Holocaust Survivors*, ed. Melvin Jules Bukiet (New York: Norton, 2002), 6.
4. Marianne Hirsch, "Family Pictures: *Maus*, Mourning, and Post-Memory," *Discourse* 15, no. 2 (1992-93): 6.
5. Ibid., 8.
6. Aliki Varvogli, "'Underwhelmed to the Maximum': American Travellers in Dave Eggers's *You Shall Know Our Velocity* and Jonathan Safran Foer's *Everything Is Illuminated*," *Atlantic Studies* 3, no. 1 (2006): 89.
7. Michael Bernard-Donals and Richard Glejzer. "Between Witness and Testimony: Survivor Narrative and the Shoah," *College Literature* 27, no. 2 (2000): 2.
8. Elie Wiesel, "A Personal Statement from Elie Wiesel: Why I Write," trans. Rosette C. Lamont, in *Confronting the Holocaust: The Impact of Elie Wiesel*, ed. Alvin H. Rosenfeld and Irving Greenberg (Bloomington: Indiana University Press, 1978), 201.

9. Menachem Feuer, "Almost Friends: Post-Holocaust Comedy, Tragedy, and Friendship in Jonathan Safran Foer's *Everything Is Illuminated*," *Shofar* 25, no. 2 (2007). Rpt. Literature Resource Center, http://galenet.galegroup.com, June 17, 2008. (para. 1).
10. Ribbat, Christoph, "Nomadic with the Truth: Holocaust Representations in Michael Chabon, James McBride, and Jonathan Safran Foer," *Anglistik & Englischunterricht* 66 (2005): 213.
11. Feuer, para. 2.
12. Feuer, para. 1.
13. Varvogli, 90.
14. Feuer, para. 35 and 37.
15. Bernard-Donals and Glejzer, 18.
16. Martha J. Cutter, "Editor's Introduction: Witnessing, Testifying, and History," *MELUS* 34, no. 1 (2009): 6.
17. Rachel Leah Jablon, "Witnessing as *Shivah*; Memoir as *Yizkor*: The Formulation of Holocaust Survivor Literature as *Gemilut Khasadim*," *The Journal of Popular Culture* 38, no. 2 (2004): 306-24. For more detailed discussion of the Trachimbrod storyline, see Menachem Feuer and Francisco Collado-Rodriguez, "Ethics in the Second Degree: Trauma and Dual Narratives in Jonathan Safran Foer's *Everything Is Illuminated*," *Journal of Modern Fiction* 32, no. 1 (2008): 54-69, both of whom link the story to the work of Gabriel Garcia Marquez.
18. Thane Rosenbaum, "The Audacity of Aesthetics: The Post-Holocaust Novel and the Respect for the Dead," *Poetics Today* 27, no. 2 (2006): 491.
19. The concept of the "presence of absence" in post-Holocaust generations is articulated by Alan L. Berger, Introduction, *Children of Job: American Second-Generation Witnesses to the Holocaust*, (Albany: State University of New York Press, 1997), 1-12.
20. Rosenbaum, 491-92.

Part 3

(Re)inscribing Jewish Text and Identity

Putting the "Jewish" Back in "Jewish American Fiction": A Look at Jewish American Fiction since 1977 and an Allegorical Reading of Nathan Englander's "The Gilgul of Park Avenue"

Adam Meyer

Almost thirty-five years have passed since Irving Howe made his famous statement that "Jewish American fiction has probably moved past its high point,"[1] and no doubt some would argue that time has proven him right, that no younger writer has yet equaled the career of Saul Bellow (with the possible exception of the not-much-younger Philip Roth). Nevertheless, it also seems safe to say that any reports of the complete demise of Jewish American fiction—such as Leslie Fiedler's lesser known comment that "the Jewish American novel is over and done with, a part of history rather than a living literature"[2]—were greatly exaggerated. Indeed, as we move further into the twenty-first century, Jewish American fiction remains a vital, important, frequently read and discussed, prize-winning literature. In fact, there seems to have been a renaissance in Jewish American fiction beginning in the 1980s, shortly after Howe's statement was published, and gaining remarkable steam in the 1990s with the works of young writers such as, to name but a few, Michael Chabon, Allegra Goodman, Melvin Jules Bukiet, and Nathan Englander.

Howe, usually a perceptive critic, failed to see this development on the horizon largely because of the assumptions underlying his definition of Jewish American fiction, a definition that emphasizes the second adjective in the phrase rather than the first. To Howe, Jewish American fiction is based on certain constants: the immigrant experience, either as a Yiddish speaker or the child of a Yiddish speaker, almost always in an Northern urban environment where the family plays a dominant role. As this way of life was coming to an end, Howe saw American "Jewishness" fading away and believed that younger writers would not have enough of a connection left to enable them to produce Jewish American fiction. Given his definition, Jewish American fiction did indeed reach its peak, and necessarily so, with Bellow, Bernard Malamud, and Philip Roth. Most younger Jewish American writers are far removed from the immigrant ethos and, therefore, depictions of such a lifestyle have in fact almost ceased to exist, except as nostalgia or historic recreation.

But Howe's is not the only possible definition of Jewish American fiction. If one has a definition that puts the emphasis on the first word in the equation, Jewish, one sees a Jewish American fiction that has not only thrived since 1977 but has in fact reached heights unscaled by the earlier writers.[3] Several factors that contributed to this renaissance were not taken into account by Howe. First of all, in the entirety of Howe's introduction to *Jewish American Stories*, which became a sort of standard textbook anthology, there is not a single mention of the Holocaust. In retrospect, this seems an amazing omission for a critic writing in 1977. The Holocaust has, obviously, become a significant area of emphasis for literary productions by many younger Jewish American writers, particularly the not insignificant number of those who are children of Holocaust survivors.[4] Second, questions surrounding the state of Israel have also become a significant area of emphasis for many Jewish American writers who came of age during or after the Six-Day War. Here, again, Howe's essay makes absolutely no reference to Israel, a subject that would soon become the foundation for a significant body of Jewish American novels and stories.[5]

Perhaps the largest and most significant body of works in the Jewish American fictional renaissance, however, falls into a third category, one that Howe does mention several times but dismisses out of hand, namely the fiction produced by the religiously oriented Jewish American writer.[6] In his introduction, Howe quotes himself as having written that Jewish immigrants to America "were left with a nagging problem in self-perception, a crisis of identity, as it came to be called, which seems beyond solution or removal, except perhaps through a full return to religious faith or a complete abandonment of Jewish identification."[7] He clearly believed that the latter, complete acculturation, was more likely to occur, and rather quickly dismissed the idea that a return to religious faith could sustain Jewish Americans and their literature. To give him his due, complete assimilation did occur in some cases, particularly at that time, and he was not alone in fearing the worst.[8] Howe may well have been right about most Jewish American writers in the mid-to-late 1970s when he wrote that they "have had only an enfeebled relationship—indeed, a torn and deprived relationship—with the Jewish tradition in its fullness" (12). Nevertheless, his own anthology gives hints of things to come in the person of one of the youngest writers represented in the collection, Cynthia Ozick, who would go on to become "the acknowledged leader of a revitalized Jewish-American literary movement" through the way in which she "self-consciously define[d] herself as a Jewish writer."[9]

Ozick, and more particularly the story that Howe reprinted, "Envy, or Yiddish in America" (originally published in 1969), did much to show how Judaism could be utilized in Jewish American fiction; her works heralded "the appearance of an American Jewish fiction which advocated the norms of Jewish tradition, although not necessarily halakha, rather than Americanism as its standard."[10] Other writers who appeared at roughly the same time as Ozick and also looked seriously to Judaism include Arthur A. Cohen, Hugh Nissenson, and Chaim Potok.[11] As new Jewish American writers appeared in the 1980s, furthermore, the idea of a return to a religious sense of Judaism came to the forefront in more and more of their works. Alan L. Berger, for example, argues that "American Jewish fiction in the eighties display[ed] an unprecedented determination to grapple with the problematic of Jewish being while struggling with the notions of covenant and chosenness[, a struggle that] involves a vigorous theological imagination"[12]; the anthology *Writing Our Way Home* (1992), easily seen as a reply to Howe's anthology, features a far greater number of stories that "are concerned with Judaism, not only Jewishness."[13] Writers representing this new group would include Rebecca Goldstein, Nessa Rapoport (one of the coeditors of *Writing Our Way Home*, incidentally), Tova Reich, Anne Roiphe, and Steve Stern.[14] The movement toward Jewish renewal became only more pronounced as still younger voices were heard from in the 1990s, such as the ones mentioned earlier. These writers, according to Andrew Furman, who has discussed them as fully as anyone in his book, *Contemporary Jewish American Writers and the Multicultural Dilemma* (2000), "have begun to assert their Jewish identities and values with an unprecedented intensity."[15] Indeed, it is this return, in many cases not just to "Jewishness" but to Judaism, not merely to *Yiddishkeit* but to Yahweh, that marks the most interesting works of the Jewish American writers who are today extending, creating, and carrying the traditions of Jewish American fiction into the twenty-first century.

This return to Judaism in Jewish American literature, although an occurrence which Howe failed to foresee completely, is rather easily explained, or at least systematized, by employing one of the founding tenets in the sociological study of American immigration, Marcus Lee Hansen's thesis (some might say law) of third-generation return. Hansen himself provided the sound bite version of his theory when he remarked that it was "derived from the almost universal phenomenon that what the son wishes to forget the grandson wishes to remember."[16] In more detail, Hansen meant that the first generation, the immigrants themselves, are bound to the old country and old ways, struggling to learn the language and the customs of their new home and to survive in it economically.[17] The second generation, born in America, see themselves as Americans and want desperately for others to see them as such; consequently, they try to distance themselves as much as possible from the old ways that identify their parents as aliens and outsiders, others. "Their motto was," according to Hansen, "Forget it all! Forget the family and community customs that the sons of the Yankees and often the Yankees themselves had delighted to ridicule."[18] And, to the extent that they are successful, so it comes to seem possible that the traits separating that immigrant group from others could completely disappear by the third generation. What happens instead, Hansen points out, is that "the grandsons of immigrants . . . do not have the same reasons or complexes that encouraged the second generation to make a complete break" and therefore they "want to know all about the beginning of the American branch of the family."[19] Because this third generation is so much "more at ease in America," according to Nathan Glazer, it "has no psychological hang-ups about exploring its past and its heritage."[20] "The third generation," Thomas J. Archdeacon concurs, "either because society is more tolerant or because the grandchildren of the immigrants come to recognize the high price paid in surrendering one's culture, embraces what the second thought it had to scorn."[21] Thus the phenomenon of return.

In terms of the history of Jewish American fiction, Hansen's theory seems to apply very well indeed,[22] as long as we employ a liberal definition of the term "generation," considering it more in a metaphorical than a biological sense. The first generation of Jewish American fiction writers would, obviously, include such European-born figures as Sholem Asch, Mary Antin, Henry Roth, Anzia Yezierska, and, above all, Abraham Cahan. This group of immigrants, in accordance with Hansen's theory, managed to make the adjustments necessary to function in American society, to earn a living at least, and to begin democratizing American literature through adding their Jewish voices to it. This generation largely gave way to the second generation in the late 1930s and was effectively ended by World War II. The second generation of Jewish American writers, those whom Hansen predicted would wish to move away from their Jewish ethnic identity, began to appear before the war years and came to dominate the field in the 1950s and 1960s, and they did indeed try to distance themselves from some of their parents' identifying traits and customs, referring to themselves as "writers who are Jews" rather than as "Jewish writers." Writers of this period would include, most notably, Bellow, Malamud, and Roth, each of whom published at least one early novel without a significant Jewish character (*Henderson the Rain King* [1959], *The Natural* [1952], and *When She Was Good* [1967], respectively). Other Jewish American writers of this time who were thought (fairly or unfairly) to be abandoning Jewish concerns included Norman Mailer, Arthur Miller, and several "major intellectuals [who] were then very distant from Jewish interests."[23] Thus *Jewish American Literature: A Norton Anthology* (2001) refers to this era as a period of "Achievement and Ambivalence"[24]; Jewish writers may have made it, but in many cases this success entailed playing down their Jewishness. It was towards the end of this second generation's reign that Howe wrote his comments forecasting the demise of Jewish American writing, as he felt that, the way things were going, the younger Jewish American writers, the third generation, wouldn't have enough Jewishness left to be able to write (meaningfully Jewish) Jewish American fiction.

What happened instead, however, as Hansen's thesis should have led Howe to expect, is that the third generation became interested in and returned to many of the traditions, in this case particularly the religious traditions, that had guided their immigrant (and even pre-immigrant) ancestors. Howe did allude to this possibility when he remarked that "tradition seemingly discarded can survive underground for a generation and then, through channels hard to locate, surface in the works of writers who may not even be aware of what is affecting their consciousness," but he again seems to dismiss this point rather quickly (13).[25] Had he been more versed in Hansen's theory, he might have seen Ozick for what she turned out to be, the precursor of the third generation of Jewish American fiction writers who would return to an exploration of their Jewish roots in their texts. Later critics and commentators, given the advantages of hindsight, of course, have certainly seen such a pattern as having emerged. Indeed, Furman writes that spiritual return "has emerged as one of the predominant themes of the contemporary Jewish American writer as increasing numbers of contemporary Jews in America (and of contemporary Jewish American protagonists) seek to rediscover the Judaism that their 'alienated' parents . . . eschewed."[26] Along the same lines, the final section of Norton's *Jewish American Literature* anthology is called "Wandering and Return," since a "determination to reclaim Jewishness as a way of organizing one's experience defines this period in literature."[27] Mark Krupnick, similarly, gives the last section of his summation of Jewish American literature the title "Modes of Return" and explains that "One major trend in Jewish-American writing of the past quarter century has been the retrieval of traditional Jewish forms and topics. If the writers of the 1930s and 1940s [and I would add 1950s and 1960s] were bent on escape, the most recent generation has been committed to a return."[28] His first example, although using nonfiction texts, makes the point almost paradigmatically in that he compares Norman Podhoretz's autobiography *Making It* (1967) with Paul Cowan's autobiography *An Orphan in History: Retrieving a Jewish Legacy* (1982), two volumes whose very titles are indicative of the transformation between second- and third-generation Jewish American writers. As Nessa Rapoport said of herself and her peers, "Having won our place in American culture, we are beginning to be confident enough to reclaim Jewish culture,"[29] just as Hansen would have expected. If we apply Hansen's thesis to the history of Jewish American literature, then, we get a clear explanation for the renaissance in Jewish-based Jewish American fiction that occurred in the 1980s and 1990s.

The return to Judaism in contemporary Jewish American fiction that has sparked such a renaissance takes many forms. Not only does the feeling of a return to Judaism mark the overall postimmigrant, third-generation ethos of Jewish American fiction in the 1980s and 1990s, but religious retrieval itself becomes the theme of many texts, particularly those wherein return is actually undertaken by one of the characters. Not only that, but the writers are occasionally aware of being returnees themselves. A perfect case in point—at least in the sense of a return to "Jewishness" if not quite to Judaism—would be one of the most critically successful novels of the past several years, Michael Chabon's *The Amazing Adventures of Kavalier & Clay* (2000). In his earlier writings, Chabon's Jewisness had played only a peripheral role at best. The main character in his debut novel, *The Mysteries of Pittsburgh* (1988), may be named Art Bechstein, and the main character in the short-story cycle that makes up "Part II: The Lost World" in his collection *A Model World and Other Stories* (1991) may be named Nathan Shapiro, but there are few other indications in either case that the works depict Jews. The protagonists of Chabon's second novel, *Wonder Boys* (1995), are not Jewish at all, although the narrator's wife is and an important scene takes place at her family's Passover seder.[30] *The Amazing Adventures of Kavalier & Clay*, quite to the contrary, relies for its success on a total involvement not only in the gentile environment of American comic books—where Jewish cousins Joe Kavalier (an immigrant from Prague) and Sammy Clay (née Klayman, a second-generation, assimilated American) have become huge successes—but in Jewish mysticism, particularly as associated with the story of the Golem of Prague, and in European Jewish history, particularly that of the Holocaust. Towards the end of the novel, Joe, who has been thought dead for ten years, is discovered by his cousin to have been spending that time working on and completing an extensive comic-book version of the Golem story. Upon reading it, Sammy says to his cousin, "You have an awful lot of Jewish stuff in here." When Joe replies merely, "I know it," Sammy asks, "What's the matter with you, did you have a relapse?"[31] In a sense Joe did, and Sammy, the second-generation Jew, might seem angry with him about it, but, in context, the tone of his question is quite different, indicating that Sammy understands that the golem comic book is not only a work of genius but that it is a work of genius which could only have been produced by Joe's reacknowledgment of the importance of Jewish tradition in his life. Chabon, in this novel, seems to have returned to some of the Jewish traditions in his own life as well, garnering rave reviews, prestigious prizes, and heavy sales in the process.

A more strictly religious return to Judaism can be seen clearly in the works of another of the most highly acclaimed younger Jewish American fiction writers, Allegra Goodman. Following in the footsteps of Ozick and Potok, Goodman has written of herself,

> I write about Jewish culture, but not merely Jewish culture. I write about religion as well. Therefore, my models are the older writers like [Chaim] Grade and Sholom Aleichem, who wrote of a living unself-conscious tradition. I write from the inside, taking, as they did, an idiom in which ritual and liturgy are a natural part of my fictional world. . . . In much of my work I use

> ritual as both structural tool and subject. In doing so I look [to writers] who treat not merely the ethnic but also the religious dimension of Judaism.[32]

This use of Jewish culture and the issue of religious return can be found at the heart of one of Goodman's best known stories, "The Four Questions," the most contemporary inclusion in Norton's *Jewish American Fiction* anthology. One of the cycle that makes up her second book, *The Family Markowitz* (1996), this story takes place at a family's Passover seder in Long Island and features three generations of the Kirshenbaums: Sol and Estelle, the grandparents; Ed and Sarah Markowitz, Sarah being Sol and Estelle's daughter, Ed being a professor of Middle Eastern Studies; and Ed and Sarah's children. One of these children, Miriam, a medical student, has become increasingly devout in her Judaism, a situation that presents difficulties for her parents and grandparents. She offends her grandmother, for example, by refusing to eat on Estelle's good (but not kosher-for-Passover) china and using paper plates instead; she offends her father by complaining that his leading of the seder, which focuses on Passover as a celebration of freedom and an opportunity to express solidarity with other oppressed peoples, makes a mockery out of the holiday by leaving out things like "the Jewish People" and "God."[33] Ed is confused by his daughter's religious zeal—"she has become very puritanical," he thinks to himself at one point[34]—but it is clear that she believes strongly in what she is doing, a stance that is only going to be reinforced by her upcoming marriage to her orthodox fiancé. In any event, the reader of the story certainly sees how "issues that had dominated the experience of second-generation American Jews," such as "offspring turn[ing] their back on the Old World obsessions of their immigrant parents, including religious rituals," now "undergo a reversal in the third generation."[35] The theme of "a return to Jewish ritual"[36] is clearly evident in "The Four Questions," as in many of Goodman's other writings.

The theme can also be found in the work of several additional Jewish American fiction writers who came to the fore in the 1980s and 1990s. Rebecca Goldstein's novel *Mazel* (1995), for example, features a third-generation character, Phoebe, a granddaughter much like Goodman's Miriam, "who represents the new Jewish American woman [and] embraces the Orthodox rituals that her mother and grandmother reject . . . thereby dramatizing the sociocultural resurgence of Orthodoxy, a revitalized resistance to the lure of secular mainstream America."[37] As with Goodman's writings, there can be no question that "Jewish scripture and practice continues to inform [Goldstein's] life [and writings] in palpable ways."[38] The same is true of Tova Reich, whose novel *Master of the Return* (1988) tells the story of Shmuel Himmelhoch, formerly a hippie now living as an Orthodox Jew in Israel. As Ellen Serlen Uffen notes, Reich's novel is "actually *about* Jewishness and Judaism."[39] Nessa Rapoport's story, "The Woman Who Lost Her Name" (1979), to cite a third example, tells of Sarah, daughter of Orthodox parents but growing up in a secularized second-generation Jewish American milieu, who becomes reenergized toward Judaism through meeting and marrying her Israeli cousin. Not only is return prevalent in the content of this story, but it also influences its form. According to Ted Solotaroff, "the narrative itself is steeped in the aggadic tradition; taking on subtle parallels to the Book of Ruth and some of its texture from the Song of Songs, Ms. Rapoport's story is closer to . . . the early A. B. Yehoshua than it is to the norms of previous American-Jewish fiction."[40] In other words, like Goodman, Rapoport has returned for inspiration to preimmigrant Jewish writers. She may thus enact return as much as describe it explicitly in the text, but the feeling permeates. The same can be said of a final example, Melvin Jules Bukiet, whose works, according to Andrew Furman, display a "mischievous theological imagination."[41] A story like "The Red Heifer and the Golden Calf" (1995), for example, which focuses on an Orthodox butcher, can be seen as "a midrash on the book of Jeremiah, an indictment against unreflective, mechanical obedience toward Jewish law."[42] Given the examples of Chabon, Goodman, Goldstein, Reich, Rapoport, and Bukiet—and more could be furnished in looking at the works of Lev Raphael and Thane Rosenbaum—we can see that Judaism as a religious idea is a prevalent concern among many of the third-generation Jewish American writers who began to publish in the 1980s and 1990s.

Another name that should be added to this list is Nathan Englander, one of the youngest of the younger Jewish American writers when his first book, the highly acclaimed collection of stories *For the Relief of Unbearable Urges*, appeared in 1999. Among the other accomplished pieces, one story in particular, "The Gilgul of Park Avenue," presents an unusual, fascinating, and quite humorous description of Jewish return. Charles Morton Luger, the protagonist of the tale, is a wealthy, WASPish, fifty-five-year-old financial analyst who is suddenly visited by the realization that he is "the bearer of a Jewish soul."[43] There is no explanation for this change, yet it is clear that Charles feels it deeply; he begins almost immediately to study with a rabbi, Zalman Meintz, to keep kosher, and to follow other Jewish scriptural laws. As the title of the story indicates, Charles is a gilgul, a reincarnated soul. According to Rabbi Allen Maller, it sometimes happens that a Jewish child is raised in some other faith but, "whatever the reason for the original separation, three, four, or more generations later, the displaced soul is reborn into the family line. . . . The yearning of the soul to return to its own people is so great that eventually it finds its way back to the Jewish religion, people, and culture."[44] A gilgul is a person within whom such a displaced Jewish soul returns to the fold. In Englander's story, not only does this concept explain Charles's "rebirth" (109), but it also accounts for the fact that he is so thrilled, "excited" he himself says (119), by these new experiences. Immediately after the revelation occurs, for example, he feels compelled to break the news to the taxi driver in whose vehicle the change has taken place: "Oddly," he says to the baffled cabbie, "it seems that I'm Jewish. Jewish in your cab" (109). The tone is one of surprise, to be sure, but also one of pride. Charles is further strengthened by learning that Rabbi Meintz is a gilgul himself, having (like Reich's Shmuel Himmelhoch) gone from hippie to Hassid. Through studying and participating in Jewish rituals (laying tefillin, keeping the Sabbath) and obeying Jewish laws (not mixing linen and wool, placing a mezuzah on the door), Charles comes to feel a calm and a sense of purpose in his life that he has never felt before, "like things, big things, are finally right" (117).

Unfortunately, Charles's wife, Sue, an art director for a slick magazine, doesn't share his enthusiasm for this lifestyle change. Quite the contrary, she believes that he is either undergoing a midlife crisis or has gone insane. Charles's rabbi, Zalman Meintz, had warned him that this would probably be her reaction when he told her of his sudden conversion to (actually his reclaiming of the lost legacy of his) Judaism, but he is determined to prove to her, not only that he is in full control of himself, but that his change needn't affect their relationship. When he refuses to eat the beef bourguignon that the maid has prepared for their dinner, however, Sue understands that their relationship cannot help but be affected. "Well, if you have to be Jewish," she asks him, "why *so* Jewish?" (122). Calling for support on Charles's psychologist, Dr. Birnbaum, whom Charles himself has spurned since his moment of revelation, Sue tries to talk him out of his delusion. Through these efforts, as well as because of problems he runs into at work, Charles begins to waver in his faith, but Rabbi Meintz is always there to prop him up. The story reaches its climax when Charles, Sue, Rabbi Meintz, and Dr. Birnbaum eat a Kosher-catered dinner on paper plates at the Luger apartment on Park Avenue. Although the exact nature of the resolution remains rather ambiguous, it seems clear that Charles would like to be Jewish and stay with Sue, but if this cannot be worked out then he will have to stay Jewish; indeed, because his soul is Jewish, he cannot *not* be Jewish, and to him being Jewish means being "*so* Jewish." As Rabbi Meintz tells him, "There is no hope for the pious" (136). Resembling the punchline of a Jewish joke, the comment indicates the humorous tone that Englander maintains throughout the text (or at least until the story's final scene), but it also expresses the difficulty of someone—and in this way, Charles is much like Goodman's Miriam—who wants to be an observant Jew when his or her loved ones do not.

Not only is Charles Luger's transformation another example of the theme of a return to Judaism as it is seen in the works of Jewish American fiction writers at the end of the twentieth century, but "The Gilgul of Park Avenue" can actually be read as an allegorical representation of such fiction, making use (again) of Hansen's theory of third-generation return. In such an allegorical reading, Charles stands for Jewish American Literature. In his WASP incarnation, he represents second-generation Jewish American writers who moved away from their Judaism, even their Jewishness, in aligning themselves with some aspect of the larger culture. Dr. Birnbaum is the obvious second-generation Jew in the story, having turned away from the torah in favor of Freud; Sue also fills this role, although she is a lapsed Christian rather than a lapsed Jew. Rabbi Zalman Meintz, on the other hand, represents a transitional figure between this second generation and the third generation, where Charles will find himself after his revelatory experience. In this sense he is like Cynthia Ozick[45] or Chaim Potok. Englander may even be alluding to this fact when he notes that the first book the rabbi instructs Charles to read is *The Chosen*, Potok's exploration of the difficulty of living an Orthodox life in a secularized society. Following his epiphany, Charles represents the third-generation Jewish American writers, the ones who want to make Judaism a focal part of their lives and writings. These are the writers, to borrow a phrase from Rabbi Meintz, who are "most open to letting take form that which is truly inside" (116), even if the larger book-buying public isn't interested in reading about it. What Englander is demonstrating, of course, is the difficulty that a religiously oriented writer faces in contemporary America. As James Francken pointed out in a review of Englander's collection, "there are risks for the writer who imagines what a devout world is like."[46] Andrew Furman makes a similar point regarding Goldstein's novel *Mazel*: "'Too Jewish,' I can only imagine an endless string of Viking Penguin editors proclaiming when they glanced at Goldstein's title on their page proofs."[47] Nevertheless, Englander and Goldstein, like Charles, stick to their guns and assert their Jewish beliefs no matter what the cost of doing so might be.

These third-generation writers, moreover, like Charles, offer little in the way of apology for what they are doing and expect their audiences (whether family members or readers) to accept it. Goodman, for example, explains that she provided a glossary at the end of her first collection of stories, *Total Immersion* (1989), but she deliberately "did not interrupt stories such as these to explain or translate religious terms or rituals."[48] This is certainly valid from an artistic standpoint, but it no doubt left many of her readers in the dark about crucial issues. Similarly, according to Sanford Pinsker, Reich's novels, such as *Master of the Return* and *The Jewish War* (1995), "make heavy demands on their readers. One needs to know a good deal about Hassidism (and especially about Nahum of Bratzlav) in the first case and about right wing ultra-Orthodoxy in the second."[49] To understand some of the other stories in Englander's collection, the reader must be familiar with Orthodox customs regarding married women's hair ("The Wig"), with the mythical shtetl of Chelm ("The Tumblers"), and with the history of Yiddish poetry in Russia ("The Twenty-seventh Man"), among many other Jewish and Judaic topics. The boldness with which these writers introduce such topics is what Pinsker admires about their works—"the assumption that Jewish fiction is, well, *Jewish*"[50]—but Charles Luger knows that following such a path is not easy, given the broader society in which one must live and work. Nevertheless, these third-generation writers, like Charles, are determined not to compromise themselves to gain approval. This is the message of the final image of "The Gilgul of Park Avenue," after the dinner party has broken up and the husband and wife are left alone together, when Englander writes that Charles "struggled to stand without judgment, to be only for Sue, to be wholly seen, wanting her to love him changed" (137). Third-generation writers are not ashamed of being "changed" from their second-generation parents, and they do not plan to change back; they merely hope that they will be appreciated as they are.

Indeed, it is this point that most separates Englander's text from a second-generation predecessor which has so many parallels to "The Gilgul of Park Avenue" that the newer work might seem merely a revision of (a midrash on?) the older one, namely, Philip Roth's "Eli, the Fanatic" (1959).[51] In that well-known story, Eli Peck, a Jewish lawyer in the progressive, modern neighborhood of Woodenton, where "he and his Jewish friends have been assimilated into the once exclusively gentile community by distinguishing themselves as little as possible from the Gentiles,"[52] is called on to deal with an Orthodox rabbi and his yeshiva which have moved into town, calling much negative attention to themselves and, by extension, to the Jews of Woodenton. Instead of convincing the rabbi to leave before he has the yeshiva closed for legal reasons, Eli becomes interested in him and his students (all of whom have been displaced by the Holocaust); instead of converting them, as he jokes to one of his neighbors, they begin to convert him. Toward the end of the story, Eli puts on the black clothes which one of the members of the Yeshiva has traded him for his own suit (so that the "greenhorn," as the Jews of Woodenton call him, can go into town and blend in). This is the final stage of his "progressive identification"[53] with the yeshiva, and he walks through town as an Old World Jew. Like Charles Luger, Eli experiences a reawakening of his Jewishness. As in Charles's case, furthermore, Eli's wife and neighbors think that he is having a nervous breakdown or has gone insane. His wife even wants to enlist his psychiatrist, Dr. Eckman, to try to talk some sense into the deranged Jew, much like Sue did with Dr. Birnbaum. For Eli, though, "he felt those black clothes as if they were the skin of his skin."[54] Like Charles, Eli has a moment of wavering, thinking that maybe he is going crazy, but he feels compelled to continue in his newfound way. For this reason, "Eli, the Fanatic" might appear to be a story of third-generation return. The ending is ambiguous, however, much more ambivalent than the ending of "The Gilgul of Park Avenue," and it remains quite likely that Eli's desire to return will be thwarted by the society around him. Having gone to the hospital where his wife has just given birth,[55] Eli is cornered by the staff and given a sedative. As he slips into unconsciousness, and as the story ends, Roth writes that "the drug calmed his soul, but did not touch it deep down where the blackness had reached" (216). The blackness (read Jewishness) of his soul seems permanent, like Charles's, but Roth also indicates that, while it cannot be eliminated, it can be calmed by outward measures.[56] Given how strong these pressures to conform are in Eli's social position, furthermore, if the soul were to try to reassert itself again it would simply be drugged into submission once more. As Jay L. Halio notes, "Roth shows that changing sides may not be so easy after all; that the mores of a community cannot be violated with impunity; that society will have its revenges."[57] Even Eli himself admits the probability that "Eckman would shortly convince him that he wanted to take off the whole business" (215). Where Roth depicts at best a tentative and very superficial return in

Eli Peck, therefore, Englander depicts a Charles Luger who stands up, makes a full commitment, and accepts whatever consequences may follow. It is this same frankness about the Jewish elements in his work that marks Englander as a third-generation Jewish American fiction writer.

In one sense, of course, both "The Gilgul of Park Avenue" and "Eli, the Fanatic" do describe the conflict between second-generation and third-generation Jewish Americans, even if that conflict plays itself out within a single individual and to different conclusions. Roth himself is quite interesting in this regard in that, having come to fame as a second-generation writer, his career (like that of Jewish American fiction as a whole) was on the way down when Howe wrote his introduction in 1977. Following this point in time, however, Roth made a remarkable comeback, largely through reemphasizing the Jewish content of his writing in texts from *The Ghost Writer* (1979), the first novel to center fully on his alter ego Nathan Zuckerman, through such acclaimed and prize-winning works as *The Counterlife* (1986) and *American Pastoral* (1997). Perhaps, after having written a number of unsuccessful novels with little or no Jewish content (e.g., *Our Gang* [1971] and *The Great American Novel* [1973]), Roth found that, like Eli Peck, he had to don black clothing more openly if he was going to let, to borrow Rabbi Meintz's phrase once again, "take form that which is truly inside" ("Gilgul," 116).[58] In any case, it seems clear that this is what many younger Jewish American fiction writers have been doing in the 1980s and 1990s, and what they seem likely to continue doing into the twenty-first century. Ted Solotaroff, looking into the future in 1988 much like Howe had done eleven years earlier, even went so far as to say that "only those writers steeped in Judaism will survive."[59] Time alone will tell if this prophecy is more accurate than Howe's proved to be, but there can be no question that recent years have seen "increasing examples of imagining Jewishly,"[60] with writers such as Nathan Englander and the others that have been looked at more briefly in this essay. Even if Jewish American fiction veers in some other direction in the future, the return to Judaism is destined to be seen as one of the hallmarks of the past quarter century or more in the history of that literature.

Notes

1. Irving Howe, introduction to *Jewish American Stories*, ed. Irving Howe (New York: Mentor, 1977), 16.
2. Leslie Fiedler, "Growing Up Post-Jewish," in *Fiedler on the Roof: Essays on Literature and Jewish Identity* (Boston: David R. Godine, 1991), 117.
3. See Stephen Wade, *Jewish American Literature Since 1945: An Introduction* (Edinburgh: Edinburgh, University Press, 1999), 194, for a somewhat less enthusiastic viewpoint. He writes that "The rebirth has its spokespeople and a few passionate advocates who sometimes make claims that exceed the evidence," although he does go on to say that "the younger writers, in all genres and conventions, are just as vibrant and innovative as the writers who occupy the status of an unofficial 'canon' of [Jewish American] literature."

4. For discussions of these writers, see Alan L. Berger, *Children of Job: American Second-Generation Witnesses to the Holocaust* (Albany: State University of New York Press, 1997); Marita Grimwood, *Holocaust Literature of the Second Generation* (New York: Palgrave, 2007); Erin Heather McGlothlin, *Second-Generation Holocaust Literature: Legacies of Survival and Perpetration* (Rochester: Camden House, 2006); and Efraim Sicher, *The Holocaust Novel* (New York: Routledge, 2005).
5. For the most complete discussion of these writers, see Andrew Furman, *Israel Through the Jewish-American Imagination: A Survey of Jewish-American Literature on Israel, 1928-1995* (Albany: State University of New York Press, 1997.
6. The identification of these three dominant issues in Jewish American fiction since 1977—"Jewish religious thought and values, the trauma of the holocaust, and the establishment of a Jewish nation in Israel"—has also been made by Lillian Kremer in "Post-Alienation: Recent directions in Jewish American Literature," *Contemporary Literature*, 34 (1993): 571. Alan L. Berger, in "American Jewish Fiction," *Modern Judaism*, 10 (1990), along almost the same lines, says that three of the most interesting areas in Jewish American fiction of the 1980s were "a reexamination of orthodoxy, an engagement with the *Shoah* and its meaning for diaspora Jewry, and the role of gender in Jewish practice" (222), although he also predicts that Israel will be an increasingly important subject in the 1990s (239). It should also be noted that the three categories are not mutually exclusive, that many texts investigate the Holocaust or Israel in a religiously oriented way.
7. Howe, introduction, 11. Hereafter noted parenthetically in the text.
8. Ted Solotaroff, in "The Open Community," in *Writing Our Way Home: Contemporary Stories by American Jewish Writers*, ed. Ted Solotaroff and Nessa Rapoport (New York: Schocken, 1992), writes of that time that "it was widely assumed, given the rate of intermarriage and the pace of assimilation, that American Jews were on the . . . road to oblivion" (xix). Andrew Furman, in *Contemporary Jewish American Writers and the Multicultural Dilemma: Return of the Exiled* (Syracuse: Syracuse University Press, 2000), also comments on the "widespread concern that Jewish Americans have all but abandoned the Jewish side of their hyphenated identities" (17).
9. Kremer, "Post-Alienation," 572. See also Mark Krupnick, "Jewish-American Literature," in *New Immigrant Literatures in the United States: A Sourcebook to Our Multicultural Literary Heritage*, ed. Alpana Sharma Knippling (Westport, CT: Greenwood, 1996), 295-308, particularly his remark that "It does appear that Cynthia Ozick's program for Jewish writing has been in the process of being carried out" (304).
10. Berger, "American Jewish Fiction," 221.
11. Berger, "American Jewish Fiction," 221; and Kremer, "Post-Alienation," 575-76.
12. Berger, "American Jewish Fiction," 221.
13. Krupnick, "Jewish-American Literature," 303-04. The distinction is Howe's; he writes that "the very term 'Jewishness' suggests, of course, a certain vagueness, pointing to the diffusion of a cultural heritage. When one speaks of Judaism or the Jewish religion, it is to invoke a coherent tradition of belief and custom; when one speaks of 'Jewishness' it is to invoke a spectrum of styles and symbols" (introduction, 10).
14. For more on Goldstein, see Furman, *Contemporary Jewish American Writers*, 82-101; for more on Rapoport and Roiphe, see Berger, "American Jewish Fiction," 223-25; for more on Stern, see Furman, *Contemporary Jewish American Writers*, 141-59.
15. Furman, *Contemporary Jewish American Writers*, 11. The subtitle of Furman's study, however, *Return of the Exiled*, refers less to these writers having returned to Judaism than it does to the return of Jewish American fiction to the multicultural canon.

16. Marcus Lee Hansen, "The Problem of the Third Generation Immigrant," in *American Immigrants and Their Generations: Studies and Commentaries on the Hansen Thesis after Fifty Years,* ed. Peter Kivisto and Dag Blanck (Urbana: University of Illinois Press, 1990), 195.
17. "The problem of the first generation," Thomas J. Archdeacon writes, "is to make the adjustments necessary to survive economically, to function within an alien culture, and to learn about democracy" ("Hansen's Hypothesis as a Model of Immigrant Assimilation," in Kivisto and Blanck, *American Immigrants,* 43).
18. Marcus Lee Hansen, "Who Shall Inherit America?," in Kivisto and Blanck, *American Immigrants,* 207.
19. Hansen, "Who Shall Inherit America?," in Kivisto and Blanck, *American Immigrants,* 209.
20. Nathan Glazer, "Hansen's Hypothesis and the Historical Experience of Generations," in Kivisto and Blanck, *American Immigrants,* 105.
21. Archdeacon, "Hansen's Hypothesis," 50.
22. Philip Gleason has argued that Hansen's hypothesis fits with the history of Jewish Americans in general more than it does with any other ethnic group ("Hansen, Herberg, and American Religion," in Kivisto and Blanck, *American Immigrants,* 85-103).
23. Glazer, "Hansen's Hypothesis," 106.
24. Jules Chametzky et. al, eds., *Jewish American Literature: A Norton Anthology* (New York: Norton, 2001), 575.
25. Howe also writes that the urban slum experience of earlier Jewish American writers comes through "even upon grandsons and granddaughters who may never have lived in or seen them" (6).
26. Furman, *Contemporary Jewish American Writers,* 174.
27. Chametzky et. al., *Jewish American Literature,* 986.
28. Krupnick, "Jewish-American Literature," 302.
29. Nessa Rapoport, "Summoned to the Feast," in Solotaroff and Rapoport, *Writing Our Way Home,* xxx.
30. This Passover scene was completely omitted in the film version of Chabon's novel.
31. Michael Chabon, *The Amazing Adventures of Kavalier & Clay* (New York: Picador, 2000), 583.
32. Allegra Goodman, "Writing Jewish Fiction In and Out of the Multicultural Context," in *Daughters of Valor: Contemporary Jewish American Women Writers,* ed. Jay L. Halio and Ben Siegel (Newark: University of Delaware Press, 1997), 270-71. For a critical assessment of these points, see C. Beth Burch, "Allegra Goodman," in *Jewish American Women Writers: A Bio-Bibliographical and Critical Sourcebook,* ed. Ann R. Shapiro (Westport, CT: Greenwood, 1994): "Jewishness has provided [Goodman] with rich material: a community and a culture to write about[,] a literary tradition that includes both scriptural and theological traditions. Goodman is keenly interested in religion, and this interest often manifests itself directly in her work" (89).
33. Allegra Goodman, *The Family Markowitz* (New York: Pocket, 1997), 198.
34. Ibid., 187.
35. Chametzky et. al., *Jewish American Literature,* 1133. Goodman's generations aren't really as clear cut as this summary makes them seem. It is actually the grandparents who are the most typical second-generation Jews; they don't even keep kosher, for example. The parents are more observant than that, not as "assimilated" (Chametzky et. al, *Jewish American Literature,* 1133) as some readers might think, but they are

nowhere near as "literal-minded," to borrow a phrase from Ed (Goodman, *Family Markowitz*, 199), as Miriam has become. It should also be pointed out that the other members of the third generation depicted in the story, Miriam's siblings, have not shared in her return to Judaism; in fact, her brother Avi is dating a non-Jew whom he has brought to the seder. Even so, the broad outlines that I have been sketching in this essay certainly do help in understanding the conflicts central to "The Four Questions."

36. Chametzky et. al. *Jewish American Literature*, 986.
37. Furman, *Contemporary Jewish American Writers*, 94.
38. Ibid., 83.
39. Ellen Serlen Uffen, *Strands of the Cable: The Place of the Past in Jewish American Women's Writing* (New York: Peter Lang, 1992), 162.
40. Solotaroff, "The Open Community," xxii. Rapoport herself has expressed an interest in Jewish American fiction that can have "a dialogue with earlier Jewish books[, that] can retrieve the materials and structures of an august and infinitely rich imaginative tradition for art" ("Summoned to the Feast," xxix).
41. Furman, *Contemporary Jewish American Writers*, 47.
42. Ibid., 51.
43. Nathan Englander, "The Gilgul of Park Avenue," in *For the Relief of Unbearable Urges* (New York: Knopf, 1999), 109. Hereafter noted parenthetically in the text.
44. Quoted in Julius Lester, *Lovesong: Becoming a Jew* (New York: Arcade, 1988), 216. For a discussion of Lester himself as a gilgul, see my essay "'Gee, You Don't Look Jewish': Julius Lester's *Lovesong*, an African-American Jewish American Autobiography." *Studies in American Jewish Literature* 18 (1999): 41-51.
45. R. Z. Sheppard, *Time*, April 19, 1999, wrote that the story "read[s] like a collaboration between Cynthia Ozick and Mel Brooks" (84).
46. James Francken, "Antic Santa," *London Review of Books*, Oct. 28, 1999, 32.
47. Furman, *Contemporary Jewish American Writers*, 101.
48. Goodman, "Writing Jewish Fiction," 271.
49. Sanford Pinsker, "Dares, Double-Dares, and the Jewish American Writer," in *The* Prairie Schooner *Anthology of Contemporary Jewish American Writing*, ed. Hilda Raz (Lincoln: University of Nebraska Press, 1997), 283.
50. Ibid., 283.
51. James Francken begins his review of *For the Relief of Unbearable Urges* with a recounting of "Eli, the Fanatic," and the first of Englander's stories he discusses is "The Gilgul of Park Avenue," but he fails to point out the striking similarities between the two texts. Another reviewer, James E. Young, "Men in Black," *New York Times Book Review*, April 25, 1999, compares the story (less appropriately, I believe) to Bernard Malamud's "The Jewbird" (7).
52. Judith Paterson Jones and Guinevera A. Nance, *Philip Roth* (New York: Frederick Ungar, 1981), 31.
53. Ibid., 32.
54. Philip Roth, "Eli, the Fanatic," in *Goodbye, Columbus* (New York: Bantam, 1981), 212. Hereafter noted parenthetically in the text.
55. Miriam Peck's pregnancy is paralleled in Englander's story by the fact that Sue Luger has just returned from having some work done at the dentist's office and is feeling less that perfect when Charles first tells her of his remarkable conversion.

56. Judith Paterson Jones and Guinevera A. Nance assert that the story's ending "implies that the spiritual assimilation Eli has achieved remains untouched by sedation" (36), but that is not to say that, symbolically speaking, Eli won't take off his black garb and put on his business suit once again, thus conforming outwardly if not inwardly. Earlier Jones and Nance had themselves pointed out that "whether Eli actually loses his balance or gains it at last depends entirely upon the perspective one chooses; and Roth has constructed the story deftly so that it supports either conclusion" (34). Similarly, the discussion of "Eli, the Fanatic" in Chametzky et al., *Jewish American Fiction: A Norton Anthology*, where the story is reprinted, ends with alternative possibilities: "Perhaps Eli has merely 'flipped,' as the slang has it. Or is a flip a conversion?" (916).
57. Jay L. Halio, *Philip Roth Revisited* (New York: Twayne, 1992), 36.
58. In this context we should note Thomas J. Archdeacon's comment that "'return' may simply refer to an emergence from a closet. . . . Ethnicity does not decline and revive; what changes with the passing decades is the willingness to acknowledge it" ("Hansen's Hypothesis," 50).
59. Quoted in Goodman, "Writing Jewish Fiction," 273.
60. Berger, "American Jewish Fiction," 239.

"Were it Not for the *Yetzer Hara*": Eating, Knowledge, and the Physical in Jonathan Rosen's *Eve's Apple*

Adam Sol

Jonathan Rosen's 1997 novel, *Eve's Apple* has not fully joined the evolving canon of contemporary Jewish American fiction that seems to be enjoying a renaissance recently. In comparison to the works of Allegra Goodman, Nathan Englander, Steve Stern, and Pearl Abraham, Rosen's work is less blatant in its references to Judaism, and thus has taken a backseat to those worthy writers whose works are clearly derived from an encounter with traditional Jewish texts, folktales, and traditions.[1] Rosen did not grow up in an Orthodox home (as did Englander, Abraham, and Goodman); however he does have a familiarity with rabbinic texts, as *The Talmud and the Internet* (2000) makes clear, despite his modest admission that he is "far from being an accomplished Talmud student."[2] On the surface, the characters in *Eve's Apple* are more heavily influenced by intellectual Western culture than by the Talmud. One reviewer even declared *Eve's Apple* to be "not an overtly Jewish novel."[3] But beneath the secular surface of the novel—with its contemporary concerns of consumerism, psychology, and eating disorders—lies a work deeply concerned with Jewish ways of looking at the world.

The central conflict of *Eve's Apple* revolves around Joseph, an underemployed teacher of English to Russian immigrants, and his live-in girlfriend, Ruth, who has suffered in the past from anorexia nervosa and who seems to be having a relapse. Joseph's attempts to help Ruth are further complicated by his own lingering grief for a sister who committed suicide. The main points of the plot, then, hardly seem to be what one might call "Jewish-Jewish" literature, despite the fact that Joseph and Ruth are both clearly identified as Jews. However, Ruth's struggle with anorexia, and Joseph's search for answers to her illness and to his grief, while influenced by contemporary ideas of psychology and consumerism, are also a compelling confrontation with Jewish rabbinic ideas concerning the body and its needs and desires. How *Eve's Apple* confronts and resolves the conflicts of its characters can be much illuminated through an examination of the rabbinic notion of the *yetzer hara*.

The yetzer hara is a familiar idea from Rabbinic literature, most frequently translated as the evil impulse. But in the Rabbinic mind this idea is more than a cartoon figure sitting on our shoulder trying to propel us towards lustful or criminal behavior. For while it is seen as the impulse which pulls us away from the path to righteousness, the yetzer hara is also associated with the natural human desires that perpetuate the world. After all, humankind is created in Genesis 2:7 by a combination of the "dust of the ground" and from the breath of God.[4] Rabbi Samuel bar Nahman, a Roman-era commentator, illustrates this idea by writing, "Were it not for the yetzer hara, a man would not build a house, take a wife, beget children, or engage in commerce."[5] In this sense the yetzer hara is seen as an essential part of human existence—without it, there is no life. Other commentaries support this notion, for while rabbinic literature constantly seeks a path to righteousness, it recognizes that righteousness can only be achieved in the context of human life as it is lived. Righteousness purged of the pleasures of the body—lust, hunger, sleep—is not a human righteousness at all. The implied lesson is that we must harness rather than deny the desires of the yetzer hara in order to live a life of goodness. The central conflict, then, for the characters of *Eve's Apple* can be seen as a struggle to balance the impulses of the body with the spirit's desire for purity, between the yetzer hara and its counterpart, the *yetzer hatov*, the impulse for good.

Rosen's novel is populated with characters all along the continuum between an animalistic acceptance of the yetzer hara and a self-destructive search for perfection. For instance, Joseph makes a meager living teaching English to Russian immigrants at a school called the English Training for New Americans (ETNA). His students are anxious to participate in American capitalism without necessarily submitting themselves to the discipline it requires, and they are the characters most influenced by the yetzer hara. Their attempts to study English are often halfhearted, and their nonchalant observance of classroom protocol is counterproductive to their own reasonable desires. Joseph frequently describes them in a animalistic terms: "A roomful of open mouths and I had to drop English into every one. The sheer weight of their wanting—to know, to be—exhausted me in a moment."[6] The image of these "open mouths," like newborn chicks, is compounded by other comparisons of the Russians to monkeys, dogs, oxen, and children. In a real sense, Joseph is teaching the animals their names, no less than Adam does in Genesis.

The Russians' submission to the yetzer hara also manifests itself in positive ways, too. Unlike Ruth, they are comfortable with their natural selves, with the basic needs of human life, and they are unashamed about attending to them, even in the ETNA classroom. While waiting for class to begin they "played chess and gossiped and filled out forms and nursed babies and ate out of their pockets and pocketbooks and smoked cigarette after cigarette" (34). The ease with which they assume their physical place in the world, along with their blunt but dogged determination to succeed in America in the most basic financial sense, is a source of strange admiration in Joseph. As he remarks, "They were practical dreamers and I envied their vitality and purpose" (291). But this ease—this submission to the yetzer hara—sabotages their ability to learn as well. For instance, it is ETNA policy to separate husbands and wives so that one doesn't rely on the learning of the other. Despite this, as Joseph reports, "Every morning I moved them and every afternoon they worked their way back to each other" (37). The students' unwillingness to follow rules of protocol, even for the purpose of learning, ultimately jeopardizes the very goals for which they are striving.

If the Russians submit too readily to the yetzer hara, Ruth's rejection of it brings her to the brink of self-destruction in a form of bulimia. Ruth is obsessively concerned with how her food is presented, and her appetite is highly susceptible to being disturbed by, for instance, the atmosphere in a restaurant or a turn in conversation. Though she maintains a normal body weight for most of the novel, it is clear that her relationship to food is unhealthy and precarious. The way she cooks, prepares, and eats her meals is precise and bordering on the obsessive. As Joseph observes, Ruth moves in the kitchen like "a temple priestess shifting among the sacred mysteries of her cult" (13). The image of idolatry here reinforces Rosen's sense of the danger of Ruth's hunger for control. Finally, as is eventually revealed, the special herbal tea she regularly drinks is in fact a powerful laxative.

Through her denial of her hunger, Ruth pursues a kind of spiritual purity to the neglect of her physical being. The rabbis recognize this temptation in terms of asceticism and admonish against it in a number of Talmudic passages, as in Tractate Taanit: "A person may not mortify himself by fasting, lest he become a charge on the community."[7] The radical pursuit of spiritual purity, from a rabbinic standpoint, is fraught with danger. One of the few texts which a friendly mentor Doctor Flek recommends unequivocally to Joseph when he seeks knowledge about Ruth's illness is Kenneth Clark's classic study, *The Nude* (1956). In the work Clark contrasts between the "naked"—the simple, "pitiful" physical body—and the "nude"—the body as it is idealized in art. As Joseph interprets Clark's ideas, "Ruth wished never to be naked. She wished only to be nude" (159). From the standpoint of this essay, Ruth wishes to deny the yetzer hara absolutely, to be a spirit rather than contend with the hungers of the human body. It is worth noting here that the majority of rabbinic commentaries about the yetzer hara derive from interpretations of Genesis, and that in Genesis it is not until after Adam and Eve have eaten the forbidden fruit of the tree of knowledge of good and evil that "they knew that they were naked."[8] Thus a discomfort with the physicality of the body is deeply connected with the beginning of human consciousness. As Doctor Flek puts it to Joseph, "'We are all overweight,' . . . tapping his broad forehead with a thick finger. 'Right here. We are all three pounds overweight'" (124).

Ruth's denial of the body is not only revealed in her eating habits, though that aspect of it is the most significant. She also cleans with a vengeance, and Joseph senses that she sees "some link between dirt and a sinful sense of the body" (142). Ruth dresses herself in sexy underclothes—not to make herself feel sexy but to disguise "the natural packaging of the flesh" (15). Her ideals can be summed up in a passage she quotes to Joseph from *Midsummer Night's Dream*: "And I will purge thy mortal grossness so / That thou shalt like an airy spirit go." When Joseph responds by declaring, "But I love your mortal grossness. It's my favorite part," Ruth's immediate answer is, "Well, I don't love it" (148). The reference to Shakespeare's play is notable for its inclusion of fairy creatures who are unencumbered by physical bodies (although it can certainly be argued that they have physical appetites). Ruth's desire to become an "airy spirit" amounts to a denial of that which makes her human.

Finally, Ruth's denial of her body causes problems with her sexual relationship with Joseph. Early in their relationship Joseph notes that Ruth has no sense of her own physical desires: "Whenever I polled her, in the midst of passion, about how she was feeling and what I might do to let her enjoy herself more, she grew vaguer and vaguer" (51). By the time the novel begins with the two of them living together, their sex life has ceased altogether, until Ruth allows Joseph to watch her masturbate. Even here, though, "her passion . . . seemed like pain" (55). Joseph is moved, but for Ruth this is just another way to distance herself from the desires of her body—even her physical intimacy with Joseph is now practiced with them hardly touching. And later in the novel, when the two actually do have sex, Joseph notes that "She wanted what she did not want. She did not want what she wanted" (224). When the condom they are using breaks, it gives Ruth reason to record in her diary only this about the event: "Sex with Joseph. Disaster" (238). The "disaster" here is never specified and seems to refer to a whole range of concerns, but all of them—abhorrence of sex itself, guilt over her reaction towards Joseph, or the fear of pregnancy—speak to Ruth's rejection of her physicality. Ruth's abstraction or abhorrence of physical passion is then just another way to control and deny the legitimate sensual desires of her yetzer hara.

By the end of the novel Ruth's radical attempts to purge herself of her yetzer hara begin to have dire consequences. She returns from a trip to Paris weighing only eighty-eight pounds and looking, as Joseph says, like she's "been in a concentration camp" (304). Joseph's anger and fear in turn reveal something about the nature of his concern for her. When Joseph accidentally calls Ruth by his sister's name, Ruth shouts, "And you can't bring me back from the dead. I'M NOT DEAD. I'm not your sister, for God's sake. I'm Ruth Simon. Do you hear me? I'm Ruth Simon." Thus in the face of Joseph's Freudian slip, it is Ruth's admission that she *is* a body, that she *is* alive, that gives her a chance to survive. Similarly it is her final admission that she has lost her sense of what her body needs—that in her attempts to control her yetzer hara she has actually denied her physical being—that Ruth concedes that she needs medical help and agrees to return to Twin Oaks, a clinic for women with eating disorders. It is her assertion of her physicality, and her recognition that she must therefore contend with its needs, her yetzer hara, that allow Ruth to emerge from the novel, if not healed, then at least on the path to recovery.

Between the animalistic submission to the yetzer hara practiced by the ETNA students and the obsessive denial of its legitimate impulses which characterizes Ruth is Doctor Flek, a former psychologist who now teaches at the New School, and who is dating Ruth's mother, Carol. If the Russians serve to demonstrate the attractions and limitations of a life at the service of the yetzer hara, Flek serves as a role model for transcending it and leading a full, fulfilling life. The doctor bears the constant reminders of being hemmed in by his body: a childhood victim of polio, Flek is bound to a wheelchair. Despite this, however, Flek is clearly a vibrant, not to mention virile, man—he has fathered a daughter from a previous marriage and is clearly involved sexually with Carol Simon. He is described as "an odd mixture of blunt directness and refined reflection that made everything he said familiar and yet somehow surprising" (78). The implication, of course, is that while still deriving strength and will from his body and fulfilling the essential needs of the yetzer hara (e.g., eating well, enjoying romance), Flek has put those instincts to higher use. The doctor accepts his physicality and the limits it has imposed upon him, but he also transcends those limits in the pursuit of intellectual and spiritual truth.

Doctor Flek attempts to help Joseph from their first meeting, encouraging him away from excessive reading (a need, as we shall see, that prevents rather than aids in Joseph's learning about Ruth), and compelling him to confront his own reasons for pursuing the "secrets" behind Ruth's illness. Throughout the novel, Flek is a voice of reason when Joseph has veered off course. At the Harvard Club Flek even has to remind Joseph to eat at one of their meetings (170). It is finally Doctor Flek who recognizes that Joseph must first confront his grief over his lost sister before he is able to truly love Ruth. Doctor Flek, then, in his recognition of the problems Joseph and Ruth are facing, serves as a secular rabbinic figure to Joseph.[9] But ultimately even he is unable to help Joseph or Ruth find the path to righteousness and well-being. In this task, as the rabbis recognize, each of us must make moral decisions on our own.

We have, then, a fairly neat constellation along the path to righteousness, with the Russians too submissive to the demands of the yetzer hara, Ruth in a self-destructive denial of its impulses, and Doctor Flek, who symbolizes an ideal balance between the needs of the yetzer hara and a higher spiritual and intellectual yearning. But where does Joseph, the narrator and "hero," fit in? While it is unquestionably Ruth's illness that drives the plot of *Eve's Apple*, it is Joseph's spiritual self-discovery and, ultimately, his recovery that mark the novel as a Jewish work of some importance. For while we sense—through Joseph's narration—that Ruth is descending again into illness, it is only through Joseph's perspective that we receive information about her, and it is thus only as his perspective widens and deepens that we begin to understand what lies beneath her illness and his confusion. Joseph wavers between a Ruth-inspired pursuit of spiritual and intellectual purity to the neglect of his natural self and a reckless abandonment to his yetzer hara.

At the beginning of *Eve's Apple*, Joseph seems remarkably well-adjusted, responding well to the strong personality clash between Ruth and her mother and carefully skirting around a direct confrontation with Ruth about her eating. While not as adept as Doctor Flek at recognizing the limits and hungers of his body while pursuing the spiritual, Joseph does have moments of insight. His relationship to food is, predictably, much healthier and more casual than Ruth's, and his memories of the beginnings of his relationship with Ruth reveal him to have been sensitive in his courtship of her. Cracks quickly open up beneath the surface, however. Joseph has been avoiding speaking to his parents, and we gradually learn that one of the reasons behind this is his unresolved grief and guilt over the suicide of his sister, Evelyn. It is easy for us to see that his legitimate fears over Ruth's relapse rapidly become a much more complicated sort of rescue mission for Joseph, and lead him close to his own sort of danger.

At the beginning of their relationship, Joseph's desire to know Ruth beyond her physicality differentiated him from other boys she dated. This represented a happy balance between the natural impulses of the yetzer hara towards sex and the higher impulse towards love and intimacy, and it was the main reason why their relationship deepened to the point it had at the outset of the novel. However, even early on there is the sense that the balance might be difficult to maintain: "And the more [information about Ruth] I coaxed out of her . . . the closer we grew. Yet the closer we grew, the less we made love" (51). Already, knowledge and physical love conflict, and where knowledge deepens, the natural impulses of the yetzer hara are suppressed, to the detriment of the relationship as a whole. Thus, when he watches Ruth masturbating, the event represents not only an attempt by Ruth to distance herself from physical intimacy, but for Joseph to observe her at her most intimate without sharing in that intimacy. In this sense even sex becomes an act of observation for Joseph, rather than an act of love.

In an attempt to keep track of Ruth's health, Joseph has been reading her diary, our first indication that his care for Ruth has sinister potential. Soon enough, Joseph decides that the best way for him to help Ruth would be to learn more about eating disorders, and he sets about reading everything he can on the subject. At first, this seems like a noble gesture, but Joseph's self-education quickly takes on the attributes of an obsession. As Joseph notes, "All knowledge has about it a pornographic lure" (102-03). His research, and subsequent hyper-intellectualizing of Ruth's health, brings about a denial of his natural instincts for love no less than Ruth's obsession with her body brings about her denial of her natural instinct to eat. He even uses the language of eating disorders to describe his quest for knowledge: "I became a binge reader . . . gorging myself on the horrific history of women and food" (153). In this sense they are both denying the impulses of the yetzer hara to their own harm. Joseph's reading rapidly has a deleterious effect on his relationship to Ruth. His first trip to the library forces him to lie to Ruth to avoid her curiosity. Later, in the full throes of a panic attack about whether Ruth is "bingeing and purging," Joseph completely misses a rare sexual advance from Ruth by deflecting her kisses so that he can have a look at her teeth to look for signs of frequent vomiting. Eventually, he confesses that he "was often quick to kiss her for the sole purpose of tasting her lips, absorbing the bouquet of her breath to see if she had in fact eaten and, if she had eaten, to tell, if I could, what had become of her meal" (175). Here his protectiveness borders on the psychotic and certainly ceases to be a helpful loving concern for her health. Joseph calls eating disorders a "mechanical detachment" from the flesh, but he is no less guilty of this than Ruth herself in his detachment from her (156). At its worst, then, Joseph's obsessive research threatens to objectify Ruth and undermine the love that the two of them have built.

Joseph's obsessive pursuit of the truth behind Ruth's illness finally takes on the aspects of a psychological disorder, affecting his own eating habits and bringing about a recurrence of migraine headaches from which he has occasionally suffered. These headaches seem to point to a literal imbalance between his mind and his body. Here is when his drive to know begins to look most similar to Ruth's self-destructive rejection of her natural impulses. As he notes, "So much reading began to shake my own sense of reality. The more I read, the more it seemed that the body itself was a problem for which there was no solution" (157). Joseph's reading threatens to stifle his relationship to his body, and in turn his natural interest in Ruth (as opposed to his intellectual interest in her illness). When he meets again with Doctor Flek he is so distracted by his questions that Flek must remind him to eat (170).

Unlike Ruth, however, Joseph demonstrates some ability, with prompting from Flek and from Ruth herself, to alter the imbalance between his yetzer hara and his higher spiritual impulses. Not that his attempts to right himself occur without their own complications, however. Eventually, while Ruth is away in Europe, Joseph realizes that his research has been leading him nowhere, and that his desire to heal Ruth is deeply linked to his lingering guilt over the suicide of his sister. Flek reminds him that "everyone makes his own choice to live or die," and Joseph attempts to make use of this advice (276). Flek's words echo those of God in Genesis, warning Adam and Eve not to eat of the "tree of the knowledge of good and evil."[10] For Adam and Eve, as for Joseph at this point in the novel, an overeagerness to know leads only to pain and suffering.

Joseph's decision to "choose life" leads him to a brief relapse in the other direction, towards an unthinking submission to the yetzer hara, represented by his affair with Felicia, a fellow teacher at ETNA. Before sleeping with her, Joseph recklessly drinks wine and eats luxuriously. (Felicia, for her part, is as comfortable with her body as the Russians, remarking "with odd knowingness" that "I like food. I like sex. I like wine" [282]). This reveling in the physicality of his body brings him little pleasure, however. The next morning, leaving Felicia's apartment, he feels "gross, physical" (288). Fortunately, Joseph's regret brings him back to Ruth, and he returns to a proper balance between the impulses of the yetzer hara and higher impulses by buying a plane ticket to join Ruth in Europe. It is a moment of recklessness that uses most of his savings (revealing the influence of the yetzer hara), but it is also an expression of love that Joseph knows to be right in a "higher" sense as well. Joseph does not end up using the ticket, because Ruth returns, undeniably sick and ready for Joseph to help her enroll at Twin Oaks, but his purchase reassures her that his love for her is unflinching, and acts as a strange token which she will carry with her to the Twin Oaks sanitarium.

Joseph, then, during the course of *Eve's Apple*, wavers back and forth between an unhealthy pursuit of intellectual knowledge to the neglect of his natural being and a brief Dionysian descent into the realm of the yetzer hara. His struggle is the human struggle, the one most familiar to us and the one explored by the rabbis in their exploration of Adam's wavering when confronted by Eve with the apple. Joseph ultimately comes to understand that his pursuit of knowledge about Ruth's condition cannot help either of them: "What magic was I expecting? The body wasn't a book. The body was simply the body. I had been misled by metaphors as much as Ruth" (307). On the other hand, he is able to use the knowledge he has acquired about Ruth and her illness to help her get to a place where she can be helped. This willingness to cede control over Ruth's illness to those who might be better prepared to help her is an acknowledgment of his limitations, but also an assertion of the positive influence he can have on her life in the long run. At the novel's end, Joseph has finally agreed to visit his parents and to therefore begin the essential healing over his lost sister that his obsession with Ruth's illness had blocked. As Joseph observes, "I had chosen Ruth to dramatize all my struggles, much as she had chosen food. We both needed to let the world back in" (309). The yetzer hara, with its interest in the physical world, must once again hold a place, albeit controlled, in the lives of this couple.

Looking at Jonathan Rosen's novel *Eve's Apple* through the lens of the rabbinic figure of the yetzer hara reveals a complex portrait of characters in various stages of struggling to balance the needs of the physical body with the desire to pursue spiritual and intellectual ideals. It is clear in the novel, as it is in rabbinic literature, that an outright rejection of the natural impulses of the yetzer hara have the potential to be just as dangerous to one's spiritual health as a complete submission to its desires. This template also reveals the novel to have a substantial foundation in Jewish philosophy, in addition to its thorough background in psychology and the history of eating disorders. While Rosen's subtle exploration of Jewish ideas may not reexamine the familiar conflicts between tradition and modernity that still seem to dominate Jewish fiction in North America, his insight into how the tradition sheds light on modernity is a welcome addition to Jewish letters, and indeed to literature as a whole. Let us hope that as his career progresses he continues to pursue these essential questions.

Notes

1. Rosen's more recent novel, *Joy Comes in the Morning* (2004), is much more direct in its references to Judaism and Jewish texts, with a female protagonist who is a rabbi.
2. Jonathan Rosen, *Talmud and the Internet* (New York: Farrar, Straus and Giroux, 2000), 7.
3. Thane Rosenbaum, *Wall Street Journal*, 25 April 1997, A12.
4. I am using the translation of the Bible published by the Jewish Publication Society of America (Philadelphia, 1955).
5. Genesis Rabah 9:7. All quotations from rabbinic commentaries in this essay use the translations provided in the William Braude translation of the *Sefer Ha-Aggadah* by Hayim Hahman Bialik and Yehoshua Hana Ravnitzky (New York, Schocken, 1992).
6. Jonathan Rosen, *Eve's Apple* (New York, Random House, 1997), 39. Hereafter cited parenthetically.
7. Tractate Taanit, 22b.
8. Genesis 3:7.
9. Early in the novel Doctor Flek even tells a parable which—in true rabbinic fashion—bears four different messages for four different listeners.
10. Genesis 2:17.

The Sweetheart Is Outside Herself: Writing the Contemporary Jewish American Writer in S. L. Wisenberg's Ceci Rubin Stories

Joe Kraus

We've all been awaiting this generation—is it the third or the fourth?—of Jewish American writers. From at least the time of Irving Howe's notorious pronouncement in 1977, the debate has raged over the death or re-birth of Jewish American literature, and it's clear that the only way to settle the question is to see what the youngsters churn out. The whole matter is freighted with anxiety. Those in Howe's camp who feel that Jewish American writing must be tied to the experience of the Old World argue that the death of the Yiddish-speaking generations means there is no longer a possibility for anything distinctly "Jewish" in American writing. You can almost hear the sigh, the wistfulness underneath that claim, that eventually found its full flower in *World of Our Fathers* (1976). At the other extreme, there seems a whole body of writers anxious to assert that, as they age, they do have literary progeny, others who will write in the tradition that they themselves extended. Cynthia Ozick's book-blurb exclamation for Allegra Goodman's *The Family Markowitz* (1996), for instance, says as much through its enthusiasm as through its denotation. Her declaration, "All the muse-fairies were present at her birth," is less the tone of an admiring fellow writer than it is of a new grandmother, one embracing the infant with the ardor that only someone who has badgered her children for years with "when will I get to see my grandchildren" can know.

That's a lot of pressure to put on Allegra Goodman, Steve Stern, Rebecca Goldstein, Thane Rosenbaum, Michael Chabon, Myla Goldberg, Nathan Englander, Jonathan Safran Foer, and the dozen or more other writers heralded as at the head of this new class. One metaphorical grandparent has disowned them and the other pins the hope of a generation on them. The result for many such writers is an extreme self-consciousness of themselves as writers. They bear the weight of their own ambitions alongside the hopes and disparagement of the writers and critics they succeed. They often, therefore, write about themselves as writers, or at least acknowledge the experience of being artists. As Tresa Grauer puts it, "What *is* unique about this literature, however, is that the debates about identity that have long circulated in the culture surrounding the production of Jewish American literature have now become its self-conscious subject. Together the array of literary texts that has emerged over the past twenty-five years should be examined less for its coherence as a body of literature defined *by* an identity as for its focus *on* it."[1] In other words, one characteristic—perhaps the central shared characteristic—of the generation of writers who came of age since the late 1960s is a sense of having to construct themselves as writers performing within a literary tradition that has chosen them as much as they have chosen it.[2]

S. L. Wisenberg embodies that concern as thoroughly as any of her contemporaries. Born in Houston in 1955 and living in Chicago for most of her adult life, Wisenberg has received less critical attention than her east-coast peers, in part because she has been less prolific but also because she has ventured increasingly into nonfiction writing. In addition, the architecture of her interconnected stories makes it difficult to recognize the ambition underlying much of her most successful work. Her single collection of fiction, *The Sweetheart Is In*, brings together twenty-one stories, many of which appeared in prominent periodicals, but it does so in two sections. While the stories in the second section experiment with form and explore a range of characters and situations, the fourteen in the first part all involve the character of Ceci Rubin or her immediate family. They compose, that is, a work with much of the complexity and nuance of *The Family Markowitz*, collectively chronicling Ceci's life from her childhood as the daughter of a bubble-bath manufacturing "mogul" to her life as a woman juggling work, love, and the responsibility of burying her parents. They do so, however, outside of chronological order, without introduction, and without anything in the text indicating that they make up this larger, interconnected work. Together, they constitute an ambitious short-story cycle, one that is virtually hidden within the book yet that announces Wisenberg as a distinct voice sharing many of the concerns of the other Jewish American writers of her generation.

The notion of "generations" of writers is vexed, of course, and what Wisenberg accomplishes through her stories is a deft reencounter with a, by now, thirty-year-old trend in Jewish American writing. In "The Complex Fate of the Jewish Author," Morris Dickstein chooses to do away with the term altogether, replacing it instead with "stages," and identifying three stages of that tradition. As he sees it, "If the second stage was debunking and satirical, even parricidal, the third stage began with [Philip] Roth's filial homage."[3] That is, once Roth, in

The Ghost Writer (1979), began to make the experience of writing as a Jew one of his central subjects, he inaugurated a new way of writing as a Jew in America. As Dickstein says of Cynthia Ozick, she "repeatedly writes stories about other people's stories. This is a latecomer's literature, almost a textbook example of the postmodern profusion of texts upon texts, or of Harold Bloom's famous theory of the anxiety of influence, which emphasizes the Oedipal tensions between writers and their precursors. We risk becoming footnotes to our forebears."[4] For better or for worse, such writing is perpetually conscious of the literature that precedes it. If the Abraham Cahans and Anzia Yezierskias of the early part of the twentieth century reflected on the novelty of their arrival in America and their children—the writers of Dickstein's stage two—ironized the recent success of the greater Jewish American community, then their grandchildren and now great-grandchildren have no unprecedented experiences to record. The novelty has worn off the Jewish American experience; what remains is a tradition of writing that offers both inspiration and the potential for feeling overshadowed.

By the time Wisenberg, Goodman, Stern, and other younger writers began their careers, the habit of looking back to their predecessors was already established as a trope within the Jewish American literary tradition. At its worst, such an impulse could generate schmaltz of the post-*Fiddler on the Roof* sort, a nostalgia for the nostalgia of an earlier generation. More serious writers, though, have found that one of their central challenges is to explore and determine the very grounds from which they can write. They cannot simply assume a distinct perspective as Jews because there are too many Jewish American writers who have preceded them. They have to explain where they, as particular individuals, have come from, and they have to distinguish themselves immediately as offering distinct and original voices. It is, in that light, surely no coincidence that Wisenberg begins her story cycle with "Big Ruthie Imagines Sex without Pain," a meditation by Ceci's mother about her discomfort when she has sex. For Ceci herself, who does not appear directly in the story, the concern is all too clear: if her mother experiences intercourse as pain, then Ceci was conceived in pain. From Ceci's perspective, the story of her conception is more properly her mother's story, not her own. She begins life—and her short story cycle—as a footnote to someone else's experience.

It is worth comparing such a story with a similar one from an earlier generation. Delmore Schwartz's "In Dreams Begin Responsibilities" (1937) is concerned with the same essential question, "How did my parents come to conceive of me?" and it also affords a child the opportunity to witness his or her parents in the uncomfortable light of a sexual creature. For Schwartz's unnamed narrator, the story is entirely about his own experience as an observer somehow afforded the opportunity to watch a film of his parents on the evening they become engaged. His parents, clumsy people who appear on a movie screen "as if it were raining when the picture was photographed,"[5] are not the center of the story. Instead, he is. The emphasis of the story lies in the way in which it affects its narrator-observer. As he shouts at one point toward the movie screen, "Don't do it. It's not too late to change your minds, both of you. Nothing good will come of it, only remorse, hatred, scandal, and two children whose characters are monstrous."[6] In other words, as he sees them together in their youth, he thinks of himself and his brother as the central outcomes of their courtship. For Ceci, the reverse is true. She is so entirely absent from the story that it is not clear until later in the collection, when we learn that Ruthie is her mother and Ruben her father, that she has any connection at all to it. Schwartz's story takes it for granted that his narrator is central; Ceci's wrestles with the possibility that her own story is insignificant in the wake of the experiences of those who have come before her.[7]

The Ceci Rubin stories turn in general on the question of how best to balance the obligation of acknowledging the past with the challenge of identifying the self in the midst of self-discovery. We meet Ceci in the middle of a range of experiences, and the stories turn on how she—or sometimes an immediate family member—comes to understand who she is in her current circumstances. There are neither conventional beginnings nor endings and, in general, little happens within a given story to change those circumstances. The stories are split between third- and first-person narration, giving the effect that Ceci is characteristically estranged from herself, somehow distant from her own experiences and left to contemplate them as if she herself were a reader of her own life. Even in the first person stories, she seems distant from the experiences she describes. It is as if there is a character, "Ceci Rubin," who mediates between the work of author Wisenberg and Ceci's fictional experiences. That is, Ceci seems more comfortable as the author of her own life than as its subject. She is, in effect, outside herself, encountering herself as a character whose experiences stand side by side with the experiences of her family and of the greater community around her.

The result is that Ceci's experiences are seldom at the center of her own narratives; instead, the stories call into question the nature of art and storytelling itself. One recurring element to the stories is the sense in which each bears evidence of itself as a specific artistic effort. Each is its own experiment, establishing its own rhythm and form independent of the ones that come before it. The title story appears on the page as a series of bold-faced statements—"What the Boys were Like" and "How the Boys Sounded," among others—followed by answers of a page or two to the implicit question behind each statement. Another, "The Crab," begins, "Situation: Your mother has cancer,"[8] announcing, as it were, the assignment the writer has set for herself. Another, the penultimate, "Rose in Her Backyard," starts by acknowledging that art can take many different shapes: "It is your art, I say. The blues and reds, hung just so, swaying or not, depending on the wind, sheets scalloped" (88). It turns out, as Ceci sees it, that Rose, Ceci's grandmother, is an artist in the way that she insists on hanging the clothes out to dry, just so. That simple vision is the entirety of the brief story; nothing happens outside of Ceci making the observation within her own mind, appreciating and writing it for her own self. The story itself is the transparent alchemy of that simple observation into something resembling traditional story, a story in which Ceci herself plays no part except as an observer.

Perhaps the central tension of the stories is Ceci's concern for the experiences of others crossed with her own uncertainty about the woman she is becoming. On the one hand, she wrestles with a sense of belatedness, one that perhaps reflects a sense on Wisenberg's own part of writing within the Jewish American tradition. For Ceci, it often seems as if she is so consumed by others' experiences that she is tempted to permit their stories to displace her own. On the other hand, Ceci is sophisticated enough to know that, without a sense of her own perspective, she cannot effectively tell anyone's story. As she puts it at one point, "The story is: we always arrive too late, never knowing what the other has seen" (32). She is aware that simply repeating what she believes has happened to others is meaningless until she acknowledges her own vantage point. As a consequence, much of what takes place in each of the separate stories is a surveying of the ground on which Ceci finds herself. She examines her own circumstances and experience, but does so with what seems an eye toward readying herself to speak of someone else. Like Delmore Schwartz's character—or like most point-of-view characters in any genre—she tries to discover who she is, but that discovery does not seem to be an end for its own sake. Instead, it takes someone aware of herself to begin to tell the story of others.

In "Living with Moranza," for instance, she reflects directly on what it means for her to be a writer when she works as a newspaper reporter alongside a colleague, Moranza, who becomes her lover and who finds ways to develop a journalistic career that ultimately eludes her. Although she begins her news-writing career with promise, Ceci loses interest when she finds that it means telling the same story over and over again. As she puts it, "I don't remember when I started feeling that every story had to be different, a statement about writing, a dazzler. I was a chef who wouldn't prepare the same meal twice, wasn't even content with variations. Everything had already been done" (59). Although the story covers nearly seven years of Ceci's life, it has less to do with her than it does with Moranza. He is the one who continues to write, who pursues the career that might have been Ceci's. As she says about a series of stories that he nearly turns into a book, "The series was almost brilliant, just a touch condescending. It was really my kind of story. Or had been" (59). In other words, it is almost as if Ceci has conceded her stories to someone else, as if she has agreed to let Moranza author what she herself would likely have written if she had continued with her career. She has willingly stepped into the background and made way for someone else.

The maneuver is neither as simple nor as self-deprecating as a mere retreat would be. Instead, while the events of "Living with Moranza" concern Moranza and Ceci equally, the story itself emphasizes how Ceci comes to be able to write about Moranza. The drama of the story, such as it is, has to do with Ceci understanding herself as a failed writer in love with another writer who does not share her burden to be wholly original or to question what it means to live and work through story. By the end, she has returned to her work as an ESL instructor in Chicago and left the formal writing to Moranza, but she has come to understand herself more deeply as someone enmeshed in the story that she is telling about Moranza and herself. In a page-long break from the rest of the narrative—one unprecedented in the rest of the collection and set off with lines at its beginning and end—she offers six quick fictions about lives that she and Moranza have not made together. In one he is a lawyer; in another he is a state senator. In the last, she writes, "I am living with Moranza. We are gypsy fortunetellers. We are 100 percent accurate" (63). It is a series of fantasies that offer her security through Moranza's accomplishments and her assistance. They culminate in the deepest fantasy of all, of her finding herself as a storyteller for whom perspective is no longer a concern. If her predictions, her stories, are always accurate, then she need no longer wrestle with who she is as she makes such predictions.

The story will not let her end on such an impossible and unsatisfying fantasy, however. Instead, the final scene shows Ceci, her future career as uncertain as ever, as Moranza joins her in a tub full of the bath bubbles that her father manufactures in his factory. In a reversal from most of the rest of the story, Moranza tends to her needs, asking her whether she wants him to give her a massage or to scrub her back. Ceci finds herself, then, in a different sort of a fantasy. She has found, for a time at least, an imperfect man who is nonetheless decent and loving, and she is temporarily complete. Literally awash in her own past, Ceci welcomes Moranza into her life, and he joins her, "miraculously, as always, without displacing the water" (65). In this more palatable fantasy, one made possible by her decision to resign as a news writer, she finds a respite from the demand to identify herself so that she can move on to the work of telling another's story. Unlike the series of six fantasies in which she diminishes herself to make Moranza the central figure, she allows him to enter her story without his needing to displace anything of it. She experiences a moment, rare enough within the collection that it stands out as a climax, in which she is so at peace with herself that she can briefly close her eyes and forget the compulsion to tell about other people.

The drama between discovering the self and displacing the self in order to recover a greater experience outside the self finds its most direct expression in "Liberator," a first-person narrative in which Ceci listens to her Alzheimer's-addled father, Ruben, tell stories that circle around his experiences liberating the Mauthausen concentration camp. Ruben will not discuss the camps directly, but it is clear that he is someone who has played a bit part in the central Jewish drama of the twentieth century. He slips in and out of lucidity. When he is coherent, Ceci reports what he has to say; when he is not, she is left with the challenge of determining who she is in the shadow of her father's experiences and the experiences of Jews more broadly. Her part in the story is to listen, but she cannot entirely shake the sense that she has more to do. As she puts it, "I get this idea and I fight it: that a piece of shrapnel of the past is lodged in his brain, damming up the currents of now, of this life, and if he could remove it—if I could remove it—his life would come flooding back to him" (32). Her description reveals both the tension she experiences as a latecomer and the sense she has of nevertheless attempting to define herself. The image of the shrapnel in her father's mind is little different from the thought of that shrapnel as something she cannot dislodge from her own brain. Both are metaphors that belong to the past; each explains a part of who Ceci and Ruben have become as she searches for a sense of her adult self and he confronts a loss of self altogether.

In the end, Wisenberg resolves the tension between Ceci's sense of latecoming and her need to understand her own life through narrative by focusing on Ruben's apparently lucid memory of how he and his wife overcame six years of infertility. In a story that seems to come out of Isaac Bashevis Singer's world, Ruben tells of a Passover Seder to which he had invited an Orthodox stranger to join them. When a girl at the Seder returns from opening the door for Elijah with blood streaming down her face, the stranger stands up and begins to shout, declaring that Ruben has "looked at death in the eyeballs." As he tells the story, Ceci reflects, "My father's eyes look to the side, as if seeing the same younger self that the old man saw. I have disappeared. I am not yet born" (29). The result, according to Ruben, is that he and Ruthie became pregnant that very evening, as if blessed by the Old World presence of their mostly Yiddish-speaking guest. The younger self that the aging Ruben seems to see is a man who will soon conceive Ceci's sister and then Ceci herself, a man who will open her life as a direct result of this strange exposure to an older style of Jewish storytelling. According to Ruth, the event never took place; there was neither a little girl nor a stranger at any of the family Seders from that time. The experience is itself nothing more than a story that Ruben has told.

There is no simple resolution at the end of "Liberator," or at the end of most of the other Ceci narratives. The story is, ultimately, about storytelling itself, whether the story of Ruben's liberating the camps, of the Yiddish stranger's supernatural influence on Ceci's own life, of Ruben's instinct to narrate even in the midst of his dementia, or of Ceci's uncertainty about her role as a daughter who has yet to find someone with whom she might conceive a child of her own. As with "Big Ruthie Imagines Sex without Pain," it is a story that culminates in Ceci's own conception, but that conception seems, again, a mere footnote to the larger narrative surrounding it. There is a deeply humane instinct at the heart of the story, and as well as in the collection as a whole. Ceci is aware of herself as a late-comer, aware that her parents and grandparents boast experiences that seem grander and more dynamic than her own. She works throughout the stories to find the proper balance between understanding herself so that she can tell those stories and discovering herself more fully through what those who came before her have known. She is a character who is outside of herself but, as a result, consciously inside a larger tradition. Her subject, apparently Wisenberg's subject as well, is that tradition itself, and her goal is to find her place within it, respectful and appreciative of what has come before, open to making it something distinctive and new.

Notes

1. Tresa Grauer, "Identity Matters: Contemporary Jewish American Writing," in *The Cambridge Companion to Jewish American Literature*, ed. Michael P. Kramer and Hana Wirth-Nesher (New York: Cambridge University Press, 2003), 269-84.
2. Several other critics have offered similar claims for the nature of contemporary Jewish American writers. Alan Berger, in "American Jewish Fiction," *Modern Judaism* 10 (1990), argues that "collectively, Jewish novels are increasingly exploring the meaning of being Jewish from within rather than from the perspective of American culture" (222). Sanford Pinsker, in "Dares, Double-Dares, and the Jewish-American Writer," *Prairie Schooner* 71, no.1, (1997), proposes that a distinctive element of contemporary Jewish writing is its "double-dare" quality, its interest in building off of the generations of writers whose earlier "daring" successes established the genre (278-85). And Morris Dickstein claims in "Ghost Stories: The New Wave of Jewish Writing," *Tikkun*, November-December 1997, that "today's Jewish writers are as likely to reach deeply into history as into memory" but that they must simultaneously "bracket their literary influences for fear of being overwhelmed by them" (36).
3. Morris Dickstein, "The Complex Fate of the Jewish American Writer," in *Ideology and Jewish Identity in American and Israeli Literature*, ed. Emily Miller Budick (Albany: State University of New York Press, 2001), 67.
4. Ibid., 73.
5. Delmore Schwartz, "In Dreams Begin Responsibilities," in *The World is a Wedding* (New York: New Directions, 1948), 188.
6. Ibid., 194.
7. Steven G. Kellman, "Tales of Jewish Houston," *The Texas Observer* 17 (2001), also draws parallels between Wisenberg's work and "In Dreams Begin Responsibilities," particularly with "The Children Who Swim from You," another story from *The Sweetheart Is In* (28-29).
8. S. L. Wisenberg, *The Sweetheart Is In* (Evanston, IL: Northwestern University Press, 2001), 66. Hereafter cited parenthetically.

Jewish American Fiction on the Border: Culture Confrontations, Double Consciousness, and Hybridity in the Work of Pearl Abraham

Bart Lievens

> What then is the American, this new man?
> —J. Hector St-John de Crèvecoeur, *Letters from an American Farmer*

> I am visible—see this Indian face—yet I am invisible. I both blind them with my beak nose and am their blind spot. But I exist, we exist. They'd like to think I have melted in the pot. But I haven't, we haven't.
> —Gloria Anzaldua, *Borderlands/La Frontera : The New Mestiza*

> Borders. To connect and to divide. Not a frontier, its deadly imagination of a line between the savages and the civilized. Not exodus, with its mirage of a promised-land to end the wandering, and not simply exile or diaspora, with its involuntary sense of never-never-home. But borders. A part yet apart, home and not-home, neither "here" nor "there" . . . Borders on the edge and on the inside.
> —Amritjit Singh and Peter Schmidt, "On the Borders between U.S. Studies and Postcolonial Theory"

From the concept of the melting pot to contemporary postcolonial and postethnic theories: the complexity of ethnic diversity and the negotiation between the notions of consent and descent in American society have preoccupied critics and scholars almost from the very inception of the New World itself. A long history of immigration has "kept in flux our understandings of assimilation and resistance, assent and dissent, descent and consent."[1] In 1782, the French-American writer J. Hector St-John de Crèvecoeur stated that "he is an American, who, leaving behind him all his ancient prejudices and manners, receives new ones from the new mode of life he has embraced, the new government he obeys, and the new rank he holds. He becomes an American by being received in the broad lap of our great *Alma Mater*."[2] The idea of shedding one's past history and former identity has been incorporated in later theories about ethnicity as well. In 1908, Israel Zangwill's play *The Melting-Pot* reflected a "perceived need to melt away differences in order to 'naturalize' the new immigrants."[3] This process would eventually lead to a "new" Americanized identity. Later on, Horace Kallen, in his article "Democracy versus the Melting Pot" (1915), recognized that an immigrant could not readily reject his past. His famous phrase, "whatever else [the immigrant] changes, he cannot change his grandfather,"[4] mirrors the central concern in the theory of cultural pluralism. In this context, ethnic difference was tolerated (but only in the private sphere). Along the same line, Randolph Bourne advocated a "Trans-National America" (1916), emphasizing the impact of and the interaction between different nationalities and ethnicities. The citizens of American were "cosmopolitan dual citizens"[5]; the hyphenated American was to be cherished, not denied. However, cultural pluralism still underscored the Anglo-Saxon facet of the American identity. In contrast, multiculturalism "challenges the priority of this monolithic identity in American history, highlighting racial as well as ethnic diversity and claiming public resources on behalf of these groups."[6] Multiculturalism, a movement that has evolved from the civil rights movements in the 1960s, can be seen in the light "of a larger transition from species to ethnos in the recent intellectual history of the United States."[7] Moving beyond multiculturalism, David Hollinger introduced the concept of postethnicity, which "favors voluntary over involuntary affiliations, balances an appreciation for communities of descent with a determination to make room for new communities, and promotes solidarities of wide scope that incorporate people with different ethnic and racial backgrounds."[8] As these various theories show, and as Amritjit Singh and Peter Schmidt point out, the "search for a single 'origin' of the 'American self' has become considerably problematic."[9] Defining the "American character" along monocultural lines is viewed with skepticism and suspicion. The concepts of ethnicity and descent continue to play a significant role. Analysts recognize that ethnic minorities maintain and honor their heritage and tradition, "even beyond the third and fourth generation."[10]

In 1987, almost exactly two centuries after de Crèvecoeur's account, a new and bold statement was made by Chicana writer and cultural critic Gloria Anzaldua. In her book *Borderlands/LaFrontera: The New Mestiza* (1987), she confidently asserts her ethnic identity and cultural consciousness. Not only is she very much aware of her ethnic inheritance, she also emphasizes the plurality of her roots (white Anglo-Saxon, Mexican, and Indian culture). Anzaldua introduced the concept of the *mestiza*, a person of mixed origins with "a tolerance for contradictions, a tolerance for ambiguity." Someone who "juggle[s] cultures."[11] Chicana culture consists of plural identities and refuses to blend indolently with mainstream American culture. Other ethnic minority groups—people marked by histories of diaspora and dislocation, such as Asian Americans, African Americans, Native Americans and Arab Americans—are characterized by the same ambivalent condition. They inhabit psychological borderlands between the tradition of their own culture and the modernity of the U.S. This condition returns as a major theme in the extensive body of ethnic literatures.

The theoretical framework of postcolonialism provides a useful system of tools for the study and analysis of (post)colonial and ethnic literatures. According to Deborah L. Madsen, postcolonial theory is a "powerful approach to ethnic literatures."[12] It both challenges the Western monocultural ideology and is concerned with the restoration of subjugated voices. This field of study examines "the effects of colonization on cultures and societies"[13] and found its main impetus in the publication of Edward Said's *Orientalism* (1978). One of the central ideas in this theory is "that the Cartesian philosophy of identity is premised upon an ethically unsustainable omission of the Other."[14] Postcolonial theory recognizes cross-cultural links, rejects the myth of group purity, and challenges authoritarian discourses and the imperialistic process of domination or constant hegemony. It acknowledges the fact that ethnicity is often "constructed and reconstructed as a dominant group defines the subordinated as outsiders, the foreigners as strangers."[15] According to Bart Moore-Gilbert, the "issue of location is a key theme. It is the whole question of belonging, and the status of the insider/outsider, that postcolonialism serves to dislocate."[16] An important symbol of postcolonial theory is the image of the border.[17] This concept can be seen in both a geographical and a psychological sense, and it can be applied to history, memory, and time. As a powerful metaphor, it "advocates the adoption of the viewpoint of people moving in and out of borders constructed around coordinates of difference and power."[18] Moreover, the border is the realm of hybridity and exile, the site of "the emergence of alternative and multiple identities."[19] In postcolonial and borders theory, the internal divisions within an ethnicity or a nation are also accentuated. The notion of a single American identity is questioned and is replaced by discourse on hybridity, contradiction, and ambiguity. Ethnicity is viewed as consisting of multiple attachments and affiliations. According to Homi Bhabha, "all cultural systems and stances are constructed in the ambivalent and contradictory space that [Bhabha] calls the 'Third Space of enunciation,'"[20] a "third space that is neither assimilation nor otherness."[21]

Postcolonial theory or borders theory can also be linked with diasporic thought, which is concerned with the idea of dislocation, displacement, and cross-cultural initiation. It finds "its apotheosis in the ambivalent, transitory, culturally contaminated and borderline figure of the exile, caught in a historical limbo between home and the world"[22] and connected with his and her ethnic past through history and memory. The concepts associated with postcolonial studies—such as "double consciousness; mobility; hybridity and revision; a 'third space' that is neither assimilation nor otherness; histories of coalition-building and transnational diasporic connections"[23]—have always been important in the study of ethnicity and ethnic literatures and are, consequently, also important for the study of Jewish American literature. However, in current multicultural and postcolonial debates in the U.S. that focus on the rise of ethnic manifestation and the emergence of subjugated groups, the Jewish literary voice has been largely neglected. Exclusion is based on the belief that American Jews are successful partners within the American mainstream establishment and therefore relinquish their minority status. However, several critics[24] have argued ardently for the inclusion of a Jewish perspective in the multicultural curriculum, on account of both the particular history that has constantly situated the Jewish people in multicultural societies and the specific (revived and intensified) ethnic identity in contemporary Jewish American literature. Moreover, critics have also argued that the Jewish American experience can be regarded as illustrative of general diaspora and multicultural experiences. For example, Paul Gilroy points to the similarities between the Jewish and the African Diaspora and argues for a recognition of these similarities.[25] Similarly, Daniel and Jonathan Boyarin state that the historical concept of the Jewish Diaspora has the potential to contribute to contemporary discussions of the term "diaspora."[26] Caught between a comfortable position in a monolithic American society and the pulls of the multicultural project that aims to preserve ethnic minority identities and save voices from subjugated groups, the Jews represent a unique, but ambivalent perspective: they are both insider and outsider at the same time. As David Biale, Michael Galchinsky, and Susannah Heshel put it, "Never before have so few barriers existed to Jews' entering the corridors of political, cultural, and economic power. Yet the path to integration has also created enormous contradictions in Jewish self-consciousness. Identification and integration with the majority stands at odds with the Jews' equal desire to preserve their identity as a minority."[27] This status gives rise to specific psychological conditions and particular cultural constructions and discourses that can be described through concepts introduced in the postcolonial context by critics like Bhabha: double consciousness, multiple and shifting identities, the hybrid condition, the symbol of the border, diasporic awareness with regard to homeland and the nation (the recognition of a collective history and the importance of memory).[28]

This unique status is also reflected in the extensive body of contemporary Jewish American literature, in which the manifest and decisive return to Jewish cultural and religious traditions shows the involvement of writers in the multicultural venture.[29] The body of recent Jewish American fiction attests to the persistence of a strong ethnic consciousness, in that its protagonists often negotiate between relations of descent and consent. As both insiders and outsiders, they operate from the border, the site where different realms unite or collide. As often as not, the American Jew is regarded as Other, as an outsider. They are located outside the Christian Western tradition. As Bryan Cheyette states, "The Jewish other is both at the heart of western metropolitan culture and is also that which is excluded in order for ascendant racial and sexual identities to be formed and maintained."[30] Although well established within American society and literary tradition, contemporary Jewish writers—such as Thane Rosenbaum, Rebecca Goldstein, Allegra Goodman, Tova Mirvis, Myla Goldberg, Melvis Jules Bukiet, and Pearl Abraham—tend to reflect in their fiction the hazy borders. Through their protagonists, they demonstrate the existence of double consciousness and the hybrid condition. The characters are at once outsider and partly rooted in the American society.

As one of these promising new writers, Pearl Abraham succeeds in translating into vivid fiction the hardship resulting from the confrontation between materialistic America and spiritual Judaism. She observes the generation gap that ensues from this competition, the conflicts experienced within Judaism, the problematic position of women in Jewish religion and religious transgression. Abraham's fiction reflects the unique position of American Jews as both insider and outsider in that it deals with the constant negotiation between tradition and contemporary society: between an ethnic, essentialist identity and an awareness of hybridity and double consciousness. In both *The Romance Reader* (1995) and *Giving Up America* (1998), the symbol of the border, psychological or physical, is a significant one, and her protagonists are situated on a border between two distinct cultures. Torn between their Jewish heritage and contemporary modern America, Abraham's characters face the tribulation of establishing an unequivocal, authentic, and independent identity. The confrontation between the two cultures results in either conflict, or in an attempt to merge the two worlds and achieve multiple affiliations, to inhabit Bhabha's hybrid third space. As a result, the psychological condition of the protagonists is often characterized by ambiguity and contradiction. The ambivalent and double consciousness of the protagonists originates from several binary conflicts: between tradition and modernity, between divergent Jewish religious beliefs, and between the limited power of women and the dominance of men. Abraham's binary systems "suppress ambiguous or interstitial spaces between opposed categories, so that any overlapping region that may appear . . . becomes impossible."[31] These oppositional structures have been "instrumental in establishing those essentialising norms of identity which, whether in terms of sexuality, class, gender or 'race,' have marginalized and oppressed increasing numbers of people."[32] As we will see, in Abraham's work, these binary systems are sometimes maintained and sometimes transcended. Instead of binary opposition, the fictitious characters in the novels seek an alternative space, a "non-binarist space of reflection,"[33] where hybrid identities are tolerated. However, the search for and creation of such as space does not always prove to be successful.

In Abraham's first novel, *The Romance Reader*, Rachel Benjamin, the daughter of a rabbi, feels constrained by the rules and regulations that make up

Jewish tradition. She encounters and opposes the limited freedom of women in a Jewish traditon that is primordially male centered and represented by an older generation. Yearning to participate in the outside world, she longs for a new definition of Jewish identity that would appreciate and liberate women to a greater extent and that would encompass secular elements as well. Throughout the novel, Rachel rebels in various ways against her tradition. She reads secular books, secretively takes lifeguard lessons, wears stockings without seams and bathing suits, and is unhappy in her arranged marriage with a Hasidic boy who is eager to please his father-in-law. Time and again, her disobedience and protest lead to conflict, but Rachel does not succeed in severing her bonds with the milieu she grew up in. Impatient to discover the outside world, she nevertheless remains confined to the stringent Hasidic household of which she is part.

In her novel, Abraham emphasizes the "outsider status" of the Jewish people. The story is situated in a Hasidic community, a peripheral environment that is located outside the ideological center of Christian America. First of all, the Benjamin family inhabits a bungalow that is located in an abandoned summer resort. It is a liminal place of transience and provisional residing. Furthermore, several images of and references to the specific Jewish history highlight a specific ethnic awareness. Jewish rituals are given a prominent place, and the memory of the Holocaust and the history of perennial persecution are rather veiled, although nonetheless present. One night, the proprietor of the resort decides to burn down a number of bungalows so as to be able to sell the grounds. As the glow and blaze of the nighttime fire illuminates the solitary bungalow of Rachel's family, images and thoughts of pogroms and persecution come to mind. The conflagration can be seen as a metaphor for an inferno that consumes or threatens the belief of the Jewish people or the Jews themselves. The image is one of an ever-present danger from which it is hard to escape. In episodes such as these, the novel substantiates the blending of a personal account with a universal and historical dimension that is inherent to Jewish culture. Personal and collective memory sustain ethnic consciousness. The incident connects Rachel to her people's past. This is important, because the Jewish experience is "grounded in the possibility of linking oneself 'with the collective and individual experience of earlier Jews.'"[34] There is also a profound distrust for goyim and secular or nonreligious Jews on the part of Rachel's father. To him, a "Jew . . . is never liked by other nations. A Jew reads only Jewish books and must remain separate."[35] Assimilation, or an attempt to combine tradition with modern elements, is unfeasible and unwanted in the eyes of the father. These examples show that the Jewish experience, as Abraham depicts it in this novel, does not coincide with mainstream, Christian America.

However, Rachel tries to overcome and escape the binary division between tradition and modernity. The memory of Jewish history is challenged and defied by the influences and temptations of American society. Ties of filiation, meaning " lines of descent in nature," are countered by bonds of affiliation, "a process of identification through culture."[36] Rachel is eager to enjoy the pleasures of American life and desires a new, more positive Jewish identity. She is fascinated by American *shiksas* and tries to imitate them, only to realize that she can never be a non-Jew herself. When Rachel tries to break loose, she always gets the same sermon from her father: "The Jews survived in Egypt because of three things. They didn't change their names, they didn't change their clothes, and they didn't change their language. Could we depend on you for survival?" (24). Rachel, or Ruchele, has neglected to do all those three things. She speaks English, surreptitiously wears modern clothes, and changes her name to Rachel. Eventually, her rebellion alienates her from the Jewish tradition, and at the same time, she still remains an outsider to the modern world. Her double consciousness is increased and leads, not to some kind of amalgamation of the two cultures, but to a double alienation and a sense of ambiguity and contradiction. Rachel remains stuck in the border. The third space, in this case, is a site of alienation and loneliness.

Also within her tradition, Rachel experiences the status of outsider. Due to the patriarchal system, she remains subjugated as a woman. Postcolonial theory is related to feminist philosophy in that both discourses "seek to decenter the hegemonic and recuperate the marginalized."[37] By analyzing the equivocal position of women within Judaism, Abraham tackles a subject that has preoccupied female Jewish American writers for a long time. They have had to cope with constraints and limitations that result from the fact that they are outsiders in two ways: as Jewish women in a male Christian American society and as women in the patriarchy of Judaism. They are also often torn between two kinds of ideals, that of the Mother of Israel and of the True Woman. The former dedicates herself completely to her household and the Jewish community, believing that on her rests the responsibility of preserving the Jewish faith in her family. The True Woman, on the other hand, embodies the white, middle-class, and Christian model of propriety. She is also connected with the desire to be independent, to be "capable of earning her own living and leading an independent life"[38] and exploring educational and professional options. This created a problem for Jewish women, confined as they were by Jewish law. The consequence is, once again, the inception of a double consciousness and ambivalent identity. In her struggle to find a proper balance between her religious background and modern society, Rachel criticizes the subversive role of women in Jewish tradition. She especially airs her critique against her arranged marriage with a pious young Jewish man.

Furthermore, there is another aspect that calls attention to the notion of difference and diverging worldviews in *The Romance Reader*. In the complex and uncertain modern world that constitutes Abraham's fiction, the diverse branches within Judaism add to the fragmented and ambivalent psyche of the Jewish American condition. Postcolonial borders theory draws attention to "internal stratification within an ethnicity or a nation."[39] Rachel's parents epitomize two very different aspects of Jewish thought: her father represents the Diaspora Jew struggling to create a renewed American Jewry in the U.S., while Mrs. Benjamin embodies the Zionist movement and is eager to return to Israel, where she can be among her own people and escape the loneliness and alienation she experiences in America.

Unhappy with the many contradictions, Rachel decides to run away to the city. There she realizes that she feels at odds in the outside world. She rents a hotel room, but the place only augments her estrangement. Like the abandoned summer resort, the hotel room functions as a liminal space, a place of estrangement and isolation. When she returns home, she feels more alienated then ever: "I'm home but not home. . . . I can never be one of the children again. I'm a stranger in this house. . . . I don't belong here" (294). However, she is still resolved to go away again: "I won't be here, on their hands, for long" (295). In the end, Rachel has no attachments and no self-understanding. Although she is impatient to drop her religious burden, she is undeniably determined by her past. This quandary leaves her without a spiritual identity. She fails to construct her own set of values and morals, and lacks an ethical and philosophical framework. She feels stranded in a no man's land, belonging neither to the world from which she wants to escape, nor to the secular world she wants to conquer, and yet belonging to both. In Rachel's case, the third space represents ambivalence, contradiction, and constant negotiation.

In her second novel, *Giving Up America*, Abraham uses de Crèvecoeur's declaration, "What then is the American, this new man," as a motto. The novel deals with the role of ethnicity and religion in American society, and, in particular, it highlights the negotiation of ethnic differences in the New World. The protagonists, Deena and Daniel, are involved in marital conflict as they try to establish their lives in America. They each belong to a different kind of Jewish religious branch—Deena comes from a Hasidic family, Daniel from a Orthodox community—and that difference causes much tension in their relationship. Moreover, Daniel's love for a gentile Miss America wannabee and the constant doubt about Jewish life in America cause an existential crises. The story exemplifies the failure of the American Dream and the difficulty of leaving behind historical differences, even within the same ethnic group. Already in the beginning, Deena's father, who lives in Israel, thinks that the marriage between Deena and Daniel is doomed: "You live in a country that believes differences among people can be overcome. This marriage will quickly teach you otherwise."[40] Indeed, the attempts to overcome internal difference fail. The promise of America to diminish all (ethnic) differences between human beings proves to be mythical.

The internal disparities are also complemented by the difference between the traditional world, symbolized in the novel by Deena's father, and the modern world, of which Deena is a part. Although a deep and personal dedication to their religion is absent, the protagonists keep the Jewish tradition alive by performing certain ethnic acts: they prepare special dinners on certain Jewish holidays and keep Sabbath. The persistence of Jewish culture is best illustrated by a powerful scene in which Deena, standing still in her house, imagines hearing her father chant and pray. At that moment, she chants with him, and thus establishes a connection with her tradition. Later, on the phone, Deena's father reassures her: "I am in Jerusalem, he said. But I am your father. I am close to you even when I am far away. I think of you morning, noon, and night" (184). The conversations between Deena and her father function as a dialogue and confrontation between the Old World and the New. Deena's father's erudite Talmudic quotes and Kabbalistic arguments are countered by Deena's citations of American presidents. In spite of the rather negative image of American society, Deena is keen on belonging to this culture. Initially, she mimics her American friends to such an extent that she becomes confused about her own personality. Because she can never be a genuine (Anglo-Saxon) American, her solution lies not in mimicry, but in fusion, in a hybrid identity. She combines notions of religion with modern symbols, and regards the *New York Times* as a prayer book. Moreover, modern dance music replaces the intimacy of prayer: "The music was a shofar calling her awake. It could do what praying and fasting were meant to" (55). This points to notions of hybridity and double consciousness that are characteristic of Deena's worldview.

In the novel, America is described as "a moving engine" (213) and as the symbol of money and professional competition, and is sharply contrasted with the endurance and solemnity of religion. Deena works as a copywriter, creating ads for consumer products, and in this way, language exists merely as a function of consumerism. This corruption of the word fundamentally differs from the sacred importance it has in Jewish religion. The advertisements—as short stories of reality—symbolize a simplistic and shallow way of representation, a deficient substitute for the complexities of the world. The novel reacts against the materialization, superficiality, and simplification of America, distinguishing this from the weight and substance of religion. Deena, in a letter to her father, quotes "comments by foreign visitors on the character of an American: *He clings to nothing. At a price, he would part with his house, his carriage, his horse, his God*" (144). Deena's father says, "Work, money, America. What do you need it for? Give it up and come home" (258).

However, Deena is not prepared to give up America just yet, realizing that she belongs to the modern world as much as she does to the religious community. She decides to visit her family in Israel, to counterbalance momentarily the arbitrariness and materialism of America with the moral and ethic foundations of her family and her faith. When Deena is in the airplane, she contemplates her situation, temporarily removed from country and nationality: "She was no longer in America; she'd relinquished her foothold there; But she wasn't in Jerusalem either. She was afloat in the middle of nowhere, in limbo, where Dante places Abraham, Isaac, and Jacob. It would be good to stay awhile, neither here nor there, not east nor west" (293). Eventually, Deena decides that she is rooted in both worlds. Her religious and ethnic background function as a strong foundation, grounded in morality, certainty, and a sense of community. But it also serves as a springboard to explore the worlds beyond the strict borders of her religion. She has to rely on both realities to make sense of her life. Deena knows that she can always fall back upon her family and her tradition: "Lost, you retraced your steps and returned to the beginning" (295). Deena crosses borders, and discovers the positive aspects of the hybrid space: "She'd gone forth, and she was coming to know herself, and she would continue this knowing. And on her return trip, perhaps she would stop in Paris" (309).

In the course of the novels, both protagonists experience a profound sense of dislocation, or *unheimlichkeit.* Rachel Benjamin and Deena belong to the group of dislocated people who, in the words of Roger Bromley,

> look in from the outside while looking out from the inside, to the extent that both inside and outside lose their defining contours. They are figures with hyphenated identities, living hybrid realities which pose problems for classification and control, as well as raising questions about notions of essential difference. The in-between zones are shifting grounds, threshold spaces, and displacement and migration have led to a struggle for space where identity is endlessly constructed, and deconstructed, across difference and against set inside/outside oppositions. . . . A process of endless locating and undermining: belonging is always problematic, a never-ending dialogue of same with other.[41]

Both Rachel and Deena try to construct a positive, nonessentialist hybrid identity out of the elements of both cultures in which they are rooted simultaneously. Rachel's attempts fail, and she gets stuck in-between and without any direction, only the hope that, someday, she will try again to break free from the rigid binary system. Deena is more confident, and, at the end, she has a clear idea of what path she wants to follow. But for both protagonists, an ambivalent and contradictory situation is the only unequivocal condition possible. Being lost, they retrace their steps in order to gain courage from the heritage they left behind, only to begin the preparation for the next exploration of modern life. They give up America only temporarily. The notion of the continuous process "involving complex negotiation and exchange"[42] is very important. These multilocational attachments and, in some cases, traveling back and forth, help to constantly refine and revise the diasporic experience as always being in motion.[43]

The protagonists evolve towards an awareness that the notion of the dialogical is more useful, because it challenges "the oppositional presumptions of border, division, exclusionary thought and absolute difference. The dialogical is an inclusive, never finalized interactivity, an opening up and a breaking down."[44] The old story of clash and confrontation is retold with an eye to the transactive or transcultural aspect. Rachel and Deena reflect the symbol of a palimpsest, consisting of layers of identity still visible, a manuscript several times overwritten, telling the story of an endless and restless revaluation of identity, struggling with dislocation and sometimes a profound sense of alienation, but at the same time able to experience the richness of multiple identification.

Both *The Romance Reader* and *Giving Up America* analyze what it means to be a Jew in America. In her fiction, Abraham explores the meaning of ethnic background and difference in contemporary America. Yet gradually, she seems to evolve towards a more constructive and more positive portrayal of cultural confrontation. She often emphasizes the similarities between the different cultures. For example, in her third novel, *The Seventh Beggar* (2005), Abraham takes the concepts of hybridity and double consciousness a little further. In this postmodern and experimental novel, a Hasidic family again stands in the limelight. Here, as in the two previous novels, the novel reflects the specific relationships, conflicts, and diverging branches within the religious community. However, although the differences between the Hasidic environment and the modern American world are unmistakably depicted, Abraham creatively incorporates positive hybrid elements and points to similarities and connections between the two cultures. The image of the Jewish outsider, although certainly present, is complemented by a more positive hybrid viewpoint. Ada, the daughter of the family, succeeds in combining her Hasidic lifestyle with her passion for fashion, as she designs dresses for Hasidic women. Joel, a sensitive young man, tries to fathom the stories of Nachman of Bratlsav and eventually attempts to create a golem. His story is mirrored by the tale about his son, JakobJoel, who wants to design a futuristic robot endowed with artificial intelligence, his own kind of golem. Traditional folkloristic aspects are merged with features from science and technology. Elements of Jewish mysticism and the Kabbalah are juxtaposed with and linked to the realm of contemporary life to compose a complex tale that contemplates the meaning of creation, life and storytelling. Abraham connects the aspects of Jewish mysticism with a more general discussion about the act of creation and artificial intelligence in modern times. This approach connects the author firmly to the Jewish tradition and at the same time allows her to get absorbed in present-day culture. With the reviving of Jewish mystical texts, Abraham honors her Jewish legacy, while constructing a very contemporary ethnic identity. In this way, Abraham also emphasizes the relevance and importance of Jewish texts, stories, myths and legends in modern times.

From these novels, it is clear that Pearl Abraham continues the complex dialogue between tradition and modern life. Moreover, the evolution in her novels shows that there is room for creative and constructive solutions and viewpoints. In this way, Abraham's fiction makes a significant contribution to the discussion of Jewish ethnic identity in contemporary American society, and highlights the existence of double consciousness and hybridity in the contemporary Jewish American psyche.

Notes

1. Amritjit Singh and Peter Schmidt, *Postcolonial Theory and the United States: Race, Ethnicity and Literature* (Jackson: University Press of Mississippi, 2000), vii.

2. Werner Sollors, *Beyond Ethnicity: Consent and Descent in American Culture* (New York: Oxford University Press, 1986), 75-76.
3. Marla Brettschneider, ed., *The Narrow Bridge: Jewish Views on Multiculturalism*, (New Brunswick: Rutgers University Press, 1996), 3. For a further discussion about the play by Zangwill, see Sollors; David Biale, Michael Galchinsky, and Susannah Heshel's collection, *Insider/Outsider: American Jews and Multiculturalism* (Berkeley: University of California Press, 1998); and David A. Hollinger's *Postethnic America: Beyond Multiculturalism* (New York: Basic Books, 2000).
4. Horace Kallen, "Democracy versus the Melting-Pot" in *Theories of Ethnicity: A Classical Reader*, ed. Werner Sollors (New York: New York University Press, 1996), 78.
5. Sollors, *Beyond Ethnicity*, 97.
6. David Biale, Michael Galchinsky and Susannah Heshel, eds., *Insider/Outsider: American Jews and Multiculturalism* (Berkeley: University of California Press, 1998), 3.
7. David A. Hollinger, *Postethnic America: Beyond Multiculturalism*, (New York: Basic Books, 2000), 65.
8. Ibid., 3.
9. Singh and Schmidt, *Postcolonial Theory*, viii.
10. Nimmi Hutnik, *Ethnic Minority Identity: A Social Psychological Perspective* (Oxford: Oxford Science Publications, Claredon Press, 1991), 33.
11. Gloria Anzaldua, *Borderlands/La Frontera : The New Mestiza* (San Francisco: Aunt Lute Books, 1999), 101.
12. Deborah Madsen, *Beyond the Borders: American Literature and Post-Colonial Theory* (London: Pluto Press, 2003), 1.
13. Bill Ashcroft, Gareth Griffiths, and Helen Tiffin, *Post-colonial Studies: The Key Concepts* (London: Routledge, 2000), 186.
14. Leela Gandhi, *Postcolonial Theory: A Critical Introduction* (Edinburgh: Edinburgh University Press, 1998), 39.
15. Rina Benmayor and Andor Skotnes, *Migration and Identity* (Oxford: Oxford University Press, 1994), 7.
16. Bart Moore-Gilbert. *Postcolonial Theory: Contexts, Practices, Politics* (London: Verso, 2000), 5.
17. Singh and Schmidt discuss a borders school. The influence and significance of this school has steadily increased, and it became a cultural paradigm for the study of race and ethnicity in U.S. studies in the 1990s.
18. Stuart Hall, as quoted in Roger Bromley, *Narratives for a New Belonging: Diasporic Cultural Fictions* (Edinburgh: Edinburgh University Press, 2000), 1.
19. Singh and Schmidt, "On the Borders," 13.
20. Ibid., 23.
21. Ibid., 4.
22. Gandhi, 132.
23. Schmidt and Singh, "On the Borders," 4.
24. See, for example, Andrew Furman. *Return of the Exiled: Jewish American Writers and the Multicultural Dilemma* (Syracuse, New York: Syracuse University Press, 2000); David Biale et. al, *Insider/Outsider* (1998).
25. See Paul Gilroy, *The Black Atlantic: Modernity and Double Consciousness* (New York: Verso, 1993), 205-12.
26. See Jonathan Boyarin and Daniel Boyarin, *Powers of Diaspora: Two Essays on the Relevance of Jewish Culture* (Minneapolis: University of Minnesota Press, 2002), 11.

27. Biale et al., 5.
28. For diasporic identities: See Robin Cohen, *Global Diasporas: An Introduction* (London: UCL Press, 1997).
29. Of course, one has to be careful to apply concepts associated with postcolonial theory to the contemporary Jewish American literary scene. Due to the successful social and economic condition of the Jews in American society, one cannot map the theory of postcolonialism unto Jewish American literature without making serious methodological errors. It would perhaps be more accurate to inscribe the postimmigrant and postassimilation experience in the framework of psychological and cultural consequences of an encounter between two or more cultures and its result on the formation of identity. And in this respect, the application of these concepts might be useful. Several critics have already made a link between postcolonial theory and Jewish culture: see, for example, Ethan Goffman's *Imagining Each Other: Blacks and Jews in American Literature* (Albany: State University of New York Press, 2000), Jonathan Boyarin and Daniel Boyarin's *Powers of Diaspora*, and David Baile et al.'s *Insider/Outsider*.
30. Bryan Cheyette and Laura Marcus, eds., *Modernity, Culture and "the Jew"* (Cambridge: Polity Press, 1998), 3.
31. Bill Ashcroft et al., 23-24.
32. Roger Bromley, *Narratives for a New Belonging: Diasporic Cultural Fictions*, (Edinburgh: Edinburgh University Press, 2000), 17.
33. Bromley, 6.
34. Ted Solotaroff and Nessa Rapoport, eds., *The Schocken Book of Contemporary Jewish Fiction* (New York: Schocken Books, 1984), xv.
35. Pearl Abraham, *The Romance Reader* (New York: Riverheads Books, 1995), 34. Further references are made parenthetically within the text.
36. Bill Ashcroft et al., 105.
37. Singh and Schmidt, "On the Borders," 32.
38. Diane Lichtenstein, *Writing Their Nations: The Tradition of Nineteenth-Century American Jewish Women Writers* (Bloomington: Indiana University Press, 1992), 17.
39. Singh and Schmidt, "On the Borders," 7.
40. Pearl Abraham, *Giving Up America* (New York: Riverhead Books, 1998), 4. Further references are made parenthetically within the text.
41. Bromley, 5.
42. H. Trivedi (1993) in Gandhi, 125.
43 Bromley, 10.
44. Ibid., 2.

Part 4

Authors in Their Own Words

Margins within the Margins: An Interview with Ruth Knafo Setton and Farideh Dayanim Goldin

Derek Parker Royal

In the fall of 2007, I was invited to Lehigh University to give a lecture on Philip Roth's fiction as part of the Philip and Muriel Berman Center Lecture Series. My host was Ruth Knafo Setton, the Moroccan-born writer in residence at Lehigh's Berman Center, the Professor of Practice in the University's English Department, and now current director of the Berman Center. During my time there, I had the pleasure to talk with Setton about her own work—her first novel, *The Road to Fez*, was published in 2001—and the state of contemporary fiction. While she agreed with me that the past several years had witnessed a flowering of new Jewish American writing, Setton was quick to point out that the authors who were capturing all of the attention were of Ashkenazi descent. There was no one in this growing list of writers, she argued, who was creating from a Mizrahi or even a Sephardic sensibility. What is more, and ironically enough, most of America's first Jews, as well as their representatives in the arts and media, were Sephardic. Setton explained to me that if Jews were still marginal voices in America, then she was part of a community that felt marginalized within that margin. I responded by inviting her to express her voice in the form of an interview. She agreed, and in early 2008 we began an engaging e-mail conversation that grew from a discussion of Sephardic authors to a full-blown exploration of her own work and aesthetics. Along the way, we invited Setton's friend and fellow author, Farideh Dayanim Goldin, to join in. Goldin's unique background as a writer—born in the *mahaleh* (Jewish ghetto) of Shiraz, Iran, to a family of Jewish community leaders and then later immigrating to the U.S.—provided a much-needed Mizrahi perspective and, along with the views of Setton, gave new meaning to my understanding of contemporary Jewish American writing.

In addition to *The Road to Fez*, Setton has written a variety of poems, stories, and essays. Her piece of creative nonfiction, "Living between Question Marks" (2010), is a lyrical and evocative expression of what it is like to live between cultures, reside among diverse languages, and inhabit a space of memory and exile. She has recently completed a new novel, *The Zigzag Girl*, and is currently working on other works of fiction as well as a poetry collection. She shared part of her novel in progress, *Darktown Blues*, with me during our interview. Setton has received a number of fellowships, has taught as a visiting writer at several colleges and universities, and has been nominated for (and winning) a variety of fiction and poetry awards, including multiple nominations for the Pushcart Prize. Goldin, a tireless advocate for Jewish women's issues, is perhaps best known for her memoir, *Wedding Song: Memoirs of an Iranian Jewish Woman* (2003), but she is also a prolific speaker, fiction writer, and essayist. Her moving "Conversations with My Father" was part of National Public Radio's *Hanukkah Lights* special in 2008, and her stories and essays have appeared in collections such as *Turnings: Writing on Women's Transformations* (edited by Louisa Igloria and Renee Olander, 2000), *To Mend the World: Women Reflect on 9/11* (edited by Marjorie Agosin and Betty Jean Craige, 2002), and *The Flying Camel: and Other Stories of Identity by North African and Middle Eastern Jewish Women* (edited by Loolwa Khazzoom, 2004). She was recently the consulting editor for a special issue of *Nashim: A Journal of Jewish Women's Studies and Gender Issues* (devoted to Jewish women writers of Iranian heritage, 2009), and she is currently at work on her second memoir, *Iran: My Homeland*.

Over the past two years both Goldin and Setton gave their time to discuss a variety of matters, including not only their own writing, but also the current state of Jewish American fiction, the place of the Sephardic and the Mizrahi literature within this community, their positions as women writers, the curses of "exoticism," and the in-between cultural status that seems to define not only a good part of their identities, but much of their art as well.

Derek Parker Royal: Over the past several years there's been increased critical attention given to the newer generation of Jewish authors in the United States, a phenomenon that has been called the "new wave" in Jewish American writing. Do you see yourself as part of this community of writers?

Ruth Knafo Setton: New wave of American Jewish writers? As far as I can tell, the new wave *is* the old wave, recycled for a new generation. It's Ashkenazi, lox, bagels, and horseradish. Not a hint of cumin. Not a scent of orange blossoms.

DPR: So you feel that your and Farideh's work isn't a part of this?

RKS: I am reminded of a comment made by Ben-Gurion in the early days of the state of Israel when he was asked about the difference in treatment accorded to immigrants from Morocco (settled in primitive camps) and those from Eastern Europe (situated in city hotels and apartments): "They are family." You can bet he didn't mean the Moroccans. The Jewish Don Corleone (Don Cohen?) stands at the front gate—yes, it's a gated community, contrary to what they'd have you believe—of the American Jewish Temple of Literature, identifying who goes in and who stays out. Russians? Family. Poles and Germans? Please. Latin Americans? Cousins. Sephardic/Mizrahi? Very suspect, the relatives you hide in the back room. There is a growing awareness of multiculturalism in Jewish literature, and I am glad to see it. But when I compare that awareness to the explosive dynamic inclusiveness of other contemporary ethnic groups writing in America (e.g., Latino, Indian, Russian, Native American), I find it woefully timid.

Do I have a Moroccan-Jewish chip on my shoulder? You bet. Am I still waiting for someone to make my day and knock it off? *Bien sur.*

Farideh Dayanim Goldin: I teach Jewish American literature at Old Dominion University. There are no anthologies that address Sephardic/Mizrahi history and literature in America. (I have to mention Mizrahi because we have been incorporated into the Sephardic culture even though we have our own distinct culture. Mizrahim are the Jews of the Middle East and the Muslim world. "Mizrakh" means "East.") Most courses on American Jewish literature recognize Ashkenazi literature in translation and Ashkenazi writers who were not born in the United States. Isaac Bashevis Singer, for example, wrote in Yiddish; he was born in Poland. Elie Wiesel was born in Romania; he writes in French. They are both literary icons. Their books are often taught as Jewish American literature at the universities. However, I am not sure if literature written in Persian by an Iranian Jewish writer living in California would be accepted under the same category. I often wonder how much of this invisibility is the fault of the Iranian community for not promoting our writers and poets, and how much of it is due to a certain prejudice against us. Hopefully, with time this will change.

DPR: And you're wondering why scholars are not bringing Mizrahi American voices into the fold?

FDG: Yes. There is not enough scholarly research on Mizrahim. Until recently, I complained that many of my articles on Iranian Jewish women writers had been ignored by American Jewish publications. One was finally published in *Jewish Quarterly* (Autumn 2005) in England. Two years earlier, I had requested membership at a Jewish women speakers' bureau. I didn't hear back. I called. I was told, "But you are not American!" Their website showed numerous women who lectured on Jewish women immigrant writers. Many Jewish women immigrants built the foundation for Jewish writing in this country. English was their second or third language after Yiddish and maybe Russian or Polish. I have lived in the United States much longer than in my country of birth. I write in English. I give my lectures in English. Why am I not American? I asked them.

But now new scholarship has been generated. The Hadassah-Brandeis Institute and the Schechter Institute of Jewish Studies, for example, devoted the 2009 issue of *Nashim: A Journal of Jewish Women's Studies and Gender Issues* to Iranian Jewish women. I was honored to be its consulting editor. I am indebted to Shulamit Reinharz for her vision, for her efforts to promote scholarship on Jewish women around the world. Additionally, both The Hebrew University and Tel Aviv University have well-funded programs on Iranian Jewry. Iranian Jews in the United States and Israel have been behind this new wave of research and scholarship. I am very excited about the publication of novels and autobiographies by authors of Iranian background both in the United States and in Israel.

DPR: Both of you give quite emphatic, and very personal, responses. How do these matters affect you as writers?

RKS: When I write I am not American, Jewish, Sephardic, female—or rather, I am all of them, and therefore, none of them. I am a writer, which I take to mean that I am a human being who explores the human condition in my particular way, through my experiences, history and dreams. In the process of exploring difference and otherness, I find (create?) connections that may not be immediately apparent. In the words of Danny, the Moroccan Jewish trumpet player in my novel in progress, *Darktown Blues*:

> He plays because he can't not play. He plays because music is his language, and he's got to talk, and this is the only way he can do it. He plays because no one else has sung his life—from Mogador to Memphis, Paris to New York. A Moroccan Jew who can't forget a thing: not the muezzin's cry . . . the tears of the Jewish children in the *fourriere* . . . his father's murderous voice, "You are nothing." . . . Django's golden laugh and his mother's silvery one . . . Prosper's gravelly warning, "*Devenir humain*: the greatest war we have to fight, against ourselves" . . . and Lili's radiant question mark aimed directly at his heart, pierced and lodged there. That's Danny's song. No one else can sing it, and he's got to sing because if he doesn't, melodramatic as it sounds, he'll die.

But after the writing is done and the work seeks a home . . . When I sent out my first novel, *The Road to Fez*, an editor responded, "You write very well. Next time write about the real Jews." Another editor: "I'd publish this book but it would be a shelf of one." A Sephardic Jewish critic: "Why tell this story now? And if you must, why tell it with so much passion?" And an Ashkenazi critic told me angrily, "This isn't the way I imagined Jews in Arab lands."

DPR: Were all critics as confining in their reactions?

RKS: No. One noted that "Setton takes risks on every page." That's more what I was after, but of course that means my writing doesn't fall comfortably into any category. *The Road to Fez* explores love in every form—from sacred to taboo—without taking a stand. If that's not problematic enough, it dives into the little-known world of Moroccan Jews and reveals highly charged pieces of their history, controversial in our politically correct atmosphere. It's not a political call to arms, not an exotic (unreal?) road trip through Morocco, not multicultural enough or too multicultural. Some of the most moving responses to the book have come from non-Jewish readers all over the world—including China, Korea, Brazil, Rumania, and Spain—who tracked me down to tell me, "This story is my story." Overall, critical responses to my first novel have been extremely favorable. And since I've begun publishing, there have been a number of Jewish critics, writers, academics who have been supportive and open to different voices.

FDG: I would like to add one more piece to Ruth's list. Our stories are often told by the elite of our societies. Iranians who read *Wedding Song* are often the byproducts of an elite English education. In Iran, they belonged to the very privileged class of Jews who studied at American, British or French schools. They mostly lived in the capital, Tehran, where they enjoyed much more freedom. They often were unaware of other Jews who lived in the Jewish ghettos, who lived in the more oppressive cities in Iran. As first generation immigrants, they would like to remember the best of Iran. They would like for their children to see the country they left behind through their parents' rose-colored glasses. I have been called a liar by privileged assimilated Iranian Jews who left Iran when they were quite young.

DPR: Are there many of your readers who find that your accounts of Iran resonate?

FDG: Yes. I have received phone calls, e-mails, messages through my website or Facebook from readers who have thanked me for telling their stories through my own. I know that there are silent people whose stories can be told through a writer like myself. I think we—Ruth, myself and other Mizrahi/Sephardic writers—keep alive stories of our people, stories that would have been otherwise forgotten.

DPR: Wouldn't you think that with such an emphasis on multicultural perspectives, both in the academy and in the general culture, there would be more readers out there wanting you to keep those stories alive?

RKS: I'm surprised that the cumin-scented chip still wobbles on my shoulder, that the growth in awareness of multicultural literature didn't knock it off. Unfortunately—as I wrote in my essay, "Ten Ways to Recognize a Sephardic 'Jew-ess'"—by multicultural, they don't mean me. To complicate the issue, I confess to having mixed feelings about the label "multicultural writer." At its worst this category invites excessive tribalism, suffocating self-obsession and political agendas that turn writing into propaganda. At its best it offers windows and insights into different perspectives and worlds. What disturbs me is that American Jewish literature, already a minority, shuts the door on the minority within the minority. In a sense I understand the resistance to a history that isn't theirs, a vision that emerges from unfamiliar traditions, voices that don't conform to their images and expectations. But it's like being doubly, even triply exiled. I expected some form of alienation from other Americans; I did not expect it from other Jews. And despite the fact that people seem to understand that we exist, we are often—still!—segregated to Sephardic anthologies and conference panels.

DPR: Farideh, what are you experiences with being, as Ruth puts it, a minority within a minority? Does this phenomenon come out in your writing in any way?

FDG: I am now working on a second memoir, *Iran: My Homeland*, with two voices: my dad's and mine, my life as a new Jewish immigrant in the United States and my father's as a refugee in Israel. I watched as Israelis mocked my father on the streets when he was a broken man, having lost his country and much of his possessions. We were both strangers within our Jewish communities.

Those early years in the United States coincided with the arrival of South African Jews. I was surprised to see our community welcoming our South African immigrants with such enthusiasm, fighting over them, wanting to be seated with them at functions, whereas I had basically been invisible for many years. Comments were made that, at best, were thoughtless. I was quite alone and new to our community. I took my three daughters to the synagogue on Shabbat, partly to make friends, to connect with my new community. A woman approached me and asked why I would attend her shul. She grew up there, had connections, but what about me? I didn't know what to say, so I stood there for a while not saying a word, and then walked away. My husband (an American-born physician) and I went to a party once. He tried to introduce me to a prominent Jewish doctor in town, "This is my wife, Farideh." The doctor said, "Oh, yes, I have met her, Fatemeh." I corrected him, "No, Farideh." He shrugged, "Okay, Fatemeh, Fa . . . whatever."

DPR: What you're describing smacks of the worst kind of prejudice.

Recently, I was at a meeting, which was set up to hear an Israeli professor as a possible candidate for teaching Jewish Studies at our local university. A rabbi, who knows me well, said that when visiting Israel, he had heard Moshe Katzoff on the radio. "His language was foul, not suitable for a President." The rabbi asked the Israeli professor, "Do you think that's because he is Iranian?" Of course if one changes the word Iranian for Jewish or Black, one can see that his statement was cloaked in the nastiness of his prejudice. When I confronted him, he wasn't apologetic.

During the Soviet Jewry exodus, my husband and I went to a meeting with the purpose of soliciting funds for the settlement of Soviet refugees. A high-ranking Israeli official was our guest speaker. We were at a friend's house; I had a glass of wine in my hand, not expecting what came next. Speaker after speaker stood up to say that this was the time to make Israel what it should be: a country oriented to the West, eschewing the growing Mizrahi influence. What was so appalling to me was the fact that the Israeli official couldn't have imagined that an Iranian would be in that room. He clearly expected that everyone would mirror his bias. I experienced much anti-Semitism in Iran, but this was the most painful since it came from a place of comfort and familiarity.

I can give many more examples about events that exacerbated my sense of alienation among my own people. However, regarding conferences, I often participate simply as a writer or an Iranian writer. I have also been lucky that Iran is a hot topic, and I have been invited to speak to diverse groups about Iran and Iranian Jews.

DPR: How do you define the voice of the Sephardic or Mizrahi Jew? Who are some of the authors you look to in your own work, or in even in your teaching?

RKS: Because our origins, histories and traditions defy easy categorization—North African? Bulgarian? South American? Middle Eastern?—I would define Sephardic Jews as any Jews who are not Ashkenazi. And because our food, music, rituals, and even our languages mingle into a Mediterranean nomadic stew, same as our foods—served twenty courses at the same time—I envision Sephardic literature as a world cafe under the sun. The opposite of a gated house, this cafe has no roof or walls; it sits on the sand, facing the sea. And because our vision of time is circular and synchronic, writers dead and alive are welcome: Primo Levi, Albert Memmi, A. B. Yehoshua, Edmond Jabes, Samy Michael, Erez Bitton, Lucette Lagnado, Edmond El Maleh, Homa Sarshar, Andre Aciman, and others. In my essay, "Living Between Question Marks," I attempt a description of the Sephardic mood:

> We are Jews with a Mediterranean accent who carry the memory of the sun in our hearts. Enter our houses in the mellah or juderia, and go directly to the soul—the tiled inner courtyard crowded with women and children—like us, hidden, secretive, restless. Dance with us: flamenco guitar and hypnotic desert oud, drums that pound like bare feet running on a beach, nostalgic and mournful yet always with a beat that circles on itself. Look at our family photos: men wearing tasseled fezzes and djellabahs, women with painted icon faces and pointed babouches beneath silver-threaded caftans. Eat with us: bstilla, with its exquisite commingling of sweet and savory, fragrant

> couscous, salads vivid with color and wit, and flaky orange-scented desserts that tingle your senses with their beauty and then melt on your tongue. After the meal join us in the salon arabe for mint tea or cardamom-spiced coffee, and discuss the destiny of the Jews, the concept of home and identity, and tell Johra stories in Arabic, French, Hebrew, Spanish and English—all in the same sentence. Laugh until you cry. Remember the sun.

Yes, it's lyrical, but there is a richness, a joie de vivre, a spicy wit and appreciation of life I find in the Mediterranean-Jewish world that I don't see anywhere else. What a shame to deprive people of it!

FDG: I have taught Andre Aciman's book, *Out of Egypt* (1996), Gina Nahai's book, *Moonlight on the Avenue of Faith* (1999), Ruth's essay, "Ten Ways to Recognize a Sephardic 'Jew-ess,'" poetry by Majorie Agosin, and interviews with Ilan Stavans, to name a few. I have to work harder to find material for this segment, and I do feel guilty for putting them in a separate category. I also include Mizrahi writings in my World Literature and Women Writers courses. I consider this a personal responsibility to educate my mostly non-Jewish students about Mizrahi, Sephardic, and Ashenazi Jews, celebrating their achievements and their literature.

DPR: What about the *American* timbre of the voices in this community? Who are some younger American Sephardic or Mizrahi Jewish authors that you feel aren't getting much attention?

FDG: Fortunately, Dalia Sofer's book, *The Septembers of Shiraz* (2007), received great reviews in the *New York Times.* I included her book and Dorit Rabinyan's *Persian Brides* (1998) in a course on Iranian Women Writers. I also managed to get an invitation for Sofer to our university's literary festival. We must be mutually supportive to one another and promote each other's works. Ruth and I have done this for each other. We must encourage new writers. For every Mizrahi/Sephardic who writes, there are thousands who are afraid, who remain silent.

DPR: Ruth, earlier you mentioned "the minority within the minority," or the margins within the margins. How does this find expression in your own writing?

RKS: This is a question about negotiating difference and otherness. For me it comes up *after* the writing. When we watch a foreign film we rely on visual cues as well as subtitles to translate the "foreign" world into one that is comprehensible. In ethnic/minority writings, unless the author is writing solely for those who are already familiar with her world, what I call the "Subtitle Factor" comes into effect. How much of her world needs to be translated and explained? Does every foreign word need to be defined? Does the work require footnotes and glossary?

How much explanation is too much? Does the work need an introduction as a gateway? A writer can plunge forward, letting the hardy reader follow her into the Steppes or the Sahara; or she can acknowledge the "Subtitle Factor," and create a bridge into the foreign world. In *The Road to Fez*, I did include a glossary; however, I did not italicize any words. Mediterranean Jews speak in a mélange of languages, often four in a single sentence, and to determine which word is the "foreign" one is beyond me.

DPR: What are the potential drawbacks in focusing on what for many readers is a "foreign" world?

RKS: Well, one drawback is timidity. Fear of penetrating the alien world without a guide. There is also the tendency to exoticize such a world, something I strenuously resist: I'm more in-your-face exotic! For a member of a largely unknown minority, the negotiating becomes a slippery bridge between what Philip Roth calls P.R. and writing the truth. I've been asked more than once by well-meaning Sephardic readers about my responsibility in describing a world that for many readers will be their only contact with it—ever. In other words, if among my Moroccan Jewish characters, I include illicit lovers, liars, and cowards, then I should balance them by including saintly rabbinic and Kabbalistic students and noble women. But what is my responsibility as a writer? Certainly the answer—for me—goes far beyond borders and minorities, and at the very least, punches holes into metaphorical and literal walls through which we can see each other and breathe each other's air.

DPR: Tell me more about your "in-your-face exoticism" and how that translates into your representation of the Moroccan Jewish experience.

RKS: It's too easy to play the exotic odalisque/Rick's Café world with Morocco. I wanted to take risks: to bite into the forbidden fruit, turn the key of the locked room, lift the veil, peer behind the curtain, become a trespasser of country, body and soul—where the exotic and the erotic become facets of each other. The exotic *is* the erotic: we desire what we don't fully know and understand. Hence, the shifting mirror of the Jew, particularly the Jewish woman, in the imagination of Muslims in precolonial Morocco, European Romantics, and men (Jewish, Muslim, and Christian).

DPR: I do see the temptation to exoticize the Sephardic experience, even within—or especially within—the American Jewish community. Have you found a similar impulse with Mizrahi concerns, Farideh?

FDG: Our culture might be exotic because it is unfamiliar. For example, no one complains when a writer mentions stopping by a deli to get lox and bagels. When

I write about gondi, an Iranian Jewish food, the smell of roasted chickpea flour and cumin permeates the story with a tinge of foreignness. Once another writer told me that I used food in my stories as a crutch, but he himself wrote about hamburgers and hot dogs. We write about the food we eat. Hot dogs and hamburgers were exotic food when I lived in Iran. Having said that, yes, you are right. I think Edward Said would have had unkind words about, for example, Dora Levy's books and the way she exploits the myth of exotic Iranian Jewish women and their sexual rituals in a Shah's harem. But that's also a genre of literature, and she obviously has a lot of readers. Readers are smart enough to differentiate between fact and fantasy—I hope.

DPR: Have critics or readers cavalierly described your work as "exotic"?

FDG: Not the critics, but definitely the readers. I am not as worried about being called "exotic" so much as being labeled "primitive." I have to constantly remind my readers that the events in *Wedding Song* cover fifty years of my life, during which Iran changed rapidly from a poverty-stricken post-World War II country to a modern, progressive state. My paternal grandmother was married off at age nine, never learning to read or write her own name; my mother was forced into an arranged marriage before puberty at the age of thirteen, barely finishing elementary education. In contrast, my sisters and I have earned graduate degrees and speak multiple languages, a testimony to the cultural evolution in Iran.

I think older Jewish readers understand this better than younger, more privileged generation, who has forgotten that their ancestors immigrated to the United States from places very similar to my background. I address this in my essay, "My Iranian Sukkah," published in *Where We Find Ourselves: Jewish Women around the World Write about Home* (2009). My husband, whose grandparents came to America from Eastern Europe, often tells me that I remind him of his Grandmother Fannie, who spoke with an accent, who listened to radio shows, who had bitter memories of her old country. She cooked food from scratch that sounded "exotic" to my ears; *Teiglach? Gribenes*? I pride myself on having these similarities with Fannie, a courageous woman who left Russia in steerage for a better life in America. However, unlike her, who wanted to forget about her life in Russia, I insist on being very vocal about my country of birth, about my own life, and the lives of the previous generations. If I don't tell their stories, who will? It saddens me that Fannie's stories are lost. Unlike her, I teach my recipes to my daughters. I serve this strange, "exotic" food to my American guests. I have also inherited Fannie's mixing bowl, chopper, and her recipe for chopped eggplant. I am passing that down the line as well. I mix our, hers and mine, "exotic" Mizrahi/Ashkenazi customs.

DPR: This kind of memory, "exotic" or otherwise, is at the center of your writing, Farideh. Your "Hanukkah in Iran: Conversations with My Father," for example, is a moving tribute. I was wondering how memories of your father define you as a writer from Iran, and as a Jew? Or another way of putting it, how does your father link you to your history?

FDG: My father and I were very close, yet we had a turbulent relationship. I wrote that essay for NPR's *Hanukah Lights*, trying to highlight the way two different generations of Jews processed our Iranian lives. My father, like many Jewish people of his generation, loved Iran and would have never left had the Revolution not forced him into exile. In contrast, I had tried to sever my relationship with everything Iranian. I was angry. My father encouraged me to appreciate our Iranian culture even though he should have been bitter, having lost so very much. I watched Persian TV programs with him in Israel. Whenever I wanted to buy something, he introduced me to Iranian shopkeepers. Those were the ones he trusted. When he spoke to me, he spiced his words with Persian poetry. My father had already passed away when I wrote "Conversations With My Father." I was still arguing with him as it had become a habit of ours.

As a side note, the NPR representative who solicited me for the article loved it. They paid me well; I cashed the check. Then the radio host who was assigned to read my article refused to do so. It was too "political," she said. I asked to have it back. They told me that I could keep the money and write another piece for the following year. I wrote something more heartwarming, more palatable this time, a story about my hopes to find a dear Muslim friend with whom I had lost contact after the Revolution. The article was later published in *The Jerusalem Post*.

DPR: So how do mothers figure your writing?

RKS: My mother was my first muse. Night after night, we lay awake in this new country of ours, America, while my father worked the night shift and my little sister slept. Huddled in my bed, both of us afraid of the foreign night sounds, my mother told me stories about Safi, the small town in Morocco where I was born and where she grew up. A born storyteller gifted with an amazing memory and the art of creating suspense, my mother recreated the wildly eccentric seaside town and breathed life into it. And like Scheherazade, she held back the harsh light of winter mornings with the fascinating soap opera that took place on the North Atlantic coast. It wasn't until years later that I understood the urgency in my mother's tales, the need to communicate her past to me, to make me see the Jewish world in Morocco that had vanished, except in her memories. And now, in mine. By transferring these stories of a vanished world to me, she imparted a sense of responsibility: to remember. To never forget the people and places that gave birth to me. When I began to write, I returned to those long magical storytelling nights in which my mother's memories became my memories and her stories mine.

FDG: Some of the articles in that special issue of *Nashim* addressed the topic of motherhood. In fact, the cover artwork depicts the artist's mother sitting in a chair, her hands folded on her lap; on the wall behind her hangs a drawing of her daughter's right hand. The voices of our mothers have not been heard, I think. They passed down their stories through the oral tradition, but they were rarely given credit for their efforts. As I have interviewed writer after writer, it has become clear to me that our mothers were our muses, our source of creativity. That issue of *Nashim* conjures that voice, giving it credibility.

DPR: Ruth, as you show in *The Road to Fez*, certain narratives, such as that of Suleika, are romanticized or revised to where they become disconnected from history and take on a life of their own. In other words, they become myths. What are your responsibilities as a writer when confronting such powerful stories?

RKS: Like Cinderella, Suleika has over three hundred versions to her story—but the difference is that Suleika was a real historical figure. A seventeen-year-old Jewish girl, her brief life and tragic death have been picked apart by the guardians of official history and reassembled as (depending on whose version you choose) Jewish cautionary tale, Arab crime of passion, or Christian holy virgin martyr legend. By the time I came to her story, nearly one hundred and fifty years after her execution, it had already hardened into myth; and by the time I visited her tomb in the Jewish cemetery of Fez, I saw Jewish and Arab women praying side by side, and European Christians kneeling before her tomb. Her story warned of the dangers of crossing borders, yet seemed to transcend every border. A Jewish girl who chose death rather than a forced conversion to Islam. Yet today, she's worshipped as a saint by three faiths. How to write a story in which every detail contradicted another? For years I was a sleuth, searching for the one ultimate version that would finally reveal the truth. Meanwhile I tried to do justice to her by squeezing crucial elements of each version into one story. Unsurprisingly, I ended up with a swollen, ungainly mess.

Years of struggle passed during which I reimagined, reshaped, and rewrote her story. I cannot describe to you the sense of responsibility I felt during that time, the absolute determination that even if my book never saw the light of day, I would not compromise by erasing and distorting portions of her life. Even if I never found out what really happened, how she crossed the border into the Arab world, whether or not the Sultan of Morocco fell in love with her (as many versions insist), I would not stop until I found the way to tell her tale that cheated neither of us. During those long years of endlessly rewriting the novel, of course, I was doing my apprenticeship as a writer, learning not only my craft but also my own code of honor. The turning point came when I understood that I would never discover the truth, that maybe there was no single truth, and that even if I'd been a member of the breathless audience who witnessed the executioner teasing the back of her neck with the point of his sword, I still might not know the truth.

The only way to be true to her—and to me—was by not choosing a single truth with which to encompass her life. Who would want to be narrowed and flattened to that extent? I rewrote the novel—for at least the fifth time in its entirety!—this time inserting fragments of Suleika's tale between the fictional story of my characters, Gaby and Brit. These paradoxical, contradictory fragments contribute an ironic commentary on the novel itself—where everyone has his or her own Suleika. Finally, imperfect as it still was, the structure of the novel sang true to me. I offered the reader the chance to examine the complex nature of identity, history and myth by sifting through the fragments of a woman— as I had—and to create her own Suleika.

DPR: Who is *your* Suleika?

RKS: Hmm. Fair enough. Suleika is a Moroccan-Jewish girl who stands on the border between Africa and Europe, Judaism and Islam, tradition and modernity, the world of women and that of men, the sacred and the profane. A girl who represents all things. People look into her story as if they're looking into a pool and see their own needs and desires reflected. As I wrote and struggled through the many contradictory versions of her life, I realized I was, in a sense, writing my own story. Suleika was my sister. She is my sister. That's why I fought the tendency to exoticize her, why I chose Iranian artist, Shirin Neshat's controversial photograph for the cover, why I refused to whitewash the forbidden love story in the novel. "The road to Fez" was quite simply the road to the heart awakening. My own heart, as well as that of others.

DPR: You've told me a little bit about how you feel as a Jewish writer, and specifically as a Mizrahi or Sephardic writer in America. But how do these ideas mesh with your thoughts on being a woman writer?

FDG: Women writers give me strength. I knew I wanted to write, that I could write, that I must write after taking a women writer's class, reading and analyzing women writers from around the world. Their stories have empowered me, strengthening my own voice.

RKS: From the very beginning my writing has been deeply imbued with a sense of what it means to be a woman. And that destiny has been interwoven with what it means to be a Jew. After receiving rejections for early versions of my first novel—most dealing with the fact that it was too foreign for them—one night I had a dream that I'd open Suleika's story with these words: "I am going to tell you a story you don't want to hear." Thinking about this today saddens me, but that is how it felt in those days of premulticultural awareness, when any foreign/ethnic writer was suspect, particularly when she challenged their world views. Looking back, I see that from the very beginning the idea of the "Jew" and the idea of "woman"—these two dangerous, unknowable creatures—were tightly, irrevocably interwoven. The question has never been fully answered: was Suleika executed primarily because she was a woman or a Jew?

For me, being a woman, a writer, and a Jew form the braided strands of my identity. I can't remove one without weakening the others. My writing is profoundly influenced by the fact that I am a Jew and a woman. Every story I write is a daughter I send forth into the world. She emerges in fragments and slivers. I gather the pieces and breathe life into them, set her on the ground, and watch as she takes her first steps. She stands on the border, always on the border: between you and me, him and her, star and cross, star and crescent, dead and living, past and future. You can't miss her: she carries her mother's memories on her back, yet she stares at you with eyes that burn like six-pointed stars.

DPR: What do you see as the particular burdens or hurdles that Jewish writers face as women in today's literary environment?

RKS: The challenges are similar: first of all, to be read; and second, to be read without prejudice. The burden is on us—Jewish writers, women writers, writers of color and ethnicities that are unfamiliar to the mainstream American readers—to write work that is enlightening, entertaining and exciting enough to capture their interest. But the burden is also on the readers to be open to new worlds and worldviews that may contradict or overturn their ideas of reality. So yes, you've got to be read, and that means publishers and readers willing to take a chance on the unknown; and yes, your work has to be good enough, powerful enough to make the reader see through the differences that separate us to the similarities that connect us.

FDG: I fear we might become a victim of our own success. At the last Associate of Writers and Writing Programs Conference, I was surprised to hear so many panelists voice resentment against Jewish women writers. There were no panels on Jewish writing. With the help of the Hadassah-Brandeis Institute, a group of us tried to put together a panel on Jewish women writers for this year's conference. It was rejected. A few years ago I organized a panel on Iranian Jewish writing. That was rejected as well. I hope I am wrong about this issue.

DPR: Ruth, your fascination with Suleika—a strong female artist figure in her own right—seems to me a fascination with borderland identity, one that transcends boundaries, one that is constructed in an in-between space that pulls from dual (or multiple) origins but rests easily in neither. Do you see this as a general characteristic of contemporary Jewish American writing, including your own work?

RKS: Yes, I definitely see this uneasy borderland identity as one shared by Jewish American writers, as well as by other minority groups. The difference between

Jewish writers and those of other groups is the slippery definition of what it means to be Jewish—and of course, who decides on the definition. Is it a religion? Race? Nationality? Historical or cultural identity? Most Jewish writers I know struggle with where they stand in terms of American literature, particularly if their own Jewish identity is not superficially evident in their work. Are they simultaneously ethnic *and* mainstream? Jewish *and* American? Is it possible to be both on the fringes and on center stage? What if they see themselves on center stage, but readers, publishers and critics move them to a smaller, ethnic stage? I love that, for Philip Roth, Jewish history begins on a kitchen table in Newark. When I first read him I was drawn to that image of solidity and rootedness—a wooden table on a solid floor, in Newark. Newark, for God's sake!

DPR: Does your history begin in a similar place?

RKS: Where does Jewish history begin for me? In a brass key that hung on my grandfather's wall in Morocco, "the key to our home," a home he described in such loving and rich detail that it was years before I realized he was describing the house of our ancestors in Toledo, Spain, before the Inquisition. And yet, brass key in Morocco or wooden table in New Jersey: maybe both symbols exist in that in-between space that Jews create wherever they go, a place they call—for lack of a better word—home. That in-between space is exactly what I explore in my essay about living between question marks:

> From the first moment I saw the Spanish question marks—one inverted and one right side up—that bracket questions, I shivered with pleasure. I thought, I can live between these question marks. There is something very Jewish about Spanish question marks. Maybe something female too. They question the very essence of the question and make concrete what is implicit: that the inner mystery is contained, almost protected, within the two question marks. Like the Moroccan courtyard, in which the truth is turned inward. Like my grandfather living between two worlds—the historical reality of Spain and the imagined reality of the future in Jerusalem—while standing on his rooftop.

I guess what I'm trying to say is that I've learned to live between those two question marks. I could live between dashes too, but never between two periods! Too final. Too sure of themselves.

DPR: You mentioned Philip Roth earlier. He also wrote about this in-betweenness quite forcefully in *The Counterlife*. In fact, the very middle of that novel takes place in flight, suspended in air and unanchored to either the turbulence of Jerusalem nor the relative safety of the West. I'm reminded of that passage that opens your novel, *The Road to Fez*. Brit, in her journal, writes about a photograph taken of her when she was six years old and about to leave Morocco for the

United States: "my patent leather shoes will be lifted from the tiles, will dangle in the air, as I hover between two worlds—the New and the Old, belonging to neither, clinging to both."

RKS: That may be why *The Counterlife* remains my favorite Roth novel: the sense of existing between countries, identities and lives, of somehow trying to remain aloft while never choosing (settling on) a single identity or life. It embodies the conflict of living on shaky ground between a nebulous future and a vanished past. When I was a child, I tried to hide all signs of my "difference" from my American neighbors and friends—the foods we ate, the music my parents listened to, their French accents, and that dim, powerful memory: Morocco. With time I've come to accept the rich complications a hyphenated identity brings, and the fact that no matter how rooted I may feel in America, the slightest breeze tilts me toward a world I can't forget.

DPR: These complications of a hyphenated identity that Ruth refers to—what do you make of this idea, Farideh, that we can best define ourselves and our writing within some ethnic or other sociopolitical context?

FDG: In my early years in America, during a dispute with an American family member, I was labeled as someone who was "different," who didn't understand American culture. Someone told me that my English wasn't good enough to comprehend issues. I internalized that conversation that went around and returned to me as all gossip eventually does. For the next five years I questioned myself; I was unsure of my identity. Who am I? Where do I belong? I asked myself. The turning point for me was a trip to Israel with my youngest daughter. My parents had a tiny apartment. I slept under their dinning room table. It was a hot summer night, and they didn't have air conditioning to cool off the suffocating air. But the air cooled off, as it does in the desert climate, a few hours after sundown. I woke up to a nice breeze coming through the window, the sound of Kol-Israel in Persian, the aroma of warm bread and hot Jasmine tea. I was transported to my younger years in Iran. It was a feeling of comfort, of belonging. That week I visited the ruins of Petra in Jordan. Persian and Arabic have similar script. I enjoyed reading the signs in the letters of the alphabet I had learned as a child. Although Iranians don't consider themselves to be Arabs, the body language of the Jordanians we encountered was all too familiar. I felt as if I could finally remove the mask I had worn since my arrival in the United States in 1975. It was liberating.

Returning to the United States, I had a different sense of myself. That family member had been right. I *was* different. I processed information and events around me differently, but that was a good thing. I knew who I was: Iranian, Jewish, American, and many other things. I didn't have to be "All-American," whatever that is. I could disagree with parts of my Iranian upbringing without having to discard all of it. I am a person of many identities, but I don't have to label myself, and I won't allow others to define me.

DPR: Both of you keep bringing up Morocco and the Middle East, for you the "Old World." I'm thinking of the significance of Eastern Europe, Poland, and the Ukraine in the works of other recent Jewish novelists such as Michael Chabon and Jonathan Safran Foer. For them, obviously, this Old World is a link to their familial and cultural past. But as several critics have noted, at times there is a tendency in them to cast a nostalgic glance and romanticize that past. Do you find yourself tempted to use your ancestral homelands in a similar fashion?

RKS: Like them I am tempted, of course. However, for me, the temptation is rather different since their "Old World" is much more widely known than mine. My first instinct is to recreate Jewish Morocco, a world that is not only unknown and vanished, but that has been largely erased by revisionists of the past. We are even denied our history! I find it curious that the Jews of Arab lands have been largely left out of the Jewish and Middle Eastern historical narrative, as if their stories are not significant in the current situation. I know that Sephardic/Mizrahi writers have been attacked on all sides when they bring up painful events in their history: for example, the Jewish refugees of Arab lands; the massacres, persecutions, and forced conversions they suffered; their dhimmi status. In Morocco, when I read an excerpt about Suleika from *The Road to Fez*, a Jewish professor asked me with genuine curiosity, "But why bring this up now? It happened so long ago."

FDG: I am almost always categorized as a Middle Eastern writer, not an American Jewish writer. I don't mind that. My Iranian culture will forever be a huge part of my identity. However, with the advance of technology, it should not be difficult to cross reference authors. I am a woman, a Jew, and an American with very close ties to Israel. My parents and my sister escaped to Israel after the Revolution. Consequently, we are not equally proficient in Persian, Hebrew, and English, the three languages we speak. My father passed away not long ago. During the shiva period, as we sat together on the floor, my two brothers, two sisters, and my mother, stumbled and fell on our words. As our various languages did not convey our feelings, we switched from one language to another, struggling to communicate. This cross-cultural experience is depicted in Ashkenazi literature as well, Henry Roth's *Call it Sleep* (1934), or Cynthia Ozick' *The Shawl* (1989), for example. Yet, it is exotic and foreign when I write or speak about it. Sometimes I feel that my shared experiences with American Jews do not bring us closer to one another. It rather separates me from the majority. I have become the voice of their grandmothers, whom they have tried to forget or to file in a "long ago" cabinet of Jewish history.

DPR: This is an interesting point, "cross referencing" authors. How do you feel about such ethnic labels being placed on your writings? And have there been any instances where you've been labeled in ways that you think might restrict or prejudice your readership?

FDG: One Jewish reviewer was irate that I would mention my devotion to America and reject Iran. In a politically correct world, maybe that's a sin. The Iranians call this *gharb-zadeghi*, West-smitten. The Iran that I rejected was the country that oppressed me. She didn't mention that I had emphatically warned the readers that this book was just a small part of my life and even a smaller section of Iranian life—and yes, I do have the right to criticize my country of birth as she has the right to criticize America. I tried very hard to make my memoirs a bit claustrophobic to show that I lived in a small city and a house that was suffocating with its old-fashioned rituals and beliefs—no sympathy there either. She was upset that the book didn't show the vast expanse of Iran, and that it had not mentioned Shirin Ebadi, who had not won her Nobel Prize when the book was finished, and I didn't know a thing about her during the time frame of my memoir. (I recently met Ebadi and have taught her book.) I felt as if the critic were appalled by a story so different, so *foreign* to her senses that she found it easier to dismiss rather than try to understand it. I wonder if she would have written the same review about a minority suffering in the United States.

RKS: Ethnic labels can be informative—such as, she's a Moroccan Jewish writer, rather than an Indian—but also restrictive—as in, does that mean she writes only about Morocco and Jews?—particularly when the label itches or chafes (e.g., but what does a serial killer have to do with Morocco? A prehispanic mask maker with Jews? How about a woman magician?). Since no label covers what I do, except exactly *what I do,* I try to ignore them and hope readers will explore with me. I've been accused by militant Sephardic activists of failing to "join the Sephardic army" in our war against the Ashkenazim. I'm not kidding. I've also been scolded for not being militant enough, for being too ethnic, for not being ethnic enough, for writing too much about Moroccans (in a novel taking place in Morocco), for not writing enough about Moroccans (in a story about Irish magicians), for being too positive, for being too negative. You name it.

DPR: How do you deal with this unfair perception?

FDG: I think a writer, Jewish or not, Mizrahi, Sephardic, or Ashkenazi, has to remain true to her words and keep on writing. I spoke to a Jewish group outside Philadelphia a few years ago. A woman raised her hand after I finished, claiming that I was not telling the truth. When I asked a few questions, it was clear that her reality was very different from mine. She had lived in a wealthy Muslim suburb outside Tehran. The neighbors were unaware of her Jewish background. She left Iran at a very young age and married an American Christian. That makes her experience different from mine. A book about Harlem doesn't tell the story of everyone in the United States, New York, or even Harlem. My book about my life in a religious family in a small town doesn't have to encompass all life in Iran, or all Jewish life in Iran, or even all Jewish life in my city of birth, Shiraz. So, I will keep on writing and talking to give a different perspective that is just that—different, maybe unusual, maybe unimaginable, maybe even exotic—but the truth as I know it.

RKS: By writing my way through it, by communicating the pain through words, by trying to show that the richer and denser the tapestry of voices in American writing, the richer and denser we become as human beings. And maybe subversively I try to blur and confuse the borders and boundaries. For example, Danny—the father in *Darktown Blues*—is a jazz trumpeter. Jazz saved his life in Morocco, gave him a dream of a place where all men's voices have an equal chance to be heard. He called it Louisland, and *that's* why he brings his family here. A fellow jazz musician in the book describes Danny's sound this way: "He's got a different groove, mixing sounds from North Africa and the Mediterranean and bop, and making them his own." Maybe that's what I'm after—taking all these influences, mixing them up and making them my own. Creating an immigrant stew that is a mix of New World ingredients and Old World memories, a stew that feeds not only your belly but your hunger for your roots. With each spoonful, you are simultaneously there and here, then and now, the you who existed across the seas and the you who walks the streets of America. Food that's a bridge. A novel that's a bridge.

DPR: What are you working on now? Where is your writing taking you today?

FDG: I am working on many different projects. My second memoir is in its final stages; I just finished a substantial article about the impact of language on memoirs written by Iranian women. Two years before he passed away, I asked my father for a list of Judi, Judeo-Persian words in the dialect of the Jews of Shiraz. The language is just about dead. My next project is to create an online Judi dictionary, making the language accessible to researchers.

RKS: I'm working on a collection of poetry, several memoirlike essays, the revision of my novel, *Darktown Blues,* and a new novel that explores the power of myth in modern-day life, particularly myths of female power. This new novel is profoundly inspired by a recent Mediterranean voyage during which I sailed and taught on a ship that stopped in Athens, Rome, Naples, Istanbul, and Casablanca, among other ports. The experience of wandering through ancient-new cities while feeling the weight and timeless presence of history and myth was very moving and inspiring on many levels. I felt I was returning to my roots, retracing the voyage my parents made when they sailed from Tangiers through the Strait of Gibraltar, and across the Atlantic to New York City. The novel I'm working on is set in contemporary America with non-Jewish characters, but in surprising ways, it's deeply Jewish—going back to our most ancient stories, myths, rituals, dreams, and yearnings. So far no Moroccans have entered the story, but they have a way of appearing in my works in progress. Usually around chapter 3, a Moroccan family will move to town and brew mint tea, cook couscous, play the oud, and serenade me with songs my mother sang to me.

DPR: What's on the horizon with Iranians and your work, Farideh?

FDG: I would like to end on a more optimistic note. There are now more Iranian Jews living in the United States than in Iran. There is a critical mass of Iranian Jews in Israel as well. The Mayor of Beverly Hills, Jimmy Delshad, is an Iranian Jew from my city of birth, Shiraz. We have found a voice, partly because of our numbers, partly because we have adjusted to life under democratic governments that do not persecute us for our thoughts, for our spoken or written words. The colossal painstaking research on Iranian Jewish life—by the Iranian journalist Homa Sarshar and her son Houman Sarshar in the United States, and by eminent scholars such as David Menashri, Amnon Netzer, and countless others in Israel—germinated hope and pride. The new generation of Iranians are mostly upbeat and proactive. For example, in 1999, when thirteen Jews were arrested in Shiraz in charges of spying for Israel, older Iranians suggested silence; otherwise, they feared, other Jews would have been in danger as well. The younger generation of Iranian Jews refused to accept humility. I believe those thirteen are still alive because of these young Iranians' decision to get involved. Similarly, there are new voices in Iranian American literature, such as Gina Nahai, Roya Hakakian, and Dalia Sofer, to name a few.

However, personally, my own fears persists as I put the last touches on my new memoir—not the fear of not being received well by the American readers, not the fear of being categorized as "other." Rather, the fear of my own Iranian Jewish community in the United States threatens to paralyze my writing hand. I face the worst fear of all for a writer, the fear of facing myself and to be as truthful as possible. But that is universal, not Mizrahi, Sephardic, or Ashkenazi—not Jewish or Gentile—just human.

Picturing American Stories: An Interview with Ben Katchor

Derek Parker Royal

One of the first things you notice when reading the work of Ben Katchor is its particularity. His comics are filled with eccentric characters who find themselves in off-beat encounters with reality. What is so ironic about these encounters is that they are set in the mundane, everyday world that is anything but atypical. Looking into an abandoned store window, leafing through the magazines in a chiropodist's office, and listening to the surrounding conversations in a neighborhood restaurant are activities in which any of us could engage. Yet, while most people would let these experiences flow right through them, never giving them a second thought, Katchor's protagonists use them as springboards into philosophical reflections, historical observations, and mystical reveries. A hotel façade is transformed into the history of urban America, a bed of lettuce generates speculations on leisure, and the sounds of digestion become keys to a higher, more spiritual reality. This is the kind of world we find in the picture-stories of Ben Katchor.

And this is what Katchor prefers to call his art: "picture-stories." Although trained in classical art within the Western tradition—having graduated from Brooklyn College and briefly attending New York's School of Visual Arts—Katchor has made a career out of wedding his art to storytelling. Not content in being a "mere" painter, he has chosen to tell stories through his drawing, creating elaborate narratives that no easel could contain. "Comics," as he reveals in our conversation, is an ambiguous label that comes with its own historical and cultural baggage. "Picture-stories," on the other hand, more accurately describes his creative intentions and gets to the heart of his medium. His picture-stories have

Figure 1. Image from the cover of *Julius Knipl, Real Estate Photographer: Stories* (Little, Brown, 1996). © 1996 Ben Katchor.

appeared in a variety of outlets, from freebie newspapers such as the *New York Press* to industry publications such as *Metropolis* (a magazine of architecture and design), from the New York Jewish *Forward* to national wide-distribution magazines such as *The New Yorker* and *Harper's*. Over the past twenty-five years these strips have accumulated and taken the form of larger collections and novellike works, published as *Cheap Novelties: The Pleasures of Urban Decay* (1991), *Julius Knipl, Real Estate Photographer: Stories* (1996), *The Jew of New York* (1999), *The Beauty Supply District* (2000), and most recently, *The Cardboard Valise* (2011).

Although Katchor's base of operation is the picture-story, he is nonetheless active in other media and occupations. He has worked in music theater, collaborating with Mark Mulcahy in such productions as *The Slug Bearers of Kayrol Island* and *A Checkroom Romance* and Moritz Eggert in *There Was a Building, or, The 58th Street Boiler*. In addition, he regularly gives lectures and coordinates artist workshops in both the U.S. and Europe. His accolades include a Guggenheim Memorial Foundation Fellowship, a MacArthur Foundation Fellowship, and a fellowship at both the American Academy in Berlin and the Cullman Center for Scholars and Writers at the New York Public Library. He taught part-time at the School of Visual Arts, has been the Harman Writer in Residence at Baruch College, and is currently an associate professor in the School of Art, Media, and Technology at Parsons, The New School for Design.

Despite his heavy workload, Katchor was kind enough to find the time, over several sessions, to talk with me about his work, his literary and artistic influences, the history of the comic strip, his views on comic art and its links to American identity, and the ways that technology and the economy are affecting his medium. This conversation began over the telephone in the summer of 2006, was carried on sporadically via e-mail over the next few years, and finalized in January 2011. Our topics of discussion developed over time, and as they evolved, Katchor revealed to me the philosophies and aesthetics underlying his unique art.

Derek Parker Royal: How do you see yourself as an artist or cartoonist working in contemporary America? Do you think of yourself as a Jewish writer?

Ben Katchor: I see myself as being very marginal to the culture. I think that there are only a few thousand people in the U.S. who would be interested in my work. I don't think of myself as a Jewish writer. The history of the Jews is a small part of my cultural make-up, mainly appreciated as history. My father was born in a traditional religious family in Warsaw at the end of the nineteenth century and so I was exposed to the Yiddish language, music and East European food as a child and young man. My father was a utopian socialist and so tried his best to discard Jewish traditions of organized religion and observance from his life. So, for the first twenty years of my life, I had this direct connection to East European Jewish culture of a very particular sort. Through my education in American schools, my literary taste was shaped by English-language literature, some written by so-called Jewish writers, but most not. I wrote one strip in Yiddish, as an exercise, but never considered working for a Yiddish-language audience. My taste in picture-making was shaped by studying world art, particularly the Western figurative tradition, mainly work by Christians, Protestants, and Pantheists. So, although I have these familial connections to old-world traditional Jewish culture of a particular sort (nineteenth- and early twentieth-century Warsaw), those connections are very tenuous and not a tradition I'm consciously trying to uphold. So, national or ethnic identity (like patriotism) is for people who are afraid of being judged for what they are making of their own life and want to ride, in a mob, on the coattails of their supposedly venerable ancestors. Racial identity is just a dangerous fantasy.

The word "Jewish" without a long string of qualifiers and explanations is a totally nebulous term, except to an ignorant anti-Semite who thinks he knows exactly what it means.

DPR: How does your cultural background come out in your comics?

BK: It comes out through historical references, linguistic usage, but mainly through first-hand observation of what I see around me. I've also written and drawn a lot

Figure 2. Image from *Julius Knipl, Real Estate Photographer: Stories* (Little, Brown, 1996). © 1995 Ben Katchor. .

about the functioning of the market economy as it developed and into the present. As I've always lived in cities and building those subjects are central to my work.

DPR: There are some authors who primarily define themselves by their ethnic backgrounds, and then there are others who just do not like that label. Do you think that "ethnic" can be a little limiting and too restrictive of a term?

BK: These terms mean nothing beyond a marketing device or jingoistic obfuscation of what's really going on. It's like a desperate film producer latching onto a literary property to give his work a veneer of quality. In any case, ethnicity and nationalism are nineteenth-century inventions of despots and deluded artists.

DPR: What, if anything, do you make of the fact that many of the innovators in American comics were Jewish? Not only are there writers such as you, Jules Feiffer, Art Spiegelman, Trina Robbins, and Sharon Rudahl (just to name a few), but there are also earlier artists such as William Gaines, Jack Kirby, Harvey Kurtzman, Will Eisner, Stan Lee, and of course, Jerry Siegel and Joe Shuster.

BK: If you're referring to the popularization of comic books around 1939, most Jews at that time had nothing to do with comics. The people who were involved with early comic books were particular youngsters with an interest in American pulp fiction and pop culture. Superman is a reworking of Doc Savage. The dominant visual influence was the newspaper adventure strips of Dick Calkins (Buck Rogers, 1929) Alex Raymond (Flash Gordon, 1933). Most of the early comic-book writers and artists started as teenagers with little education. I like to think that the more common impulse for Jews at that time was the one taken by Saul Bellow, a near contemporary of Siegel and Shuster.

Because of all the chauvinistic Jewish cultural boosting of Superman, etc., some people believe that comics were invented in 1939 by Siegel and Shuster. The best American newspaper comic strip artists at the early twentieth century—Chester Gould, Windsor McKay, Harold Gray, and George Herriman—were not Jewish, and the tradition goes back to at least the early nineteenth century in Europe. The man who ran the King Features syndicate, Moses Koenigsberg, was Jewish, but the best cartoonists were not. In any case, if there was some vital connection between Jews and comics, why were there so few comic strips in the Yiddish press? For the most part, Jews had to leave the Jewish cultural milieu in order to make comics. The quality of work that appeared in these early comic books—a low level of commercial art directed at children and adolescents—set the comic strip back 100 years. Yiddish humor had a great effect on the American entertainment business, but more in humor writing, film, and vaudeville than comics. The Yiddish socialist/communist milieu of New York, with its wholesale distrust of American culture, spawned the satire of Kurtzman and Feiffer. This one specific aspect of Jewish culture *did* have an influence on comics in

Figure 3. Image from *The Jew of New York* (Pantheon, 1998). © 1998 Ben Katchor.

the 1950s. It took sixty years to shake off the subliterate/artistic stigma the early comic books imposed upon the form, and for that we can thank Robert Crumb and Bill Griffith, whose work starting appearing in underground newspapers in 1968-69.

DPR: So you don't consider yourself a Jewish graphic artist?

BK: No. I just say I live in New York city, I write in English and draw in a style inspired by Nicolas Poussin.

DPR: Have you ever felt any pressures from the Jewish community? And I'm thinking in particular of your book *The Jew of New York*. Was there any kind of reaction or any kind of expectation that you perceived, maybe from yourself, or maybe from critics or outside readers in the way you were representing the various characters, primarily Jewish, in nineteenth-century Manhattan?

BK: Other than a few historians, most people have no idea of what sort of Jews were living in New York City in 1830. Most of those Jews, if you were able to identify them as Jews, were further removed from old-world Jewish culture than I am today.

Mordecai Noah, who's at the center of *The Jew of New York*, was the first professional Jew in America. To jump-start his floundering political career he dreamt up the idea of founding a Jewish state on Grand Island in the Niagara River. He claimed that he was being directed by God, but, in fact, it was largely a real estate scam. Somebody else of that time could say he was of Hebraic extraction and not make much of it. He was somewhat delusional and carried ethnic identity to an insane length. But, on the other hand, he was willing to accept anyone who said they were Jewish into this "Jewish State," including the American Indians who were supposedly one of the lost tribes of Israel. Noah had the most widely inclusive idea of who might be considered a Jew.

DPR: How did your readers react to the book and these kinds of issues you address?

BK: Many readers enjoyed it, rabbis recommended it as a bar mitzvah gift, but it has as much to do with theater and the beginnings of the market economy in America as with Jewish American history. It was a comic strip that I created for the English-language *Forward* in New York. The editors didn't want to run the weekly strip I was doing at the time, *Julius Knipl, Real Estate Photographer*, because they felt that it was not specifically Jewish. So I said, "Well, I'll come up with a strip that's specifically Jewish." And I called it *The Jew of New York*.

DPR: So that was the birth of your graphic novel?

BK: Yes, at that time I was struggling to make a living doing comic strips. My main goal was to evoke the atmosphere of Jacksonian New York, with all of its strange obsessions, and the exotic nature of Jews in New York City at that time.

DPR: Well, in *The Jew of New York* and in your other strips like *Julius Knipl*, you have a series of interesting characters, and they find themselves in absurd and even grotesque situations. It's fascinating. Given the diverse mixture in these strips of yours, do you see yourself as a socially conscious comic artist, or a politically conscious writer?

BK: Well, I don't think you can avoid being a political artist. These things are just there whether you plan them or not. I'm not a political cartoonist in that sense of drawing cartoons about current politicians, but all of my strips question why the world is set-up as it is and not another way, and that's political. I'm not attacking current political stupidities. My strips are more of an analysis of situations. Ev-

Figure 4. Image from *The Jew of New York* (Pantheon, 1998). © 1998 Ben Katchor.

eryone can read it and enjoy it. No one will pick up my strip and say, "Well, this is a biased left-wing political cartoon." They just don't know where it's coming from until they've read it and by then, it's too late. Hopefully, they've understood it and had some sort of revelation.

DPR: When I first encountered your work was when I was living in New York in the 1980s. And I would always pick up the *New York Press*, and there I would see your strips. That was definitely an independent, maybe even alternative, paper. Would you consider yourself, let's say, an alternative comic writer, an inheritor of the underground cartoonists of the 1960s and 1970s?

BK: Well, I've also worked for Condé Nast.

DPR: And that's the other end of the spectrum.

BK: And I now mainly work for an architecture/urban design magazine called *Metropolis*. Those alternative weeklies were an outgrowth of underground newspapers and featured weekly comic strips. It's where Matt Groening and Lynda Barry started their strips. They had miniscule editorial budgets. They were read mainly for horoscopes, comics, sex advice columns, and classified ads.

DPR: Well, what kind of role do you see for publications like that, alternative or underground papers, and then the comic strips in them, in today's culture?

BK: Recently, most of those weeklies have dropped their comics even more. The comics in daily newspapers are a moribund vestigial form of syndicated comic strip not worth preserving. We're seeing the severing of comics from newspapers for the first time since 1895, when The Yellow Kid began.

DPR: Do you think that alternative or independent publications, and the comics that go along with them, are migrating or finding a different audience online? Has the Internet sapped a lot of the potential audience for those kinds of publications?

BK: For good reasons, the Internet will bring about the end of mass-market printing. Ecologically, print is a disaster; culturally it was available only to people with the capital to underwrite it. Since the advertising base of newspapers and magazines may soon be gone, comic-strips artists, like journalists, will have to find a new source of income. To move print comics online doesn't seem to be taking advantage of the technological possibilities of digital imaging, sound, and motion. It may all end up having to be subsidized by taxes on the sale of material goods or nonprofit educational institutions.

DPR: Well, you have your website. How has the Internet changed your work?

BK: It's more digital imaging that's changed the way I work. About a year ago, I began drawing on a Cintiq—a digital drawing board. It made no sense to digitize images on paper, once a decent physical drawing interface was invented. I have access to a vast picture and text archive 24/7. Since there's a lot more to read and look at online, the visibility of my strips has decreased. People would pick up one of those weekly newspapers because they were looking for an apartment and, by chance, they would come across my strip. The online world is the ultimate in specialty publishing, where you can look up the blog that's exactly what you want to read about. At the moment, I make most of my living from teaching, not from selling reproduction rights for print or online publishing and that's how most writers have always subsidized their work.

DPR: In your art, whether it is in print or online, do you find yourself writing for a specific audience or a specific community?

BK: I write and draw out of an obsessive need to make poetic sense of the world. The readers who stumble upon my work share this need, and so it's quite utilitarian. There's no shortage of senselessness that needs explaining.

DPR: I think you're on target when it comes to your audience and the kind of interest people find in your strips. Your comics are filled with eccentrics, and your characters are fascinated with minutiae and the non sequitur. How do you come up with your ideas for the various story lines? I'm thinking, for example, of your strips *The Shoehorn Technique*, *The Cardboard Valise*, or especially the various strips in *Julius Knipl*.

BK: How do I do it?

DPR: Yeah how do you come up with these offbeat ideas?

BK: Inspiration driven by the necessity of a deadline. There's always some kind of structure, some form I want to write about that week or that month. I try to give my strips some kind of form. I start off with some nebulous idea, then I try to narrow it down to what it really is or what it's about. That's sort of how it works. Most of my ideas come from extrapolating upon an observation. When you work in a serial form, you can't think about how it's done. It's just like asking someone who makes pizza, "How do you do this every day? How do you get this taste?" There is a kind of formal requirement in my mind that I have to match every week, or surpass, a kind of poetic form. Some weeks it's more inspired than others. But that's the way serial writing works. I mean, everything I do goes into print. I don't get to put it away if it's not completely successful. On the other hand,

Figure 5. Image from weekly installment of *Shoehorn Technique* © 2006 Ben Katchor.

because I do so many strips, I arrive at a high number of successful ones. I come up with ideas that I wouldn't have come up if I produced less material.

DPR: Well a lot of your work is individual one-shot strips, but there are some, like for instance, the storyline of *The Jew of New York,* that you've carried out in a novelistic way. Do you think more in terms of longer story lines or just one-shot strips?

BK: My main interest in the picture story is the short form. I mean, I think in a page you can do a lot. It's a really concise form. In one panel you can reveal your worldview, in two panels you can comment on that view, and in eight, or nine panels, you can set up a complex dialectic. Originally, *The Jew of New York* ran as a weekly strip. Each page was a self-contained episode. So even if you weren't following the entire story, you'd hopefully be entertained by that week's episode.

DPR: When you were conceiving *The Jew of New York*, did you think that it would end up being a long novelesque work?

BK: It was invented week to week, with only a vague idea of were it was going. It ran in the *Forward* for fifty-two weeks. Then I went back and expanded upon elements that were hinted at but not fully developed in the original series. So, it became a book by accretion. *The Jew of New York* is one of the longest strips that I've done. Most of my strips begin and end in single-page. My most recent weekly strip, *Shoehorn Technique*, is also kind of a vaguely connected narrative. But again, each week's episode functions as a self-contained story.

DPR: Do you have any plans now of collecting your work on *Shoehorn Technique* into a longer book, like you did with *The Jew in New York*?

BK: Hopefully, all of my strips will be collected in book form. A collection of *The Cardboard Valise* was published in March 2011. Next will be the *Metropolis* series, then *Hotel & Farm* and eventually *Shoehorn Technique*. I have only a year's worth of *Shoehorn Technique* and I've put it aside to work on other projects.

DPR: A lot of your work takes place in an American setting, whether it's New York or otherwise. To what degree do you consider your work and what you do as defining American or Americanness?

BK: It's more East Coast urban culture than American. America is this vast place I know very little about. I have always lived in an East Coast city. Although New York is becoming a strip mall like the rest of the country, it's the Asian and Latin American influences that make it bearable. With the exception of a few major cities, the rest of the country feels pretty alien to me.

DPR: Even though they seem to be American or East Coast urban settings, there is something almost detached about your settings, as if they're in another time and another place, divorced from the current events that surround us today.

BK: My series in *Metropolis* magazine deals specifically with contemporary architecture and urban design, and it's been running for more than ten years. Those stories are definitely set in this time.

DPR: Do any recent cultural events or political events—current issues like, for instance, arguments surrounding American immigration—find their way into your work?

BK: Those are not current issues—they're endless variations on a theme. My series, *The Cardboard Valise*, is about an American's obsession with the exotic qualities of foreign cultures, mainly as they exist in his mind. I'm not interested in competing with the superficial drama of the evening news.

DPR: Not like *Doonesbury*, in other words.

BK: No, definitely not.

DPR: How much of an impact has the underground comics of 1960s and '70s had on your own work?

BK: I grew up reading comics, and then in the '60s when I saw underground comics, it confirmed my feeling that you could write and draw serious fiction in the comic-strip form. I kept coming across things as a kid, such as Edward Gorey and a few *New Yorker* cartoonists who did extended picture books and I saw that the possibility was there to do something of more substance than I found in the comic books I read as a child. The best of the underground cartoonists, Robert Crumb and Bill Griffith, seemed as subtle and complex as the prose fiction I was reading.

DPR: You mention Crumb and Griffith. Who are the other influences when it comes to your art? Not necessarily underground comic artists, but any artists.

BK: Probably early European figure draftsman: Poussin, Rembrandt. That's what I was attracted to in art school, the tradition of Western figurative art. Once I discovered the larger Western tradition, cartoonists were no longer a model for me. The way I draw is the result of aspiring to work in Western figurative tradition.

DPR: So at what point in your career did you think, "I'll try my hand at cartooning"?

BK: I always drew comics as a child, and I published them in fanzines. I stopped doing that when I went to college and studied painting. At some point I realized that being a painter and showing in galleries did not appeal to me. I loved the

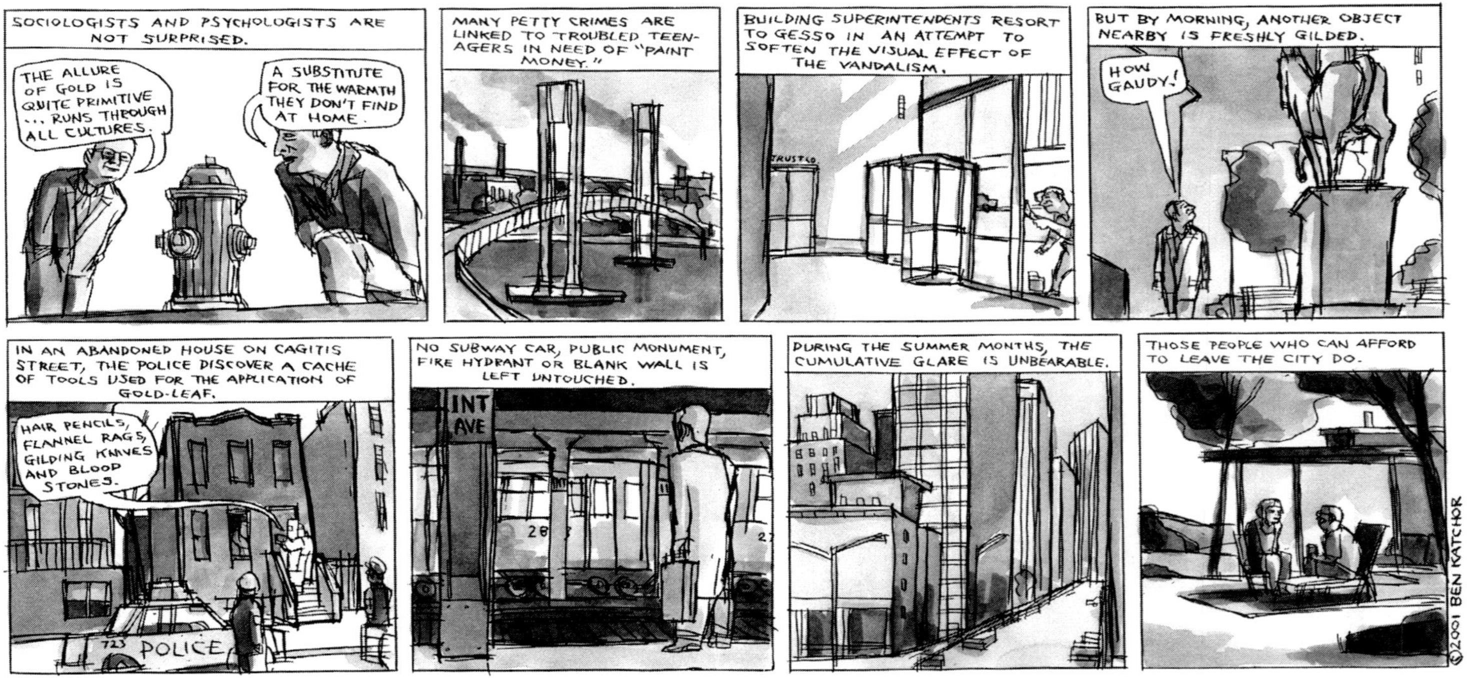

Figure 6. (pp. 236-37) A full-page story in *Metropolis* magazine entitled "The Decorative Impulse." Originally appeared as a single color image. © 2001 Ben Katchor.

AS ONE VISUAL MANIFESTATION OF THE CITY'S TEENAGE POPULATION FADES FROM THE PUBLIC'S MEMORY . . .
ONE BOY ACTS AS THE LOOKOUT WHILE THE OTHERS SET TO WORK.
A NEW FORM OF EXPRESSION TAKES ITS PLACE.
WHO DID THIS?
WHO DO YOU THINK?
BOYS WITH A SURFEIT OF ENERGY, WIELDING CHEAP BRISTLE BRUSHES AND PAILS OF 14-CARAT GOLD PAINT . . .
GIOTTO
ROAM THE STREETS LOOKING FOR OBJECTS AND SURFACES OF A NEUTRAL COLOR.
THE AUTHORITIES CONSIDER WAYS OF CHANNELING THIS DECORATIVE IMPULSE INTO A MORE PRODUCTIVE DIRECTION.
LET THEM PAINT CLOCK HANDS, FINIALS, PICTURE FRAMES...

idea of art made for reproduction as opposed to the "original" hanging on a wall. In the back of my mind I had this perfect print form that I knew as a child; this form that everyone could afford to buy and take home. I aspired to make paintings with the narrative content of a short story, and as there was this ready-made form—the comic strip—that allowed me to combine both impulses. I simply returned to what I knew as a child.

DPR: Will Eisner said at one point that he felt that he wanted to be a writer and a painter. But he felt like a mediocre painter and like a mediocre fiction writer. However, in the medium of comics, he could combine his mediocre talents into something he could excel in. Do you feel the same way?

BK: I don't buy that theory. A successful comic strip needs a strong literary sensibility coupled with a matching visual sensibility. I think when you have a weakness it shows up in that combination. I think every writer should draw and every draftsman should write. The continuum between pictures and words should be reestablished. The text is constantly corrected by the image, and the image is corrected by the text. When a comic strip really fails, it fails on both counts.

DPR: What are your thoughts on the cross-fertilization between comic art and other mediums, for instance, between comic books and film, or between comics and painting, or comics and traditional novels? Because there have been a number of films over the past several years that have been adaptations of comic books. And then you have comics inspiring Michael Chabon's *Amazing Adventures of Kavalier & Clay*, and then that novel spawning a new comic book series.

BK: Each form has its own qualities and demands. Because prose fiction doesn't deal with spatial drama, an adaptation into film or comics has to completely invent this spatial drama. When those spatial qualities are extraneous additions, the film is a failure. The adaptation of comics into film usually dispenses with the handwriting of the artist—the one element that's at its core. Adding the element of motion in a meaningful way to a static form is also a difficult thing to pull off. It's usually a case of a desperate businessmen/artist hoping to leverage some quality and reputation of a successful work of art into a second product. The result is usually a watered down, ill conceived mess.

DPR: What about the way that other media have informed comics, or even how comics have influenced other kinds of narrative, like film or novels?

BK: Eisner was highly influenced by film and in some ways brought the storytelling in his early strips up to the level of sophistication found in film of the time. That same 1940s film sensibility made his later work seem very limited and melodramatic. Alain Resnais was influenced by the freedom of storytelling structure found in early newspaper comics to rethink the conventions of film. The low cultural stigma attached to comics made them appealing to "fine art" painters.

DPR: What do you think of comics as literature? For instance, I work in the academy and I teach, and many times I will use comics or graphic novels in my literature classes.

BK: Comic strips can be as poetic and literate as anything I've read in prose fiction or poetry. The technique of combining text and images goes back to theater and went on to cinema. It was only in those archaic forms of writing and drawing that a purification of disciplines took place in the academy and that purification lead to a sterility that doesn't exist in the worst comic strips.

DPR: What are some examples of comic writing that, you think, are the best, that stand out?

BK: One of my favorites is a cartoonist who worked in England named John Glashan. He did a strip in the *Observer* called *Genius*, as well as many other things. They are highly literate and they're beautifully drawn. Peter Blegvad, who lives and works in England, did a long-running strip called *Leviathan*. It ran in the *Sunday Independent*. It's pure visual and literary poetry. The concrete visual dimension gives his text a depth and meaning it would not otherwise have. Bill Griffith's picture-stories, *Zippy the Pinhead* and others, are perfect expressions of the surrealist sensibility. They produce effects that even the French surrealists couldn't achieve, because they were either writers or picture makers, but rarely both.

DPR: What do you think of the current state of comic art today? At times you reside in France, so maybe another way of asking the question is this: What is the state of comic art in the United States, compared to the state of comic art in Europe?

BK: I'm only in France for the summer. We're in the midst of a golden age of handmade comics. It may be a reaction against computer-generated art and boring 3D animation. On the other hand, the literary recognition that comics have received has given people a license to do long and boring fake-literary-feeling graphic novels. Previously, comic strips had to be at least mildly entertaining and sometimes reached the level of art. Today we have people trying to make art, and foregoing the entertainment value, and the result can be reminiscent of the worst literary fiction or the most pretentious poetry. Overall, there are more things being published and more people trying to do serious work in the comic-strip form than ever before.

Figure 7. (pp. 240-41) A full-page strip in *Metropolis* magazine entitled "The Call of the Wall." Originally appeared as a single color image. © 2003 Ben Katchor.

SUDDENLY, AFTER HUNDREDS OF YEARS OF JUST LOOKING...
MORRIS ?
I'LL BE RIGHT BACK.
A NUMBER OF OTHERWISE UNATHLETIC INDIVIDUALS
PLEASE, TAKE OFF YOUR SLIPPERS.
FEEL COMPELLED TO CLIMB THEIR LIVING ROOM WALLS.
ALLEY-OOP!
BY MEANS OF CLINGING TO THE PICTURE AND DADO MOLDINGS...

DPR: Where do you see your work now? You mentioned your current work on *The Shoehorn Technique*. What else you are working on?

BK: Well, I've done four shows for music theater in the last few years. They're collaborations with the composer/singer Mark Mulcahy. I write the libretto and design projected images that serve a scenic and storytelling function. Historically, theater is the first place in history where words and pictures were put together—the stage pictures combined with the words uttered by actors. Some early European proto-comics were just an attempt to record that kind of synthesis. There is definitely a basic connection between those forms. Picture-stories are the pre-cinematic method of notating theatrical events. Today, most people who want to tell picture-stories go into film, because there's something of an industry and you may be able to make a living. There's the glamor assorted with living actors and movie stars. But the thing that interests me about this handmade form of the picture-story is *handwriting* as an extension of the written word. I'm interested in the cultivation of an autographic voice that's the physical expression of my thought.

DPR: You refer to your work as "picture-stories." Do you prefer "picture-stories" over "comics" or "graphic narrative"?

BK: Picture-story seems like a more descriptive term, and that's what they are called in German. Comics, or comic strips, is American term that came about with newspaper comics where a lot of the strips were intended to be humorous. In France they're just *bande dessinée* or strip-drawings. Mine are more like "comic-tragedy strips."

The problem with the term "comics" is that if someone asks, "What do you do?" and you say you make "comics" they'll think *Garfield*, not John Glashan. Then you're forced to explain what *you* mean by comics. But if I tell people I make "picture-stories," they have no idea what I'm talking about and they'll ask, "What do you mean by that?" And then I can show them.

DPR: Then you can draw a picture. And we're back to the ambiguity of words like "picture-stories," "comics," and "Jewish."

BK: I will explain to them what a picture-story is. But, you know, these terms, like "Jewish" need a lot of defining to have any meaning, otherwise it's just a slogan, maybe racist slogans, or a jingoistic slogans, like "I am an American" or "I am a Jew." They don't mean too much.

DPR: Some have argued that this emphasis on ethnic identity, the hyphenated identity, is very American, an American obsession that you don't find this in other places around the world.

BK: Polish Jews I know who immigrated to France from Eastern Europe before World War II became very French. They spoke French. They began eating French cuisine, and so, culturally, adopted many of the aspects of the French culture of 1930s. Today, in this very small world, there are young people living in France who are more involved with American pop culture than I am. So in some ways, you can say they are more American than I am. I think that today, everybody invents their own "ethnicity" and everybody is their own little country, and no one can speak for much more than what's going on in their own kitchen. Anything more than that is just nationalistic baloney. It doesn't mean anything. It could mean enough to go to war, but it does not mean anything really. It just means slogans and generalizations. I don't know if you're going to get people in the world of comic strips who feel these strong ethnic identities in their work. I think there's too aware of a world culture of visual storytelling.

DPR: That's one of the differences between what goes on in the American academy and what goes on in the world of art. Those who create the works that we discuss and teach, as professors, may not be concerned with defining or pigeonholing what they do. Especially when it comes issues like ethnicity. Take, for example, one of the first questions I asked you: "Would you consider yourself an ethnic or Jewish writer?" Maybe you do, maybe you don't. Because on the one hand, you have someone like Toni Morrison who has said that she considers herself more of an African American writer than an *American* writer. And then you have Phillip Roth who absolutely dislikes the term "Jewish author" and will get rather defensive about that. So I think that's something that those of us in the academy are more concerned with than the authors themselves, at least to some degree.

BK: There's a history or a story behind the work, but it's a very *particular* story. So just saying "I'm a Jewish American writer" doesn't tell you much. To me, it means almost nothing. To my father, a Yiddish-speaking Jew born in Warsaw, the comics he saw me reading as a child were the epitome of American culture regardless of the fact that they might have been made by the children of Eastern European Jews. They were written in English, were full of violent imagery and so had a frivolous American quality to them. To a Hasidic Jew, you're either a free Jew or an observing Jew. And if you're a free Jew, you've gone your own way outside of the Jewish community. When it comes to language, you've got to clarify these terms and make them more concrete—and that's where pictures come in.

Questions for Discussion

1. How has Jewish American fiction changed over the past fifty years?

2. What lead to Irving Howe (and Ruth Wisse and Leslie Fiedler) predicting the eventual passing of Jewish American literature? How might his forecast have been short-sighted? What cultural and literary conditions have changed since Howe's prediction?

3. What are the problems of ascribing only one or two causes behind, or reasons for, the flourishing of Jewish American writing? How might such a limited perspective frustrate our understanding of, and appreciation for, Jewish American fiction?

4. In what ways might contemporary scholars, trying to explain the "new wave" of recent Jewish American fiction, be performing a critical act similar to that of Irving Howe in 1977?

5. How do you define Jewish American literature? Does a text have to have "Jewish" content to be called Jewish? How do you define that content? How might it be possible, if at all, for an American writer of Jewish heritage to create a work of fiction that is not "Jewish"? What about the inverse, a non-Jewish American author creating a "Jewish" text?

6. What cultural, political, and historical conditions underlie the post-1980s wave of Jewish American fiction?

7. How has the most recent generation of Jewish American writers benefitted from the dominant presence of such authors as Saul Bellow, Bernard Malamud, and Philip Roth? What have been the potential liabilities to this inheritance?

8. In what ways has Jewish women's literature changed since the days of Anzia Yezierska, Mary Antin, and Gertrude Stein?

9. What are some of the general themes defining Jewish American writing today?

10. How might visual narrative (in the form of comics and graphic novels) challenge our conceptions of contemporary Jewish American writing? What kind of cross-fertilization has there been between Jewish American fiction and other media?

11. What kinds of writers tend to garner the most critical interest within Jewish American literary studies? How much does the marketplace determine our definitions of Jewish American writing? What writers, or what kinds of writing, might be marginalized in our common definitions of Jewish American literature?

12. You are given the task of creating an anthology of contemporary Jewish American fiction. What writers would you include, and why? What texts would you unquestionably anthologize, and which ones would you exclude? Is there the need to make your anthology comprehensive, and if so, why? Who is your audience for this anthology?

Contemporary Jewish American Fiction: A Selected Bibliography

Anthologies
(with significant contributions from contemporary authors)

Bukiet, Melvin, ed. *Neurotica: Jewish Writers on Sex*. New York: Norton, 1999. Reprint, New York: Broadway, 2000.

———, ed. *Nothing Makes You Free: Writings by Descendants of Jewish Holocaust Survivors*. 2002. Reprint, New York: Norton, 2003.

Bukiet, Melvin Jules, and David G. Roskie, eds. *Scribblers on the Roof: Contemporary Jewish Fiction*. New York: Persea, 2006.

Chametzky, Jules, John Felstiner, Hilene Flanzbaum, and Kathryn Hellerstein, eds. *Jewish American Literature: A Norton Anthology*. New York: Norton, 2001.

Raz, Hilda, ed. *The* Prairie Schooner *Anthology of Contemporary Jewish American Writing*. Lincoln: University of Nebraska Press, 1998.

Shapiro, Gerald, ed. *American Jewish Fiction: A Century of Stories*. Lincoln: University of Nebraska Press, 1998.

Solotaroff, Ted, and Nessa Rapoport, eds. *The Schoken Book of Contemporary Jewish Fiction*. New York: Schocken, 1996. Reprint of *Writing Our Way Home: Contemporary Stories by American Jewish Writers*. New York: Schocken, 1992.

Stavans, Ilan, ed. *The Oxford Book of Jewish Stories*. New York: Oxford University Press, 1998.

Zakrzewski, Paul, ed. *Lost Tribe: Jewish Fiction from the Edge*. New York: Perennial-Harper, 2003.

Critical Sources

Aarons, Victoria. *A Measure of Memory: Storytelling and Identity in American Jewish Fiction*. Athens: University of Georgia Press, 1996.

———. *What Happened to Abraham?: Reinventing the Covenant in American Jewish Fiction*. Newark: University of Delaware Press, 2005.

Baskind, Samantha, and Ranen Omer-Sherman. *The Jewish Graphic Novel: Critical Approaches*. New Brunswick: Rutgers University Press, 2008.

Berger, Alan L. *Children of Job: American Second-Generation Witnesses to the Holocaust*. Albany: State University of New York Press, 1997.

Berger, Alan L., and Gloria L. Cronin. *Jewish American and Holocaust Literature: Representations in the Postmodern World*. Albany: State University of New York Press, 2004.

Berger, Alan L., and Naomi Berger, eds. *Second Generation Voices: Reflections by Children of Holocaust Survivors and Perpetrators*. Syracuse: Syracuse University Press, 2001.

Biale, David, Michael Galchinsky, and Susannah Heschel, eds. *Insider/Outsider: American Jews and Multiculturalism*. Berkeley: University of California Press, 1998.

Boyarin, Jonathan. *Thinking in Jewish*. Chicago: University of Chicago Press, 1996.

Brettschneider, Marla, ed. *The Narrow Bridge: Jewish Views on Multiculturalism*. New Brunswick: Rutgers University Press, 1996.

Brook, Vincent, ed. *You Should See Yourself: Jewish Identity in Postmodern American Culture*. New Brunswick, NJ: Rutgers University Press, 2006.

Buhle, Paul, ed. *Jews and American Comics: An Illustrated History of an American Art Form*. New York: New Press, 2008.

Bukiet, Melvin Jules. "Crackpot Realism." *Tikkun* January/February 1995. Reprint in "Crackpot Realism: Fiction for the Forthcoming Millenium." *The Review of Contemporary Fiction* 16 (1996): 13-22.

———. "In the Beginning Was Auschwitz." *The Chronicle of Higher Education* 8 March 2002, sec. 2: B10.

Burstein, Janet Handler. "Recalling Home: American Jewish Women Writers of the New Wave." *Contemporary Literature* 42 (2001): 800-24.

———. *Telling Little Secrets: American Jewish Writing since the 1980s*. Madison: University of Wisconsin Press, 2006.

———. *Writing Mothers, Writing Daughters: Tracing the Maternal in Stories by American Jewish Women*. Urbana: University of Illinois Press, 1996.

Dickstein, Morris. "The Complex Fate of the Jewish American Writer." *Ideology and Jewish Identity in Israeli and American Literature*. Ed. Emily Miller Budick. New York: State University of New York Press, 2001. 57-78.

Flanzbaum, Hilene, ed. *The Americanization of the Holocaust*. Baltimore: Johns Hopkins University Press, 1999.

Freedman, Jonathan. *Klezmer America: Jewishness, Ethnicity, Modernity*. New York: Columbia University Press, 2008.

Fried, Lewis, Gene Brown, Jules Chametzky, and Louis Harap, eds. *Handbook of American-Jewish Literature: An Analytical Guide to Topics, Themes, and Sources*. New York: Greenwood Press, 1988.

Furman, Andrew. *Contemporary Jewish American Writers and the Multicultural Dilemma: Return of the Exiled*. Syracuse: Syracuse University Press, 2000.

———. *Israel through the Jewish-American Imagination: A Survey of Jewish-American Literature on Israel 1928-1995*. Albany: State University of New York Press, 1997.

Gilman, Sander L. *Multiculturalism and the Jews*. New York: Routledge, 2006.

Goffman, Ethan. *Imagining Each Other: Blacks and Jews in Contemporary American Literature*. Albany: State University of New York Press, 2000.

Goodman, Allegra. "Writing Jewish Fiction In and Out of the Multicultural Context." *Daughters of Valor: Contemporary Jewish American Women Writers*. Ed. Jay L. Halio and Ben Siegel. Newark: University of Delaware Press, 1997.

Grimwood, Marita. *Holocaust Literature of the Second Generation*. New York: Palgrave, 2007.

Hirose, Yoshiji. *Shadows of Yiddish on Modern Jewish American Writers*. Osaka, Japan: Osaka Kyoiku Tosho, 2005.

Hirsch, Marianne. *Family Frames: Photography, Narrative, and Postmemory*. Cambridge: Harvard University Press, 1997.

Hirsh, Marianne, and Irene Kacandes, eds. *Teaching the Representation of the Holocaust*. New York: Modern Language Association, 2004.

Hungerforg, Amy. *The Holocaust of Texts: Genocide, Literature, and Personification*. Chicago: University of Chicago Press, 2003.

Kaplan, Arie. *From Krakow to Krypton: Jews and Comic Books*. Philadelphia: Jewish Publication Society of America, 2008.

Kessner, Carole, and Ann Shapiro, eds. *Studies in American Jewish Literature in Honor of Sarah Blacher Cohen*. West Lafayette, IN: Purdue Univesity Press, 2010.

Kramer, Michael P., and Hana Wirth-Nesher, eds. *The Cambridge Companion to Jewish American Literature*. Cambridge: Cambridge University Press, 2003.

Kremer, S. Lillian, ed. *Holocaust Literature*. New York: Routledge, 2003.

———. "Post-alienation: Recent Directions in Jewish American Literature." *Contemporary Literature* 34 (1993): 571-91.

Lambert, Josh. *American Jewish Fiction*. Philadelphia: The Jewish Publication Society, 2009.

Lang, Berel, ed. *Writing and the Holocaust*. New York: Holmes and Meier, 1988.

McGlothlin, Erin Heather. *Second-Generation Holocaust Literature: Legacies of Survival and Perpetration*. Rochester, NY: Camden House, 2006.

Rosenbaum, Thane, ed. "Literary Symposium: The Jewish Literary Revival." *Tikkun* November/December 1997. (With commentary by Melvin Jules Bukiet, Morris Dickstein, Rebecca Goldstein, Sanford Pinsker, Nessa Rapoport, Mark Shechner, and Steve Stern).

Roth, Laurence. *Inspecting Jews: American Jewish Detective Stories*. Brunswick: Rutgers University Press, 2004.

Rothberg, Michael. *Traumatic Realism: The Demands of Holocaust Representation*. Minneapolis: University of Minnesota Press, 2000.

Royal, Derek Parker, ed. *Jewish Comics*. Special issue of *Shofar* 29, no. 2 (Winter 2011).

Rubin, Lois, ed. *Connections and Collisions: Identities in Contemporary Jewish-American Women's Writing*. Newark, DE: University of Delaware Press, 2005.

Shandler, Jeffrey. *Adventures in Yiddishland: Postvernacular Language and Culture*. Berkeley: University of California Press, 2006.

Sicher, Efraim. *The Holocaust Novel*. New York: Routledge, 2005.

Sundquist, Eric J. *Strangers in the Land: Blacks, Jews, Post-Holocaust America*. Cambridge: Belknap-Harvard University Press, 2009.

Wade, Stephen. *Jewish American Literature Since 1945: An Introduction*. Edinburgh: Edinburgh University Press, 1999.

Weingard, Michael. *American Hebrew Literature: Writing Jewish National Identity in the United States*. Syracuse: Syracuse University Press, 2010.

Whitfield, Stephen J. *In Search of American Jewish Culture*. Hanover, NH: Brandeis University Press, 1999.

Wisse, Ruth R. *The Modern Jewish Canon: A Journey through Language and Culture*. New York: Free Press, 2000.

Contributors

Lee Behlman is an assistant professor of English at Montclair State University in New Jersey, where he teaches courses on Victorian literature and the Hebrew Bible in translation. He has published a biographical entry on Michael Chabon for the *Routledge Encyclopedia of Holocaust Literature* (2002) and is currently writing on the representation of Jews and conversion in Victorian historical fiction. He has published essays in *The Journal of Victorian Culture, Victorian Poetry, Nineteenth-Century Gender Studies, Nineteenth-Century Prose,* and in the book collections *Antiquity Recovered: The Legacy of Pompeii and Herculaneum* (Getty Museum, 2007) and *Mothers Who Deliver: Feminist Interventions in Public and Interpersonal Discourse* (SUNY Press, 2010).

Tracy Floreani is Chair and Associate Professor of English at Oklahoma City University, where she teaches American literature and contemporary "minority" literatures while also pursuing initiatives to get students involved in social justice work. Her research focuses on ethnicity and immigrant identities in American culture since World War II.

Farideh Dayanim Goldin is the author of *Wedding Song: Memoirs of an Iranian Jewish Woman* (2003). She was born in Shiraz, Iran, to a family of *dayanim*, judges and leaders of the Jewish community. Her family moved out of the *mahaleh*, the Jewish ghetto, to a Moslem neighborhood when she was eight years old. There, she experienced both friendship and anti-Semitism. Later, attending an American-style university in Iran, she was torn between her loyalty to her family, who obeyed strict social, cultural and religious mores, and her western education that promoted individualism and self-reliance. *Wedding Song* reveals Farideh's struggle in balancing her two worlds. She is a prolific essayist, speaker, and advocate who confronts issues of identity as she searches for a place in American society as an Iranian immigrant.

Susan Jacobowitz is an associate professor of English at Queensborough Community College, CUNY. Her recent publications and presentations include work on second-generation literature and performance art, Australian Jewish writers, graphic genres, and the conflicts and challenges of modern Jewish identity. Her articles have appeared in *Shofar, Studies in American Jewish Literature* and the *Australian Journal of Jewish Studies*; she has also contributed essays to *Jewish Women's Writings of the 1990s and Beyond in Great Britain and the United States* (2004), *Parenting and Professing: Balancing Family Work With an Academic Career* (2005), *Companion to Australian Literature since 1900* (2007), *Art Spiegelman: Conversations* (2007), and *Reading Down Under: Australian Literary Studies Reader* (2009).

Ben Katchor's picture stories and drawings have appeared in the *Forward*, *Metropolis Magazine*, and *The New Yorker*. His books include: *Julius Knipl, Real Estate Photographer* (1996), *The Jew of New York* (1999), *The Beauty Supply District* (2000), and *The Cardboard Valise* (2011). He was the recipient of a Guggenheim Memorial Foundation Fellowship, a MacArthur Foundation Fellowship, and was a fellow at both the American Academy in Berlin and the Cullman Center for Scholars and Writers at the New York Public Library. Katchor's libretto and drawings for *The Carbon Copy Building*, a collaboration with Bang on a Can, received an Obie Award for Best New American Work. More recently, he has collaborated with musician Mark Mulcahy on *The Rosenbach Company*, a sung-through musical biography of Abe Rosenbach, the preeminent rare book dealer of the twentieth century, *The Slug Bearers of Kayrol Island*, which won an Obie Award in 2008, and *A Checkroom Romance*, a love story about the culture and architecture of the coat-check room. He is an associate professor at Parsons, The New School for Design in New York City. For more information visit www.katchor.com.

Joe Kraus is associate professor of English & Theatre at the University of Scranton, where he directs the honors program and teaches creative writing and American literature. He is the coauthor of *An Accidental Anarchist* (2001), and his scholarly and creative work has appeared, among other places, in *MELUS*, *The American Scholar*, *Centennial Review*, *Southern Quarterly Review*, *Oleander Review*, and *Moment*.

Jennifer Lemberg teaches at The Gallatin School of Individualized Study, New York University, and serves as Co-Director of the Holocaust Educators Network, a professional development organization for middle school, high school, and college faculty. Her work has appeared in *Studies in American Indian Literatures* and *Women's Studies Quarterly*.

Bart Lievens has written a dissertation on the importance of Europe in contemporary Jewish American Literature at Ghent University, Belgium. His work focuses on writers such as Dara Horn, Melvin Jules Bukiet, Steve Stern, and Jonathan Safran Foer. He currently teaches English at Artevelde University College, Ghent, Belgium.

Michael J. Martin is an associate professor of English at Stephen F. Austin State University in Nacogdoches, Texas, where he teaches courses in contemporary American fiction, postmodern fiction, literature of the road, and literary theory. He has published his work in such journals as *Peer English*, *Children's Literature Quarterly*, *Shofar*, and *American Book Review*.

Adam Meyer is Associate Professor of Jewish Studies at Vanderbilt University. In addition to the full-length *Black-Jewish Relations in African American and Jewish American Literatures: An Annotated Bibliography* (2002), he has published articles in such journals as *Studies in Short Fiction*, *MELUS*, *Modern Jewish Studies*, *Prospects*, and *African American Review*, as well as entries in several reference volumes.

Monica Osborne teaches in the Department of Germanic Languages at UCLA, where she was also recently a Mellon Postdoctoral Fellow in Jewish American literature. She has written for *Tikkun*, *Studies in American Jewish Literature*, *Religion and Literature*, *Shofar*, *Modern Fiction Studies*, and *Jewcy.com*. She teaches courses on Jewish literature, Holocaust studies, ethics of representation, and midrash in a modern context. She is finishing a book manuscript called *The Midrashic Impulse and the Literary Response to Trauma*.

Derek Parker Royal has taught as an associate professor of English and director of Liberal Studies at Texas A&M University-Commerce, and he is the founder and executive editor of *Philip Roth Studies*. His essays on American literature and graphic narrative have appeared in a variety of scholarly journals and edited collections. He is the editor of *Philip Roth: New Perspectives on an American Author* (2005) and the recent special issue of *Shofar* (Winter 2011) devoted to Jewish comics and graphic novels. He is currently working on three book manuscripts, *The Hernandez Brothers: Conversations* (2012), *Coloring America: Multi-Ethnic Engagements with Recent American Comics*, and *More Than Jewish Mischief: Narrating Subjectivity in the Later Fiction of Philip Roth*.

Ruth Knafo Setton is the author of the critically acclaimed novel, *The Road to Fez* (2001). Born in Safi, Morocco, she is the recipient of literary fellowships from the National Endowment of the Arts, Pennsylvania Council on the Arts and PEN, and writers' colonies including Yaddo and MacDowell. Her poetry, fiction, and creative nonfiction have appeared in many journals and anthologies, including *Best Contemporary Jewish Writing* (2001), *The Schocken Book of Modern Sephardic Literature* (2005), *Becoming Myself: Reflections on Growing Up*

Female (2006), *Common Boundary: Stories of Immigration* (2010), *Israel Short Stories* (2011), and *The North American Review.* She is the Writer in Residence for the Berman Center for Jewish Studies and a Professor of Practice in the English Department at Lehigh University. She often gives lectures, creative writing workshops and readings. She just completed her third novel, *The Zigzag Girl,* and is working on a new novel and a collection of poetry.

Michael Schuldiner is Professor and Chair of English at the University of Akron. His publications include a new book, *Contesting Histories: German and Jewish Americans and the Legacy of the Holocaust* (2011), and *The Selected Writings of Mordecai Noah* (1999), a collection of the best writing by the early American Jewish playwright, journalist, and statesman. He is the recipient of awards from the Folger and Huntington Libraries, fellowships from DAAD (the German American Exchange Service), and the Center for Advanced Holocaust Studies of the U.S. Holocaust Memorial Museum, and he has been a Fulbright Senior Lecturer in Israel.

Maya Socolovsky is an assistant professor of English and Latin American Studies at the University of North Carolina, Charlotte, where she teaches classes in ethnic American literature, Latino/a literature, literary theory, and American literature. She has published on issues of memory and history in Latino/a literature and Jewish American literature. Her articles have appeared in journals such as *LIT, PMLA, Contemporary Literature, Shofar,* and *JAC.* She is currently at work on a book about place, nation, and geopolitics in contemporary Latina literature.

Adam Sol teaches at Laurentian University's campus in Barrie, Ontario. His writing on Jewish literature has appeared recently in *The Forward* and *Studies in American Jewish Literature*, but he is better known as a poet, having published three collections of poetry, including *Jeremiah, Ohio* (2008) and *Crowd of Sounds* (2003), which won Ontario's Trillium Award for Poetry in 2004.

Alexis Wilson is a Ph.D. candidate at Indiana University. She specializes in American Literature from the late nineteenth century to the present, and her critical interests include crime fiction, law and literature, psychology, gender and sexuality, and Jewish American literature.

Index